The Selected Models of American Fiction

R.N. Sarkar

ATLANTIC
PUBLISHERS & DISTRIBUTORS (P) LTD

Published by
ATLANTIC
PUBLISHERS & DISTRIBUTORS (P) LTD
7/22, Ansari Road, Darya Ganj,
New Delhi-110002
Phones : +91-11-40775252, 23273880, 23275880, 23280451
Fax : +91-11-23285873
Web : www.atlanticbooks.com
E-mail : orders@atlanticbooks.com

Branch Office
5, Nallathambi Street, Wallajah Road,
Chennai-600002
Phones : +91-44-64611085, 32413319
E-mail : chennai@atlanticbooks.com

ISBN: 987-81-269-1816-4

Printed in India at Glorious Printers, A-13, D.S.I.D.C.,
Jhilmil Industrial Area, Delhi-110095

Preface

I prefer a self-explanatory title for this work—*Selected Models of American Fiction*, which, I think, could be immediately helpful to Indian readership and all those whose English is a second language anywhere, and could yet warm up a new interest in an Indian appreciation of literary values of those selected writers who belong to non-Indian English speaking areas.

America has a recent settlement history beginning with European migration as early as 1607. This migration character is different from the early Wandering of Nations in the whole of Europe, a splinter of pre-Christian nomads (Jute, Angles and Saxons of Gemanic origin) down to Britain across the British waters. English migration across the Atlantic was a part of the renascence explosions due to the adventurous navigators' all out attempts for new discoveries. Their El Dorado expedition, a non-existent El Dorado only made real after their own dream, thus America faced up. Sir Raleigh is the last of their progenitors. Raleigh was frustrated, but they were not. They fought the wildness of nature, and man, a mere autochthon, fought the unknown forays and withstood their stubbornness, and made his settlement secure.

The early period of these formative activities marked out a phase of romance, in Irving Babbit's idiom 'quixotic romance', an essential urge that engaged the immigrants in feverish activities, left them hardly time enough to consolidate even stray ideas and feelings for a consistent communication except for a relief from tension, and no definite form followed or evolved. Phillis Wheatley a Negro slave, originally of a Boston master, as early as 1773, at her nineteenth year of age adopted or innovated due forms of literature; her experience, under her master's appreciative care and by observation of life around her, were enough material for her work. She had no reason to be an adventurer like the migrants from across the sea, if adventure, it was of a different kind, and as, at a later stage of settlement, it could be; the writers from amongst the settlement were more or less variants of their homeland legacy already rich in literary forms and styles, particularly in fiction. Foremost among them must have been Nathaniel Hawthorne.

In American settled life there were new problems one after another, their post-Elizabethan forefathers had never to face in the same form, for example, plantation and slave problems and the problems of a mixed population of different culture, faith and speech, and even colour. The Unity-attempt was a protracted progression. A problem that gave rise to a prolonged Civil War of 1861-65, in addition to their War of Independence in 1776, the geographical position of the riverine South and the industrial North led to two different styles of life and accommodations of the population—black and white both. Though Independence gave them a sense of unity, internal differences of interest continued long. Reasonably, they adopted a federal system of democracy, with regional administrative independence under an overall central control of the President, everyone's President elected by everyone, a United States for all the common concerns.

American fiction, as literature generally, can hardly ignore these major issues of their life. Mark Twain's adventure stories represent models of characters, styles of life, in a sense of a selected region, as Hardy's Wesex, in a different sense of a nation in general, striving for a settled unity in future. The first batch of settlers were true adventurers, later adventure itself formed a part of the national spirit and suggested a literary type, an art intellectually to be cultivated, which Twain's Tom adopted and Huck inherited. British adventure stories are not as deeply associated with their life—Swift's Gulliver, De Foe's Robinson, Lewis Carroll's Alice really are not. America is by itself an adventure, consolidated and united.

Faulkner is more inclined to experiment in modern innovative styles than a consistent picture of life, yet life is inescapable, when he concentrates on a family saga of the Compsons in the South, particularly Yoknapatawppa area, in its degeneration with a lot of black servants in the household, degeneration from the glorious days of the civil war (1861-65). Faulkner is not exactly the British model of 'stream of consciousness' as a principle of delineation of life. He kept 'watch' only as a reminder of time to undo the sequence in a situation of unavoidable consequence, which is purely American. When Morrison follows this method, consequence seems to rule with a lucid variation of a monologue, deliberation in a pseudo-supernatural atmosphere and extreme agony of soul under one-sidedly adopted mechanism of suppression with all the attendant cruelties perpetrated in the process.

What Phillis Wheatley could not pursue at so early a stage of African-American literature in America, Alice Walker does, giving the inside story of the Negro world, slave and non-slave both, the transitional stage of their freedom, and their uninterfered homes and unpeeked closets. The picture suggested a self-responsibility on their part of the erstwhile slaves to improve their lot, slavery a symptom of the disease undetected, buried deep in their character and customs. They are weak because they did not grow strong, they remained satisfied in their own area of darkness. Harlem Black did not, they struggled out of darkness into light. Black and white mere colour, no manifesto of superiority or inferiority, if we don't deserve by an attained distinction. Walker drives at a human basis of distinction, yet further deep towards a divine source of support we know commonly by the name of God. If argued beyond our reach, the reachable alternative still remains love. We can love Him in everything in His creation.

American democracy is stronger than original British democracy, with individual right of freedom ensured, not under a monarchic unity, but by the direct choice of the Head of the United States, to ensure unity of the nation composed of disparate diversities of autonomous units. Walker in her masterpiece seems to suggest a further unity prospect, a little above the mundane discipline, unity under Godhead.

Faulkner seems to be less burdened by his stylistic interest in his short stories, particularly one selected here, an over-sized short story; for that perhaps he could, like the Old Testament 'Genesis', present a consolidated history of a composite culture and evolution of a nation, from the woods and unowned common partnership of vast lands inside and on the outer fringe, men and beasts living together in perpetual cooperation and conflicts, to a gradual development of a mix-breed white and coloured inter-related unity, though not conflict-free, yet silently; white master's authority unchallenged, secret understanding obeyed—just in a situation like this white and colour blood-mix stage by stage unplanned reckless a way racial purity was lost on the one hand, on the other unknowingly unforeseen an inter-racial integrity slowly developed. Faulkner stops short of highlighting the tragic side of this secret story and lets it pass, as in the Old Testament, to show how the nation reached its New Testament stage, metaphorically to say, nation with its pets, free-hold coloured citizens, with all their common independence struggle and internecine conflicts ended.

Back home, Hemingway's no more the old man of the sea, but a clean well-lighted home, if not possible, at least a place like that to spend the time at night. The young waiter of the café had no problem, he was for leave 'to go to bed', his family waiting, clean or not, well-lighted or dim-lighted, no matter. India is different, home their moorings, nation and Uncle Sam still not an adequate substitute, so a step behind yet a true democracy of American style, the lack of which Rabindranath too lamented even before India had freed herself from alien rule.

The book will be useful to the students and teachers of English literature, particularly American literature, and researchers in these fields.

R.N. Sarkar

Contents

1

An Idiot's Tale

[1]

A tale told by an idiot full of sound and fury, should we say 'signifying nothing'? William Faulkner's tale discards this part of Macbeth's realization. The tale here signifies, as does Dostoevsky's story of *The Idiot.* This part of Faulkner's novel *The Sound and the Fury* (1929) sets the pattern of his telling, an idiot's tale cannot be well-arranged in a proper time-sequence, which was Macbeth's meaning, time was not in plausible order seemed to him. It was a shocked realization for him that death did not keep up proper time-sequence. It was ordered by some other order, which Shakespeare knew. Faulkner respects Shakespeare's known order, so meaningful.

You are expected to do away with normal course of narrative when an idiot is the narrator, he has to narrate in his own way, you cannot question it; what you can is to follow his role as narrator to get at his meaning, beware, not your own or what you want it to be. The Compson family is an ill-fated American family with a negro house-staff, a family of three sons and a daughter, one parent ailing the other soon to die, oddly homogeneous with an incestuous strain. Though the action covers 1910-28, long eighteen years, no movement to that remarkable extent. The story opens with 7th April 1928, then immediately a shift to 2nd June 1910 and back again to 6th April 1928, and then to April 8, 1928, only a day after. Within these eighteen years whatever the story unfolds happened. Time-shift too frequent and too anomalous to get the picture clear.

The three consecutive dates of the same year, 1928 April 6, 7 and 8 are not relevant to the events on those specific days, neither is the date June 2, 1910 to corresponding the events on that day, alone. Why this is so is because:

> ...I give it to you [Grandfather's watch] not that you may remember time, but that you might forget it now and then for a moment and not spend all your breath trying to conquer it. Because no battle is ever won he said. They are not even fought. The field only reveals to man his own folly and despair, and victory is an illusion of philosophers and fools. (Section June Second, 1910 opening)

Father's gift to the narrator son, then a Harvard scholar, with the above reminder is definitely a variation of Jamesian 'Stream of Consciousness' psychology. But Faulkner's is more a philosophy than psychological interest. The gift-watch is a reminder to Quentin of the unnoticed passage of time otherwise altogether lost. Its tick-tock and position of the hands are only indicator, past present and future are human adjustment, time is free from such constraints. Faulkner has made his characters free from the artificial division of time. Time not definitive, events not time-bound, timing only human choice, relevance, if sought for, is only artificially made to human advantage.

This is done in Faulkner's narrative, in which time remains as free as ever, only narrators' choice makes the difference. Every narrator unlocks their own minds in their own stories, all inside the same family, roles different, all taken together unfolds the family, to which they all belong. Finally the story of Faulkner's own knowledge of a representative 'Yoknapatawpha county family', a white family conglomeration with a lot of black servants inside and white neighbours outside.

[2]

The family itself is full of 'sound', a crybaby the initial source of sound and 'fury' around, a number of negro attendants trying to hush up to relieve an ailing worried mother upstairs in her sick room. The crybaby to some extent deprived of normal power of speech with an extended power of smell is the narrator of the first part. He is the youngest member of the family, a curse to the family itself an idiot, a source of added worries. Three other children, two male, the third a female proved a thorn to their flesh. Benjy (short for Benjamin a Biblical name), earlier name Maury changed for better luck, a born idiot, introduced in the story at the age of five, grown to thirty-three, is posed as the narration. His sound is no speech. His movements, mannerisms repulsive, yet his narrative is a part of the family history, particularly his incestuous closeness to Candance his sister who was an emotional support to his life. Benjy is one problem in the family, Caddy another, undoubtedly more serious. Exactly in the same year (1929) Ivy Compton-Burnett wrote *Brothers and Sisters* to delineate an English home with the possibility of such a problem gradually developing. She only stopped short, Faulkner did not.

The Compsons have only one daughter Caddy; born before Benjy an idiot, in spite of his lack of usual speech capacity his body and mind cannot remain idle and inactive, so his narrative is more a rumination of his mind. Faulkner is assured a free access to that obscure area, the record is not exactly 'Stream of Consciousness' like, the narrative has an external target—the family itself, Caddy is older than Benjy and Quentin than Caddy, and nearer their age and not absolutely a neglected beauty. Mother warns her: "He's too big for you to carry. You must stop trying. You'll injure your back. All of our women have prided themselves on their carriage. Do you want to look like a washerwoman" (p. 40). Caddy and Benjy are from their early years very close to each other, her closeness to Quentin must have been a later development and of a different nature, initially caused by an adolescent preference. Benjy's really out of a loving dependence and Caddy's out of a loving care for love-dependence.

Neither Caddy's nor Benjy's was essentially a 'need'-based dependence save love and protection; Quentin-Caddy closeness was need-based, easily adolescent need (a romance of association innocent though) developing further into inevitability. Benjy's negro-attendant Luster was an officious oppressive type, Dilsey's grandchild, under her constant watch yet not mischief-mended. She was a long-serving negro, head of the servant staff virtually, though a cook. Versh her son a kind of factotum. For Luster's carelessness Benjy once got his hand burnt, timely of course Dilsey detected and spared a major harm. Of the children Jason, the eldest, left the other three early to form a homogeneous group amongst themselves, a little away from parental protection and care amidst negro servants and outside the residential complex on the open-sky lawn gardens and pasture, plenty of space for freedom and mischief. Crossed crib-stage Benjy and Caddy shared a single bed, mother in her sick room, father a 'congregational minister' (p. 90) a disinterested philosopher. They were left alone to servants' care or entirely to themselves.

From porch to pasture—this vast area of the family property is their Kingdom. Benjy the growing boy is the Sound and all of them, negro servants and Caddy, then joined Quentin, all around him the Fury, to hush him, to keep the ailing mother in peace and the house peaceful. Before Quentin joined, Caddy was Benjy's onliest support. Quentin never was. Jason was not in the flock, Mrs Compson claimed him a Bascomb, and repeatedly distinguished him as of a different breed. She may have her own reason, as she constantly lamented his neglected upbringing.

Disley is the second layer of control in the family, with her long service in the family authoritarian among the children and servants (six in number). She duly pointed out the impropriety of sleeping together: "You too big to sleep with folks. You a big boy now. Thirteen years old. Big enough to sleep by yourself in Uncle Maury's room" (p. 27). Rushdie's Moor is a deformed child, bodily overdeveloped for age, to that extent virility developed early. Faulkner's Benjy is not deformed but demented, premature virility left him still closer to Caddy; Luste, Versh these two niggers were engaged constantly to attend him, but more and more he developed beyond their control, and more and more Caddy's attendance and attention were required, and perhaps Caddy too was willing to discharge her unscheduled responsibility. Here is an early scene, Benjy uncontrollable, 'bellering' 'hollering', crying slobbering, and taken out by two negroes to keep peace at home; Caddy returning from school, she met them outside:

Caddy was walking. Then she was running, her book satchel swinging and jouncing behind her.

"Hello, Benjy," Caddy said. She opened the gate and came in and stooped down. Caddy smelled like leaves. "Did you come to meet me", she said. "Did you come to meet Caddy. What did you let him get his hands so cold for, Versh" (pp. 4-5).

So long Benjy was attended by servants, now Caddy was bent on taking him out again. Benjy was trying to say something "What are you trying to tell Caddy", she knew he was unable to speak. She asked mother, 'can't he go out again, Mother. I want him to go with me'. Uncle Maury ruled he must be in, already cold, but "She's in school all day. She needs the fresh air. Run along, Candance" (p. 6).

Caddy pleads: "Let him go, Mother," Caddy said. "Please you know he'll cry."

Maury's interdiction first, then intercession for Benjy to go with Caddy, were calculated steps, to send a letter to Mrs Patterson, when Caddy would not go without Benjy, better they go together to deliver the letter. Though Benjy had less of language and much of sound and slobber he had a keen responsive body and physical senses, all stray and unorchestrated though. He is then Faulkner's right kind of narrator. Caddy could not make out what he wanted to tell her, but he told all the same; only she could not read. She took him out and preferred to take him all to herself "You needn't go, Versh. I'll keep him for a while" (p. 6). Versh was relieved, yet made a pert comment. Benjy described: "Caddy knelt and put her arms around me and her cold bright face against mine. She smelled like trees." Caddy confirmed her special care: 'You're not a poor baby'. Are you. Are you. "You've got your Caddy, Haven't you got your Caddy" (*ibid.*).

Caddy was still not of the age to understand the meaning of Maury's secret letter to Mrs Patterson; she knew only what Maury their uncle (Mother's brother) told her: "Uncle Maury is going to surprise Mrs Patterson with it. We got to give it to her without letting anybody see it...we cant even tell Mother and Father. You know what I think it is. I think it's a surprise for Mother and Father and Mr Patterson both, because Mr Patterson sent you some candy" (p. 7). For Benjy's reason the children and nigger attendants got often to keep outside home on the sprawling pasture with plants and trees around and shallow rills and scalable hills here and there, cowshed, pigpen, cellar and livery stable all on twenty-acre land; among themselves quarrelsome and sportful; if wickedness, that is also freely indulged. One parent always sick, the other indulgently aloof, philosophically intellectual, though both pious. Among the children the eldest Jason even in his playing days keeps a healthy distance though constantly quarrelsomely critical, bitterly Caddy's antagonist. He is a born critic of the family, when grown up a practical responsible member. A healthy American model.

Mr Jason junior Jason's father, head of the family made Caddy his favourite child, he ordered all his children including Jason 'to mind Caddy' for home discipline inside and out, but Jason was not ready to oblige and obey. Caddy a mere school going child then insisted he should obey her. An air of conflict prevailed. Extra fondness for Caddy, so clearly shown estranged Jason further from the whole lot too early in the family. He felt himself further neglected when Quentin, Jason's immediate younger, was sent to Harvard at the cost of Benjy's share of the pasture. Their long-ailing mother, instead of protracted illness, outlived their father. A lady proud of her family afterwards constantly lamented this injustice done to Jason. Proud of Bascomb blood she reminded Jason frequently he was more a Bascomb than Compson. But that could not heal Jason's secretly nursed sore.

Caddy and Benjy grown-up adolescent, one thirteen the other fourteen, are duly in their intimacies not really sibling kind, not merely loving and quarrelsome, but age-induced physical proneness, as suggested in several passages in the story, though because of the author's adopted method of frayed time sequence and frequent shifts requires unshifted attention to note. Benjy's speechless ruminations presented here in his possible recorded language:

> Caddy came to the door and stood there, looked at Father and Mother. Her eyes flew at me, and away. I began to cry. I went bud and I got up. Caddy came in and stood with her back to the wall, looking at me. I went toward her, crying, and she shrank against the wall and I saw her eyes and I cried louder and pulled at her dress. She put her hands out but I pulled at her dress. Her eyes ran.
>
> We were in the hall. Caddy was still looking at me. Her hands were against her mouth and I saw her eyes and cried. We went up the stairs. She stopped again, against the wall, looking at me and I cried and she went on and I came on, crying, and she shrank against the wall, looking at me. She opened the door to her room, but I pulled at her dress and we went to the bathroom and she stood against the door looking at me. Then she put her arm across her face and I pushed at her, crying. (p. 44)

Unlike many modern writers Faulkner in his restrained language describes an insane speechless idiot's carnal impulses, who had only physical senses for response and physical organs for activity, no moral sense or sanity of judgement. For Caddy a bizarre aberration all. A child overindulged and over-confident in her ways, womanhood early ripening, Benjy-Caddy undue special closeness did both of them to grow faster than they could manage. Isolated from parental association all the children grew up among servants, most of the time outside home on the pasture, quarrelling fighting in their unchecked wild ways, intimacies too reckless, Caddy among them most inventive of the kind of sport they would play, always Benjy in tow. Caddy and Quentin landed in the shallow water of the branch, she left her upper garment on the bank and only bodice and drawer on she provoked Quentin to slap, yet threw water whomsoever she could get at.

Jason threatened to tell at home and get her whipped, but she was desperate enough to declare she didn't care. Quentin began to be closer to Caddy, only Jason remained apart their accuser, and critic. Perhaps as the only girl child she found favour with her parents, an overindulgent child often does. Faulkner does here a feat, the most heinous evil to reveal in the most restrained language, a long passage inescapable to justify, Miss Quentin's name and Compson mother's lamenting agony elaborate:

"I wanted you and she get along with one another", she says. "But she has inherited all of the headstrong traits. Quentin's too. I thought at the time, with the heritage she would already have, to give her that name, too. Sometimes I think she is the judgement of both of them upon me."

"They were both that way", she says. "They would make interest with your father against me when I tried to correct them. He was always saying they didn't need controlling, that they already knew what cleanliness and honesty were, which was all that anyone could hope to be taught. Now I hope he is satisfied".

"They deliberately shut me out of their lives," she says. "It was always her and Quentin. They were always conspiring against me. Against you too, though you were too young to realize it. They always looked on you and me as outsiders, like they did your Uncle Maury. I always told your father they were allowed too much freedom, to be together too much. When Quentin started to school, we had to let her go the next year, so she could be with him. She couldn't bear for any of you to do anything she couldn't. It was vanity in her, vanity and false pride. Then when her troubles began I knew that Quentin would feel that he had to do something just as bad. But I didn't believe that he would have been so selfish as to—. I didn't dream that he—" (p. 163).

[3]

Caddy's closeness to Benjy, an idiot without speech, in the early stage was withheld, in her further grown up stage, for a more intimate closeness to Quentin, which their mother noted and warned the father for a check, but he took pseudo-philosophic stand. He sent him to Harvard, gifted him a family souvenir, grandfather's watch, philosophized over it, watch not time, it is our mind that makes—a theory that Faulkner seems to follow in his narrative pattern. We live in Time but Time does not live in life, he quoted "the good Saint Francis that said Little Sister Death, that never had a sister" (p. 49). Father's philosophy formed often a part of Quentin's monologue, perhaps influenced him too, one here on virginity: "And Father said it's because you are a virgin: don't you see? Women are never virgins. Purity is a negative state and therefore contrary to nature. It's nature is hurting you not Caddy and I said That's just words and he said So is virginity and I said you don't know. You cant know and he said yes" (pp. 73-74).

Really it is 'nature' that asserted in Caddy in time as well as in Quentin her brother. Caddy's early developed womanhood created a trouble, in her and in the family, her closeness to Benjy more than its due measure must have confirmed her in future closeness to any male partner from outside, Cherlie is one who demanded her alone to himself and insisted she should leave Benjy home or send him home by a nigger attendant. He knew "He can't talk", but Caddy warned him, "He can see. Don't. Don't" (p. 30). They planned something not to be talked out or seen. Quentin, at Harvard, did yet struggle against himself, brooding on his past and present unethical deeds, memories curiously seeking support, immediately from his father's philosophic interpretations, here a fragment: ...In the South you are ashamed of being a virgin. Boys. Men. They lie about it. Because it means less to women, Father said. He said it was men invented virginity not women. Father said it's like death: only a state in which the others are left and I said. But to believe it doesn't matter, and he said, what's so sad about anything: not only virginity and I said, why couldn't it have been me and her who is unvirgin... (p. 50).

So far as Quentin brother is concerned the incident is not matter much but its incidence is, hogging him to Oedipal remorse. Snatches of his tormented soul float upon the surface of his mind, and give the true character to his author's style, mind reacts not timed by the tick of the clock, it cannot. Faulkner frees the mind from artificial trappings of Time, a thing that it has not. Has not because Father Time is untrapped eternal. Trappings our creation. Quentin recounts in his brooding mind how, no past and present not even future demarcated, cannot be. In this process Caddy is a contrast, Faulkner could provide her with no such monologues as he could with Quentin. Quentin's all fragmentary, he recalls: "Saint Francis talking about his sister. Because if it were just to hell; if that were all of it. Finished. If things just themselves. Nobody else there but her and me. If I could just have done something so dreadful that they would have fled hell except us. I have committed incest I said Father it was I it was not Dalton Ames" (pp. 50-51).

Father 'put the pistol in my hand I didn't'. It was not Dalton Ames. Father wrong. The shot is reserved for him, not due to Dalton Ames. Quentin knew a hard truth from his experience: "when you don't want to do a thing, your body will try to trick you into doing it, sort of unawares" (p. 53). Quentin not Caddy, her body's urge left no scope for such hammer to knock, if at all weakened by headstrong will. She survived the shock but Quentin could not. Caddy grew up an overindulgent young lady, free-spirited, for sometime at home caused envy between Benjy and Quentin, naturally Quentin won, an unworded shock to Benjy. She was expelled from her club, and from school for an offence in the Examination hall. Now herself her own mistress. Her marriage too failed very soon. Left home too, as she vowed she would. She had no self-control, her body-urge overmastered everything else. Already she had Charlie outside, Dalton Ames whom their father suspected, could even others; inside the family Quentin at last. Father's most indulged child spurned mother's warning, her cherished special fondness for Jason offended every other child especially Candance (Caddy), another excuse for slighting her control, among the servants oldest Disley was always on the side of Caddy, sometime aggressively due to her privileged position of old age and long term continued service, and the mistress's prolonged illness and confinement in the sickroom, upstairs.

The nature of quarrel and fight between brother and sister in the family differs from one set to another on the basis of who fights and quarrels with whom. Caddy is always a party, when it is with Quentin it is not real anger but sport, when it is with Jason it is anger, rage and conflict. Benjy is always dependant, sometimes an object of pity, only occasionally an object of annoyance. Caddy's fight with Jason over Benjy's paper dolls destroyed by him was terrible and tearing, Caddy even provoked to take the scissors to slit his throat. Caddy more secretly raging when she suspected Jason was following her movements outside home for ill-chosen guys. She must have accused even mother, because she thought she set Jason on her. Mother's lament a long string of allegations against Father Compson her husband:

> Jason [husband Jason] I must go away you keep the others I'll take Jason and go where nobody knows us so he'll have a chance to grow up and forget all this the others don't love me they had never loved anything with that streak of Compson selfishness and false pride Jason was the only one my head went out to without dread. (p. 65)

Compson Mother's indictment of her husband was true, he innocently by his usual indifference and disinterested philosophy made Quentin's fund of knowledge replete, which like the Tree of Knowledge in Eden bred sin. Quentin recounted what he knew and responded to that knowledge:

> Because so delicate so mysterious Father said. Delicate equilibrium of periodical filth between two moons balanced. Moons he said full and yellow as harvest moons her hips thighs. Outside outside of them always but. Yellow. Feet soles with walking like. Then know that some man that all those mysterious and imperious concealed. With all that inside of them shapes an outward suavity waiting for a touch to. Liquid putrefaction like drowned things floating like pale rubber flabby getting odor of honey suckle all mixed up. (p. 81)

Quentin met Natalie an Italian poor ill-clad unwashed girl, called her sister, took care of her safety and want, she must have been Caddy's age; called sister but behaved subtly otherwise. His over-care was noted by the store owner woman who warned him: "Take my advice and stay clear of them, young man." The girl, otherwise uncommunicative, when alleged 'what did you let him for kiss kiss', told them the truth "I didn't, let him I made him watching me getting mad" (p. 84). It is Quentin's mind talking, "What do you think of that? Red print of my hand coming up through her face like turning a light on under your hand her eyes going bright."

"It's not for kissing I slapped you" (*ibid.*). Yet it remains "a fishbone in your throat", he remembered his father said. "Girl's elbows at fifteen. Father said you swallow like you had a fishbone in your throat what's the matter with you and Caddy across the table not to look at me. It's for letting it be some dam town squirt I slapped you you will will you now I guess you say calf rope" (p. 85). In his mind Natalie and Caddy got mixed up, both sisters, one formal the other real. In spite of father's warning knowledge, just like God's warning against knowledge in Eden, Quentin could not withhold his interest, Natalie-Caddy turned his Eve, who intensified his knowledge-interest, made it irresistible to him. Away from Harvard he enjoyed apparently innocent sport with her in the pastoral scene, sometime in muddy water, as he did with Caddy away from home on the family pasture, their Eden.

Knowledge by itself innocent, but it can lead, even tempt to sin. It did and that resulted in a family tragedy. Natalie's brother Julio could rudely resist, but at home none was there to do, Jason could not act the role of Julio, their culture and position different. At home it was resented, Julio could rudely impose "Git on home", Julio shouted at her. "I beat hell out a you" (p. 90). Culture imposed refinement, father Compson more an emblem of this refinement, so he could hardly restrain Caddy and Quentin except by philosophically imparting knowledge. Mrs Compson too failed. Sin invaded Eden because God left them free unprotected save in their faith in Him, in what He said (decreed). In a human way Compson Father depended on their faith in him, his knowledge of life. Quentin had the benefit of this knowledge most, but it inflamed his curiosity as it did in Eden, so they, in exactly the

Biblical sense, 'Knew', Quentin-Caddy, like he did many other sisters', Natalie a stranger whom he knew in so minute a detail as here:

> ... You know what I was doing? She turned her back I went around in front of her the rain creeping into the mud flattening her bodice through her dress it smelled horrible. I was hugging her that's what I was doing. She turned her back I went around in front of her. I was hugging her I tell you. (p. 86)

It is adolescent love, calf-love, Natalie responded negatively only apparently 'I don't give a damn what you were doing'. Quentin was given the knowledge, so retorted, 'you don't you don't I'll make you give a damn'. 'She hit my hands away I smeared mud on her with my other hand', he could not feel the wet smacking of her hand.... The other boys saw them so scuffling "They saw us from the water first heads and shoulders..." (p. 87). The boys objected, "Take that girl away! What did you want to bring a girl here for?" (*ibid.*).

They took a different path 'curving along beside the water'. 'We lay in the wet grass panting the rain like cold shot on my back. Do you care now do you do you.' Quentin knew his father's warning, though in a form of philosophy psychology included, now just an Eden scene, he knew, so just like Adam repented "My Lord we sure are in a mess get up" (*ibid.*). Only in the Bible not worded. Away from Harvard, a way beyond the river and the bridge across it, the scene is a modern American Eden. The story is adolescent innocent love, very refined in Faulkner's language. Very similar the scene in Compson family pasture, love too innocently quarrelsome, only finally a consanguineous sin. Natalie and Caddy love episodes sisterly, only one consanguineous and sin. The other breach of moral laws and attracts conventional legal procedures, sin is beyond the scope of legal procedure, it does not require law to punish, it has punishment within itself unimposed. Oedipus its example.

[4]

Natalie-episode is a natural adolescent aberration, a breach of law and is immediately punished, put under arrest, charged and realized compensation six and one dollars, and released by the intervention of his friends, Gerald, Shreeve and Spoade. Quentin could take it lightly. But he could not be so light when it was Caddy, it had to pass through many unforeseen, unthought-about hurdles, finally when the crime was committed sin-sense haunted him, he could not help it. Caddy-Quentin relation awfully complex. Almost the whole night they are outside home in their Eden, not in public view of boys to complain, why a girl there to disturb their games! Here is jealousy to fray their cool. Quentin could not forbear to tell Caddy, "did he make then he made you do it let him he was stronger than you and he tomorrow I'll kill him I swear I will father needn't know until afterward and then you and I nobody need ever know we can take my school money we can cancel my matriculation Caddy you hate him don't you don't you" (p. 95).

In Eden there was no Benjy, no onlookers to object to bringing a girl, but in post-Eden life there is jealousy, hatred and even rage. Caddy's 'poor Quentin' is more than a brother, sometime threating to kill her, sometime himself. It is their Eden all to themselves in the dead of night:

> I didn't look back the treefrog didn't pay me any mind the gray light like moss in the tree drizzling but still it wouldn't rain after a while I turned went back to the edge of the woods as soon as I got there I began to smell honeysuckle again I could see the lights on the Court house clock and the glare of town the square on the sky and the dark willows along the branch and the light in mothers windows the light still on Benjy's room and I stopped through the fence and went across the pasture. (p. 98)

He lay on the bank thinking, then not thinking about anything at all when "she came along the bank and stopped I didn't move" (p. 99). He told her, 'its late you go on home'.

She sat on the ground her hands clasped about her knee, 'go on to the house like I told you'. She said, "yes I'll do anything you want me to anything yes" (*ibid.*). At the steps he did not forget to ask her, 'Caddy do you love him now'. Caddy's answer ominous, 'I don't know'. When the same answer repeated to repeated queries, Quentin got infuriated, "I'll kill you do you hear" (p. 100). When urged repeatedly to disclose, Quentin crossed the limited area of jealousy and felt stunned. Caddy's main role in the family is not a myth, real life cannot be myth though myth can be made of it. Faulkner has done it, which has not blurred hard realities of life.

Benjy is an idiot, his subtle human sense blunted, his body develops with all natural urges latent in it, sex healthy body's natural evolution regulated by moral sense and higher engagement, an essential part of humanity. Education in its wider sense for every child is an adjustment system of latent qualities getting potent, this adjustment mechanism begins at least with the birth of a child derived from the kind of marriage of the parents and the kind of adjustment in their conjugal life. An idiot male child bereft of even formal education thrown into an almost constant company of a girl child wilfully made herself unworthy of schooling, idling at home and outside, only attended by a number of negro servants. The lay-out of the story like this is consistent with the developments afterwards. Benjy a booby, if cheated cannot complain in communicable language, Caddy's closeness to Quentin may not have been a calculated game, but it must have worsened his lunacy, more Jackson-worthy than ever.

Quentin was the only child who was sent to Harvard, but his studies, though taken care of, even at the cost of other members' comfort, were interrupted by his intemperate 'sister'-seeking, at home Caddy, in Boston-suburb Natalie, if Shreve accurate, Spoade's surmise not wrong—"Well, bud, I reckon you'll do your girl chasing in Boston after this."

"You damned fool," Shreve said "What the hell do you mean any way, straggling off here, fooling with these damn wops?" (p. 92).

Quentin could not form immediately a reply for all of them, his rescuers, Mrs Bland, Gerald and Shreve Spoade. But had one for himself: away from Natalie "following us with unwinking gaze. Then we ran beside the wall, our shadows running along the wall, and after a while we passed a piece of torn newspaper lying beside the road and I began to laugh again. I could feel it in my throat and I hooked off into the trees where the afternoon slanted, thinking of afternoon and of the bird and the boys in swimming. But I still could not stop it, and then I knew if I tried too hard to stop it I'd be crying and I thought about how I'd thought about I could not be a virgin, with so many of them walking along in the shadows and whispering with their soft girl voices lingering in the shadowy places and the words coming out and perfume and eyes you could feel not see" (p. 93).

This is the kind of adolescent response, semi-sisterly which Caddy must have intensified, as Eve did in Eden and could persuade Adam to disobey God's decree against knowledge (of good and evil), he knew Eve and sin bred sin. Quentin's new role in modern America, thereafter repented and early finished his career, life as well. Natalie-relationship negatively amusing, but Caddy-relationship positively tragic, to himself as well as to the family. Mother lamented the folly of the father, and the father a congregational minister got so much shocked that he turned a whisky-addict to forget everything that could every moment prick his conscience. That was his early end. Quentin came one day bleeding, Shreve had to nurse his wound, he did not know who he had to fight and why. Spoade yet a joking critic: "Oh, the champion of dames. Bud, you excite not only admiration, but horror" (p. 106). They made humour of his position, the Natalie-episode is entirely Faulkner's humour, but in sharp contrast Caddy-episode deepest possible irony. Sophoclean trilogy of *Oedipus Rex* had no scope for humour, modern life alone could provide Faulkner the occasion to explore the prospect.

American society around 1929 cannot be expected to repeat the incestuous birth in a Christian society without modern fun and fury associated with it. Here incest is neither out of a curse (or disobedience to an Oracular prophecy) nor uninvolved in the complex social disgrace and repercussions. Incest here is not curse-imposed eventuality, but a nature-provoked unguarded intimacy. The difference between sin and morality so delicately made by the Compson father made no sense to the mother. She was on the side of morality and did not know the difference it made from sin he accused. He was indulgent enough to the extent of natural human misadventure. Natalie-episode natural breach of human sense of morals, but not incest a sin. Sin unsettled him, his philosophy could not protect him and keep him cool.

The birth of a child remained a living evidence what was going on before, the quarrel began when the Compson Father brought home the child: Father went up there and got it and brought it home and would not tell anything about where she was or anything and mother crying and saying "And you didn't even see him? You didn't even try to get him to make any provision for it?" Father says "No shall not touch his money not one cent of it" and Mother says "He can be forced to by law. He can prove nothing, unless—Jason Compson", she says, "Were you fool enough to tell" (p. 124).

Father Jason had nothing to say to his wife, he only said, "Hush, Caroline", then he sent Jason to help Disley get that old cradle out of the attic. Miss Quentin came home, mother in unknown whereabouts 'cast off by her husband' (p. 125). Father Jason could not restrain her, she raised objection to the baby's accommodation in a room, where, Disley said, 'I put her maw to bed ev'y night'. Mother unwittily disclosed her reason to avoid being "contaminated by that atmosphere. It'll be hard enough as it is, with the heritage she already has" (*ibid.*). Quentin's suicidal death left the Mother further to recount in her mourning the whole history of the sin committed, she was powerless to prevent, constantly in her sick bed. In spite of his harsh criticism of his mother Jason knew her "a Christian forbearing woman like Mother" (p. 136).

Jason felt himself a deprived child, mother too sometimes felt, like that, Quentin was sent to Harvard but his elder he was not, he grew up a practical man with an acute sense of self respect. He could advise but would not hurt mother's sentiment. Sending Benjy to Jackson and leave Caddy and her daughter alone and forget all about it was his suggestion for peaceful life at home. But that appeared cruel to mother and he let her have her way. It is possible Caddy's incestuous tendency was formed and natural repulsion-barrier scaled down by unnatural closeness to a brother in whom moral senses were deadened and to that extent physical senses intensified, Caddy's formed tendency reached a finale with Quentin. Mr Compson sought to bury the sin under a deep layer of silence within home, Caddy away and Quentin dead made it rather easy. When Mr Compson was dead in less than two years daughter Quentin remained the daily reminder of a disaster in the family to the surviving Mrs Compson.

On the very day of Quentin's burial Caddy's secret visit to the grave was the beginning of fresh worries, herself a shameless sin, for the family salt upon sore. Caddy's life obscure, forsaken by husband, where how living life not known, living honest or dishonest a matter of guess, who provided money husband or anybody else not clear. Caddy's visit to Quentin's grave must have been contemplated a secret visit, planned so as to escape eyes, but Jason accidentally met her there when uncle Maury and Mother drove home leaving him at the funeral site, leaving him thus alone he explained to himself as their loveless selfishness. However he saw Caddy just withdrawing, the grave seen at least 50 dollars worth of flowers bestrewn all over. The meeting led to an exchange-deal:

"A fine lot you care, sneaking in here soon as he's dead. But it wont do you any good. Don't think that you can take advantage of this to come sneaking back. If you can't stay on the horse you've got, you'll have to walk", I say, "we don't even know your name at that house". I says "Do you know that? We don't even know your name, you'd be better off if you down there with him and Quentin."

"I know it," she says. "Jason," she says, looking at the grave, "if you'll fix it so I can see her a minute I'll give you fifty dollars" (pp. 129-28).

She rose then to hundred and Jason took the money and fixed one minute only and immediate dispersal. He arranged to take the baby out of home secretly and showed her the baby at the back window of hack and asked immediately to take the train, no more sneaking here around. He reminded her: "I thought you promised her (Mother) you wouldn't come back here. I thought you had more sense than that" (p. 127).

[5]

Jason is an upright American young man, apparently he can be considered a money-grabbing type; but better say a money-earning kind, he is not expected to be Maugham's Lotus Eeater (Wilson). Money to be earned honestly otherwise you cannot honestly spend, his idea is a model American idea, money is for use, one must earn it to keep up a respectable standard. But he sometimes tells harsh truth, as one here:

> We'll, I reckon those eastern Jews have got to live too. But I'll be damned if it hasn't come to a pretty pass when any dam foreigner that cant make a living in the country where God put him, can come to this one and take money right out of an American's pockets. (p. 121)

He would not allow Caddy and Mother to pamper Caddy's daughter, now their keep, to go recklessly free. If that means to divert the excessive flow of money to his pocket he will not hesitate. Caddy and Quentin were pampered children at home, the result is Caddy's daughter, their Mother too apprehends her 'heritage' but cannot act upon it. Jason can and will. If he is called a thief he is a well-meaning upright thief. He accuses his parents of a timely failure: "...because how can the hell can I do anything right, with that dam family and her not making any effort to control her nor any of them like that time when she happened to see one of them kissing Caddy and all next day she went around the house in a black dress and a veil and even Father couldn't get her to say even a word except crying and saying her little daughter was dead and Caddy was fifteen then..." (p. 144).

Father Compson gave Quentin knowledge of a fifteen year old girl, an irony of knowledge—a Biblical theme. This knowledge with Caddy brought about the tragedy of the family, as in Eden it did to whole mankind—sin. Sin here in a worldly way, a little different from the ancient Greek world. Caddy's daughter a well-nursed snake in the family. Jason just wary of this sin-spell. Two lives already lost, fury's claim. Jason is a natural critic of everything around, home and the immediate world around including even himself. His mother understands things but often carried by softness of heart too often. Her brother Maury exploits this softness of the heart. Jason does not like him at all, a hanger-on in the family. Jason legally enjoys the benefit of fluctuating money market. He serves in a country store in which his mother had a thousand dollars share, the Store head Earl always takes exception to Jason's spirit of freedom, often threatens to fire him but his independent adequate service keeps clear of this threat, his repartees are of Congreve-Wilde tradition, more evident in Earl's raging dialogue with him, his rage always transferred to ready wit, one scrap here:

> "You go home to dinner?"
>
> "I had to go to the dentist..."
>
> "You might have told me," he says. "I expected you back right away."
>
> "I'll trade you this tooth and give you ten dollars to boot, any time", I says. "Our agreement was an hour for dinner," I says, "and if you don't like the way I do...." (pp. 142-43)

Faulkner along with severed time-linkage method of narrative introduces sparkling vernal grace, mainly through Jason, his metaphors too bear witness to a rare glow of his mind not acquired by education. This power made him perhaps a modern man firm in his judgement, less overpowered by emotion end passion, which appeared sometime on occasion rude, Disley must have seen it when Luster was denied the benefit of a Pass for the band show, instead of charity he preferred it thrown into the stove fire. A little too mercenary and thrifty. Love quite regulated, tenderness of feelings judgement-guided. More intellectual than emotional. This side of his character often offended his mother and he too was unready to allow indulgence and indiscipline. His visit to Lorraine regulated by principle of conduct and decency. He is not ready to hold a person's religion against him, but holds the person responsible for unkindly repulsion. Faulkner's Jason the neatest approach to Shaw's John Tanner so far as in a mercantile society like modern America possible.

For a man like that Ben a booby can expect no compassion, neither Caddy, nor her daughter, who all violate all natural laws of social decency, he thinks Ben for Jackson island out of social order, Caddy and her daughter better elsewhere outside home, just to allow others to live in peace—almost a Shavian stand. Mother at home cannot accept it. She is for accommodation inside, a sharp contrast. Jason is not inconsiderate, but afraid of chaos, mother's consideration and kindness created chaos, and still more of it awaited. He was only to resist further evil. Uncle Maury almost a nuisance in spite of his decent standard English in which he wrote him a confidential letter, better with the Pattersons where he had already dropped a bait for Mrs Patterson. The fun is Mr Patterson preempted the delivery. Uncle Maury is not Uncle Toby, he is a dud, in spite of his chaste English.

The difference between mother and son is clear in relation to Miss Quentin, now their protégée; mother for soft dealing Jason for strictly disciplined dealing; but the young lady was born of serious disruption of discipline: Mother made no secret of it, though father wanted complete 'hush' over it when he was alive: "But she has inherited all of the headstrong traits. Quentin's too. I thought at the time, with the heritage she would already have, to give her that name, too. Sometimes I think she is the judgement of both of them upon me" (p. 163). Not only the difference was sharp but also the long drawn blunder was out from their disagreement long after. Jason pointed out: "You've got Ben to depend on". Mother missed the point. They allowed Ben to depend on Caddy, even when Caddy thirteen they slept on the same bed, they grew up together too closely, his carnal propensity unchecked for lack of healthy development of moral senses made him more intimately dependent on Caddy. Jason suggested check at that stage, otherwise Ben's accommodation in Jackson island. They had ultimately to send him to Jackson, but not before they were compelled:

> I don't reckon he even knew what he had been trying to do, or why Mr Burgess knocked him out with the fence picket. And if they'd just sent him on the Jackson while he was under the ether he'd never have known the difference. But that would have been too simple for a Compson to think of. Not half complex enough. Having to wait to do it at all until he broke out and tried to run a little girl down on the street with her own father looking at him.... (pp. 164-65)

The same dependence mired the healthy relationship between Quentin and Caddy. Mother took note of only Quentin-Caddy closeness, missed the seed and counted the seedlings: "They deliberately shut me out of their lives" she says. "It was always her and Quentin" (p. 163). Father Compson assured the mother philosophically, expecting his children, particularly Quentin—whom he gave knowledge of things—, to observe Christian ethics: "they didn't need controlling, that they already knew what cleanliness and honesty were" (*ibid.*). They had knowledge, but not really 'cleanliness and honesty', knowledge includes both 'good and evil', the Tree of Knowledge to bear both the kinds in Eden, God only knew, Father Compson did not. Caddy's early knowledge Quentin shared, a secret compact. Finally Caddy had to leave protected Eden, only leaving a 'note' behind. A chapter closed another opened.

[6]

The Compsons are a kitchen—controlled family, all the negro servants, as many as six, are really under control of the longest serving negro woman named Disley, three other members of her family are also there to serve, her grandchild Luster engaged to attend Benjy the idiot. Disley is the kitchen in charge. Disley asserts her power frequently interfering in the family's dealings with daughters, Caddy first then her daughter Quentin. Jason resents her interference and makes a characteristic comment: "That's the trouble with nigger servants, when they've been with you for a long time they get so full of self-importance that they're not worth a dam. They run the whole family" (p. 130).

Jason had immediate proof, ill-reputed Caddy barred against entry home now sneaking around to see her daughter, her re-entry could be more scandalous in the neighbourhood. She left home of her own accord. He warned Disley to act, but she argued: "I like to know whut's de hurt in letting dat po chile see her own baby. If Mr Jason was still here hit ud be different" (*ibid.*). A bit of explanation of the problem: Benjy's wild furies at her sight, provoked her still harsh a word: "You's a cold man. Jason, if man you is. I thank de Lawd I got mo heart dan dat, even ef hit is black".

She created more problems by ignoring Jason's authority, flouting it claiming often she raised them all. When Caddy's baby was brought home she eagerly acknowledged the pleasure of raising it too. In spite of her emotional response to Christianity she would hardly understand their folly, their sin and blatant violation of discipline, and disobedience. Her interference is a sort of foolish indulgence to immoral tendencies, which duly lent incentive to evil. Faulker seems to trace moral graph of modern American life, at the centre a family, in spite of his adopted quirks of frequent time-shift. Even an upright model American like Jason faulted in fraudulently grabbing another's money though as a restraining measure to check proliferation of evil. Jason explains his stand: "But to have been robbed of that which was to have compensated him for the lost job, which he had acquired through so much effort and risk, by the very symbol of the lost job itself, and worst of all, by a bitch of a girl" (p. 191).

It is Caddy's daughter who grew under the overindulgence of grandmother and Disley at home and outside by the overflow of money from her mother predictably ill-earned. Jason accuses Caddy's daughter as a great source of evil: "I wouldn't lay my hand on her. The bitch that cost me a job, the one chance I ever had to get ahead, that killed my father and is shortening my mother's life every day and made my name a laughing stock in the town..." (p. 189). Faulkner takes note of the other side of the deal: "Of his niece he did not think at all, nor of the arbitrary valuation of the money. Neither of them had entity or individuality for him for ten years: together they merely symbolized the job in the bank of which he had been deprived before he ever got it" (p. 190).

The story has a complex development, half known outside and half concealed even in the filmy figuration of the author's minute particulars, a trick that claims close attention to appreciate. Jason is the personal constant witness to covert sin allowed to flourish that destroyed not only his prospect but turned the whole family to a sin-loaded sinking ship. Neither the mother of the child nor the child herself obeyed discipline of devout life, they cheated their school and home as well, yet adopted a profligate style of expensive life. At her mother's age she turned a regular truant, cheated her grandmother herself signing the Progress Report for her, only a Professor's telephonic call to grandmother disclosed her deceit. It is a model of her unregulated mischief, veiled pursuit of evil. Benjy and Luster saw her with a red-tie stranger at night in the pasture, a show man whom "Luster approached if he could get inside: Luster came back. Wait, he said. Here. Don't go over there. Miss Quentin and her beau in the swing yonder" (p. 30). He marked, "He had a red tie" (p. 31).

Jason took up the responsibility of disciplining Miss Quentin, the ailing mother wanted to be relieved of worries but wanted Jason to be a loving uncle. But he wanted to impose discipline all on a sudden on a girl already outrageously steeped in lawlessness, obviously conflict arose. Her mother too sent her money much more than she needed, though through Jason by cheque, and always doubted she was properly looked after. Her letter to Jason is an evidence (p. 120). But she hardly cared for her proper schooling, at least not as much as for her comfort. Quietly she fell into low company, in Jason's language 'drummers' and 'squirts': Really she had already picked up a show man with a red tie then performing in the neighbourhood.

Caddy, since her visit only for a sight of her baby daughter, kept sneaking around and met Jason at his Store to plead for her daughter. Now Quentin is in the grave, so shamelessly pleaded for re-entry into the family to be with her daughter, but Jason is a practical man, he believed 'once a bitch always a bitch', Quentin gone but Benjy was there. Even when Father was willing Caddy back he resisted. Mother still argued in favour of Caddy's coming home. He believed it would then turn to a pig-pen. Caddy finally appealed: "Don't lie to me now. About her. I wont ask to see anything. If that isn't enough. I'll send more each month. Just promise the she'll—that she—you can do that. Things for her. Be kind to her. Little things that I cant, they wont let.... If you will get Mother to let me have her back, I'll give you a thousand dollars" (p. 131).

Caddy's daughter also came to visit him obviously for money and mother's letter, more for money. She could not trust him. His explanation and information failed to convince her. When Jason turned a few steps away to the front to attend a customer she dipped her hand into the drawer and rummaged out the letter and annextures. It is quite unmannerly, her need for money so urgent that she forgot everything else. A heated debate followed. She asked, "Is there some money in it?... She said she would send me some money. She promised she would. Give it to me" (p. 133). A significant query: "What do you want with money?" Jason gave her the letter. She said she borrowed money from a girl, he would not give her more than ten dollars, she haggled for fifty, she thought it was no less, but he insisted either ten or nothing. Apparently he told a lie. He deceived even his mother, asked her to burn a cheque valued two hundred dollars, he meant a hoax. He knew money sent in mother's name would surely make her more indulgent to Quentin and allow her to spend more. And Mother was more soft-hearted than she should have been, really to anybody's good.

She did not like Miss Quentin's disobedience, neither could she appreciate Jason's rudeness, nor could control Quentin.

Though Jason took her in his car to school in the morning she escaped lessons and fled for a ride abroad with that red-tie stranger. Jason in spite of his arduous efforts even during his duty hours hunted them to see who it was, but failed. He visited home thrice even in the face of his partner employer Earl's obvious dissatisfaction and irritating comments. At dinner Quentin absent, Disley waited for her and would not mind Jason, she delayed dinner for Quentin until he insisted he would be out to the Store if any further delay. At supper that evening he wanted Mother and Quentin at the table. Disley always on the side of Quentin, she would not come. Unwilling Quentin was persuaded by Mother. Disley's comment justifies Jason's view: Disley came back to the door, "Come on," she says, "fo you kin think up some mo devilement. You just trying yoself tonight" (p. 160).

The supper table turned into a heated quarrel scene, Mother too arbiter of peace, always repeating 'I wanted you and she to get along with one another', 'I wish you could be kinder to her'. But Quentin practically revolted. Mother had already been reported by Quentin innocently 'she did not go to school, only "went for a car ride with one of the boys this afternoon and you followed her" (p. 163), she held out an accusing finger at Jason at the same time. She in her revolt took grandmother on her side, "Grandmother Grandmother. Why does he treat me like this, Grandmother?" (p. 162).

She never said a word to restrain her, even when she accused incorrectly "Whatever I do, its your fault," she says. "If I'm bad, it's because I had to be. You made me...." She ran up the stairs and the door slammed. Still the Mother pleaded, "She did not go to school today", and hardly took note of Jason's question, "How do you know?", rather insisted "she didn't go to school today", on the next page noted. Without restraining her she spoke of her 'heritage' as if that was enough for indulgence, and pleaded her inability to control them, including this child. When she found that Jason could not be brought in line with her tolerant treatment of Quentin without making her repent her follies, she duly fell upon the line of self-reproach and her failed attempt at protecting Jason's interest:

> "You say things like that to hurt me," she says. "I deserve it though. When they began to sell the land to send Quentin to Harvard I told your father that he must make an equal provision for you. Then when Herbert [Caddy's husband] offered to take you into the bank I said, Jason is provided for now, and when all the expense began to pile up and I was forced to sell our furniture and the rest of the pasture, I wrote her at once because I said she will realize that she and Quentin have had their share and part of Jason's too and that it depends on her now to compensate him. I said she will do that out of respect for her father. I believed that then. But I'm just a poor old woman: I was raised to believe that people will deny themselves for their own flesh and blood. It's my fault. You were right to reproach me." (p. 164)

The above is essentially her self-justification, which does not relate to the present situation; she trying to stigmatize Jason's following her the whole day and justify Quentin's not attending school and having a car ride with a boy, encouraged the girl on her adopted course and discouraged Jason's course of correction. She never said a word clearly against Quentin's uncivil manners and outrageous revolt against a person in respectable position in the family and outside, her grandmother's eldest child. Everything she told her she uncritically believed and virtually she wished Jason to compromise. She did not know what Luster a nigger boy every night saw, her climbing down a pear tree within the reach of her back window. If Jason told her she would not believe, rather believed what Quentin would have told her. Only she could not clearly tell Jason that she did not believe him. She had chosen rather a course of laboured self-justification concluded by a devout tag of 'Judgement'.

[7]

Jason is all along in a critical role. His language is often beyond Mother's head. Every character in the story is subjected to his critical judgement, Faulkner makes him his eye and ear and withdraws his own save only Jason's own situation and his failings beyond his perceptions. Mother must have thought she and Quentin required relief after so unpleasant a situation created by Jason's over jealous corrective methods. Next morning a new scene opened. Disley preparing breakfast, it was Jason's day of rest as everyone's except the household staff. As usual Jason would have everyone at the breakfast table. Mother came, Quentin was awaited, Disley would not have Quentin early awakened. Mother too wanted to avoid Quentin's presence, but Jason insistent. Jason could easily realize Mother and Disley had never taught her manners courtesy and obedience. What they wanted with her they did not know, one shrewdly and the other openly only wanted to shield her from apparent rudeness, even if corrective. What Jason earlier suggested, to keep them away, would have been prudence. Both mother and daughter perverted and perverting.

When in this family she cannot be allowed to tarnish the good name of the family and create an air of open enmity—this is Jason's stand. Mother's veiled support and self-justification, more irritating when meandering, are provocative to American straightness. So he was already disturbed in mind. He wanted Quentin at the table, Mother to avoid it trickily, Disley openly. She began to shout at Quentin's door: "Now, now," Disley said. "What kin happen? I right here. I aint gwine let him hurt her. Quentin," she said, raising her voice, "dont you be skeered, honey, I'se right here" (p. 175). It is like Rushdie's India-defendant Olga Volga the darkie defends Quentin. On the stair Mother and son harrying for the key. A funny fury. Mother wailing 'in my own house!'

The door opened, swang inward. Jason stood guard outside and allowed mother in, the bird fled already, but the mess is there, the evidences of "crude and hopeless efforts to feminize it but added to its anonymity, giving it that dead and stereotyped transience of rooms in assignation houses" (p. 176). The window open, the pear tree close beside. Disley's remark, "Dar now", ... "Didn't I told you she all right?" Fun cannot continue long in a story dealing with 'Fury' too, though it can a little longer in the servants' quarter, as here: "Me and

Benjy seed her climb out de window last night. Didn't us, Benjy?" "You did?" "We sees her doing hit ev'y night", Luster said. "Climb right down dat pear tree" (p. 178).

Jason immediately out of home, only they saw him telephone, breakfast remained uneaten. Mother took to bed, her litany of helplessness and 'judgement', and a Bible on one side of her bed, the usual scene left behind. Disley and Luster could uninterruptedly attend their special Easter service along with Benjy. Complete silence at home when Jason was twenty miles away meeting the law officers, Sheriff and all, for the recovery of his money, three thousand dollars. The two concurrent scenes, an Easter Sermon a serio-jocular scene and Jason's pleading for Police help and personally pursuing the absconder a sad failure, are together a sharp contrast.

The Sheriff politely but strictly told him he could not help him, a girl fled out of tyranny at home vengefully with a sum of money, a failure in family adjustment. A big sum holding at home also irregular, the Police unwilling to interfere. When he impulsively tried to find the absconder and her red-tie show-man it created more trouble and aggravated his headache, car too required refilling; all these made him more ill-tempered in queries at the already dismantled show-site. He was saved from further trouble by the owner of the troupe who reported:

> "I told him to get the hell out of these, both them", "I wont have nothing like that in show. I run a respectable show with a respectable troupe." Jason asked, "you don't know where they went ?" To which he answered: "No. I don't want to know. No member of my show can pull a stunt like that. You her...brothe?" (p. 194)

Jason completely frustrated took the road back home, now unable to drive, his head hurt, long outside home on a Sunday, hired a negro driver for four dollars. When very near home he saw Luster with Disley and Ben driving the surrey close to an accident. He promptly sprang out of car, crossed road and fisted Luster's head and took the rein in time. "He jerked Queene back and jumped down" (p. 199); warned "Get to hell on home. If you ever cross that gate with him again, I'll kill you". The story comes to an end.

[8]

Faulkner delineates the degeneration of an American family in the South, which could once boast of a governor and three generals, in spite of an intricate time shift. Inside the family itself a model of American Common man is upreared, his spirit of self-independent freedom, a Common man's sense of justice and good life. The Sound and Fury of the home made him feel suffocated and turn critical. His money-making, apparently sly method, cannot be completely isolated from a good will to drive a check upon too lavish a perverted life that immediately did greater harm to the standard of the family itself, caused loss of life and bred sin.

Caddy and her daughter are better out of home for the peace of others inside. They wanted sin-nursing desperate freedom, they had better enjoy it outside and get crushed under its own weight, why should they force others to succumb? It is no American concept of personal freedom. It is a Free State in the sense your freedom is okay but not at the cost of another's freedom of comfortable life. The story comes to a reasonable end. Caddy is out already, that her own choice, now her daughter out, her choice was a red-tie showman fired by the owner to keep his troupe free from scandal. Now Mother should not repent. Both Father and Mother were unpractical unrealistic good people. American approach to even Faith is realistic. Jason asked a relevant question "You did not resurrect Christ, did you?" Mother did not react, because she could not understand the question.

Disley was going to attend their special Easter Service. If one is to appreciate Christ's resurrection one must know how Christ attained this power, only un-understanding emotional or customary observance cannot ensure human improvement. Disley stood guard against any harm to Quentin from Jason, but did she guard against her perverted life almost open knowledge? Mother too, knowing full well her evil tendencies, did not try to correct her. If it is explained as love, it is at least expected it should not be given a human colour, far less a religious colour. Jason is clear he must not hold a man's religion against him. It is a plain human approach. American life does not allow anybody to cause another's inconvenience. So Jason asked them to accommodate Ben to Jackson. They had to finally.

Disley shed tears at the Easter Sermon, a mere cunning emotional approach to Calvary, the priest made a drama; at home she pampered sin, all against the Gospels. Father relied upon his children's 'cleanliness and honesty', yet made the first mistake, knowledge of evil before they had knowledge of good. Mother's Bascomb-pride unaccounted for. If Uncle Maury is a specimen her pride is hollow. He is a sort of holy cow in the Compson family. Mother's another pampered protégé. Whoever enjoyed Mother's love grew up a poison tree much to human harm. Mother pleaded her ignorance of modern freedom of women and their ways, virtually an excuse for her indulgence to her daughter and granddaughter. Jason is not a man to condone it. Their sins visited upon her, it is true she rarely enjoyed health, and always complaining. Her curious sympathy for all those who sought to be indulgent offended Jason. For all her protestations of love and thankfulness "you are only hope. Every night I thank God for you" (p. 126), he had reason to doubt when Mother and Maury left in a car leaving him in the drizzle exhorting "you can come in with somebody, they'll be glad to give you a lift", "Little they cared how wet I got, because then Mother could have a whole of a time being afraid I was taking pneumonia" (p. 127).

Jason did not like Uncle Maury, his father too did not but could conceal it, Jason could not and did not. In the story Jason is the standard by which every other is measured up, where he apparently faulted it was mainly due to forced involvement in others' follies or undue indulgence. After all he is a human being with a limited power of endurance. Mother created, by her true or pretended softness and proclaimed innocence, the house a mad house, a scene of the Sound and the Fury. Jason a true American to live a peaceful life. His language has attained an unusual shapness, most of which were beyond her head. Jason speaking to her mother on the night of Quentin's breaking away from home and Mother's replies together in view of the next morning's detection clearly revealing:

"Do you think I need any man's help to stand on my feet?" I says "Let alone a woman that cant name the father of her own child."

> "Jason," she says.
>
> "All right," I says. "I didn't mean that. Of course not."
>
> "If I believed that were possible, after all my suffering."
>
> "Of course it's not", I says. "I didn't mean it."
>
> "I hope that at least is spared me," she says,
>
> "Sure it is," I says. "She's too much like both of them to doubt that."
>
> "I couldn't bear that," she says.
>
> "Then quit thinking about it," I says. "Has she been worrying you any more about getting out at night?" (p. 164)

The old lady told him, no, she studied after she locked the door and she saw the light. When Jason asked how she could be sure she was studying she brushed it aside "I don't know what else she'd do in there alone. She never did read any".

She knew next morning, yet one had reason enough to doubt that she did. Jason back home in the evening exhausted yet alert enough to avert an accident at the door step almost. What happened thereafter let one write a short story if one likes, Faulkner would not, though he can write a good number reviving therein his Yoknapatawpha reminiscences.

2

The Scarlet Letter: A Puritan Parable

[1]

Dickens's contemporary in New England, Hawthorne deals with a sort of Exodus and new settlement in a sort of Canaan, England their Egypt, from there to the assured land in the early modern age around 1630. Over two hundred years later Hawthorne recounts a story of that early age in the new settlement where they came with a Bible in one hand and a sword in another. Hawthorne's remote progenitor did. The Puritan saga of the family gave him a close view of a tradition they established in their new home, the story of *The Scarlet Letter* is a skeleton that tumbled out the cupboard of that olden time, the author only gave it a new life. How the skeleton came into his hand he describes in his 'Introductory'. It was a neglected personal document of Salem Custom House Surveyor Jonathan Pue of Governor Shirley's time. During his stay at the Manse Hawthorne, while burrowing the rubbish in one corner, found a small package, in which he found the Scarlet letter. 'A' designed and embroidered on a fine piece of cloth and a roll of paper with a skeleton account of a woman Hester Prynne by name.

Hawthorne's Salem Custom House account recalls Lamb's South sea House account of his cronies of the establishment. He is only a little more exhaustive with a fling of humour more amusing and more to purpose. Style too differs from Lamb's, rather reminds one of 18th century Fielding's style, a little lavishly metaphoric. His instant response a model:

> ... With his own ghostly voice, he exhorted me, on the sacred consideration of my filial duty and reverence towards him—who might reasonably regard himself as my official ancestor—to bring his mouldy and moth-eaten lucubrations before the public.... (p. 26)

Further how he had got to people his story world: "My imagination was tarnished mirror. It would not reflect, or only with miserable dimness, the figures with which I did my best to people it. The characters of the narrative would not be warmed and rendered malleable, by any heat that I could kindle at my intellectual forge..." (p. 27).

Hawthorne had more acutely Lamb's experiences in the Counting House, and he in the Custom House. Lamb felt he had grown to the wood of his desk and the wood had entered into his soul, Hawthorne felt dry and dead. Now release, not in Lamb's myths and metaphors unaccustomed unlimited freedom in 'The Superannuated Man', is not exactly an unblemished joy of freedom but a shock of 'rusty intellectual machinery' requiring time to refurbish. He took time, like Shakespeare, to enflesh the bones of his find, endue them with blood, heart with sensibility; and finally to place them as living men and women in their society and their natural background. The world that was thus created was a world of the first batch of Puritans in New England towards the close of seventeenth century, raw in the zeal of their faith and flushed in the hegemony of their new conquest of a heathendom; so flawed in every detail.

The story draws to a lesson that bespoke a volume against the rawness and rankness of their deal, out of a faulty idea of Puritanism. The story duly serves as a Parable, which does not, of course, arrest its luxuriant human side in its natural richness. Nature too not less bounteous. Nature never withdraws her bounty for man's sin, if it is. But man's society does, though in the name of faith or discipline of law. A Puritan and a Methodist are one cousin to the other. Hawthorne's *Scarlet Letter* and George Eliot's *Adam Bede* are almost in the same order, though their genius different, time and milieu too. Weal or ill life has its own course though it is constrained by law and faith. Hetty Sorrel and Hester committed almost the same sin, a child's birth beyond wedlock, Human laws later changed on either side of the Atlantic to accommodate the vagaries of life less cruelly. This accommodation began long long before since the dawn of life, which ultimately shaped into what we call civilization.

One such mechanism of accommodation at a much later stage was marriage to make natural man and woman relation healthy, marriage is after all a match which requires selection, which woman could match which man. In India all negotiated marriages target that. It is a fulfilment. Still in the English word wifman (woman) there is an echo of the earlier stage 'man's wife', man's choice of a woman, bond of marriage could be precluded. Civilization imposed a love bond and fidelity, for such a prospect selection must needs be scientifically and ethically sound.

Hester's sin had its seed in a wrong selection, George Eliot's Dorothea could escape that sin mainly for Casaubon's early death, society too different, character herself too, then finally Ladislaw too of a different character. Dr Chillingworth committed the same sin Dr Casaubon did, and Hester made the same mistake Dorothea made. This mistake led to a sin. Mr Dimmesdale is not Ladislaw, whose Victorian society, and Dorothea's widowhood, did not forbid a fresh alliance. Hawthorne harks back to Elizabethan age and the first British settlement in Boston wood and wasteland, all adventurers like Defoe's Robinson Crusoe, with a zeal of their faith carefully guarded against adulteration from inside and out.

[2]

Pue-written those six pages mouldered over the years Hawthorne must have had the skeleton of his story there. The story in this novel is professedly his own making. Hester's genealogy his own construction, she is given a heraldric descent, to suit her independent chivalric spirit, tall stature and handsome appearance and finally her romantic passion. More a Renascence heroine than Dorothea's Victorian soberness and blooming peace. The two Queens' representations of their time as it were. Hester's sin with her majestic appearance on the scaffold is a high romance, which Hawthorne's tricks of metaphors and sharp contrast in lush detail bring home to a sensitive heart. Her misery of a sin, scarlet letter its symbol to bespeak it, by its contrast seems to intensify her personal romantic glamour. The whole community of Puritans, high and low, by their dull purity cult, and external display of hate can neither bedim her personal glow nor can add a whit to their personal dignity:

> The young woman was tall, with a figure of perfect elegance, on a large scale. She had dark and abundant hair, so glossy that it threw off the sunshine with a gleam, and a face which, besides being beautiful from regularity of feature and richness of complexion, had the impressiveness belonging to a marked brow and deep black eyes. She was lady-like, too, after the manner of the feminine gentility of those days; characterized by a certain state and dignity, rather than by the delicate, evanescent, and indescribable grace, which is now recognized as its indication.... (p. 39)

Her spectators around and above in the gallery were "dimmed and obscured by a disastrous cloud, were astonished, and even startled, to perceive how her beauty shone out, and made a halo of the misfortune and ignominy in which she was enveloped" (*ibid.*).

Hawthorne paints a time of Puritan justice in their new settlement in New England, but his accused heroine scales far beyond history in her appeal and seems to bedim the wisdom of her accusers, hers is a human sin and theirs apparent wisdom inhuman, and ultimately the whole piece a wisp of irony, only streak of humour lithely twining it inside and around to keep the romance in its proper shape. Hester is a heroine of a romance more than Rowena and Rebecca. Her marriage itself a romantic misadventure. Herself, accused of iniquity, exposed to public shame on a scaffold in a marketplace; a subject of aghast Medieval torture. Hetty Sorrel lacked Hester's majesty, her other qualities, her sin was more repugnant with a child-murder-tag, while Hester's three-month old child under the same open sky so loved by the mother nestled on her arms made to share the same pedestal of shame, a Papist could have been reminded of 'the image of Divine Maternity' (p. 41), should have at least softened the measure of justice.

Hester's sins is a sequel to another sin, sin of incompatible marriage like Dorothea's with Casaubon. Chillingworth fresh released from Heathen captivity is now among the crowd of spectators around Hester with baby on the scaffold. Her husband described, a white man beside an Indian red lately his captor master, "by a seeming careless arrangement of his heterogeneous garb, he had endeavoured to conceal or abate the peculiarity, it was sufficiently evident to Hester Prynne, that one of this man's shoulder rose higher than the other. Again at the first instant of perceiving that thin visage and slight deformity of the figure..." (p. 44) she seemed to shudder and take care to protect herself and the baby, as if he were her evil spirit.

The skeletal story of her separation from this husband and some other necessary details came out of conversation between Chillingworth and a knowledgeable spectator in the crowd, two passages here to speak out:

> You say truly. I am a stranger, and have been a wanderer, sorely against my will. I have met with grievous mishaps by sea and land, and have been long held in bonds among the heathen folk, to the southward; and am now brought hither by this Indian, to be redeemed out of my captivity....
>
> Truly, friend, and methinks it must gladden your heart, after your troubles and sojourn in the wilderness...to find yourself, at length in a land where iniquity is searched out, and punished in the sight of rulers and people; as here in our godly New England. Yonder woman, Sir, you must know, was the wife of a certain learned man, English by birth, but who had long dwelt in Amsterdam [it was then safe sanctuary for separatists and Puritans—1608], whence, some

> good time agone, he was minded to cross over and cast in his lot with us of the Massachusetts. To this purpose, he sent his wife before him, remaining himself to look after some necessary affairs. Marry, good Sir, in some two years, or less, that woman has been a dweller here in Boston, no tidings have come of this learned gentleman, Master Prynne. (p. 44)

The local informant did not know that he was speaking to learned Mr Prynne. Chillingworth's immediate response was not at all sympathetic, his face a 'bitter smile', then with no less bitter a gibe, a smile played upon his lips: "The learned man should come himself to look into the mystery" (p. 45), he means the mystery of this child's birth. He missed altogether the deplorable present predicament of the woman he loved and married, and the unlucky baby's sharing its mother's misery, and the mother's unsupported life alone among strangers. At first sight after about two years of separation from a loved object, however iniquitous the act may be, in a miserable condition of infamy and mental torture should have been one of shock and compassion. But Chillingworth felt bitterly amused. His interview in Hester's prison cell, purported to her and babe's cure, his stay there needed for the settlement of ransom with the sagamores of the Indians.

[3]

Hester-Chillingworth relationship is more complex than Dorothea-Casaubon relationship. Chillingworth and Hester as characters are more complex though representations of two centuries agone. Their relationship involves double sins, Chillingworth is as much a sinner as Hester, but he is not repentant though intellectually understands where he sinned. His seeming repentance is an intellectual verbose. He agreed he had sinned: "It was my folly, and thy weakness. I—a man of thought—the bookworm of great libraries—a man already in decay, having given my best years to feed the hungry dream of knowledge—what had I to do with youth and beauty like thine own! Misshapen from my birth-hour, how could I delude myself with the idea that intellectual gifts might veil physical deformity in a young girl's fantasy! Men call me wise. If sages were ever wise in their own behoof, I might have foreseen all these..." (pp. 52-53).

He admits his bookish dead knowledge could hardly extinguish his desire for a 'household fire' to remove "the chill of a lonely life", and acknowledged, "Hester, I drew thee into my heart, into its inmost chamber, and sought to warm thee by the warmth which thy presence made there!" (p. 53). But Hester had already told him she did not feel warm: "thou knowest that I was frank with thee. I felt no love, nor pretended any". The exchanges ensued from their interview in her prison cell, where Chillingworth told Hester if revenge were his wont to what extent he could go: the measures were then cold bloodedly calculated—almost like Heathcliff in the early 19th century could have planned: "Dost thou know me so little, Hester Prynne? Are my purposes wont to be so shallow? Even if I imagine a scheme of vengeance, what could I do better for my object than to let thee live—than to give thee medicines against all harm and peril of life—so that the burning shame may still blaze upon thy bosom?" (p. 52).

Hester is neither Dorothea nor Catharine Earnshaw, she critically represented her husband frustrated in all his efforts at professions of love for her: "Thy acts are like mercy. But thy words interpret thee as terror!" (p. 54). His threat and decision to disclose in no way his identity as her husband and unflaggingly to pursue the course of revenge upon the undisclosed interloper, as Shakespeare's witch pursued the unobliging wife's sailor husband: "I will drain him dry as hay/ Sleep shall, neither night or day/ Hang upon his pent-house lid;/ He shall live a man forbid...."

Hester would not disclose the partner of her sin though it meant for her to bear the burden of her sin alone; she willingly took the burden because she loved him. The partner also was not Lady Chatterley's lover Mellors, neither was Chillingworth Sir Clifford who loved Constance and was yet ready to accommodate her even with that unborn burden of sin and would not agree to a divorce considering Mellors' low position. He was hell-bent for witchy hunt, but determined not to encounter the dishonour "that besmirches the husband of a faithless woman", further reasoned, "it is my purpose to live and die unknown. Let, therefore, thy husband be to the world as one already dead.... Recognize me not, by word, by sign, by look! Breathe not the secret, above all, to the man thou wottest of. Shouldst thou fail me in this, beware! His fame, his position, his life will be in my hands. Beware!" (p. 54).

Hawthorne depicts a world of Puritan extremism. He got her to swear and finished with a banter and a curious smile: "I leave thee alone, alone with thy infant, and the scarlet letter! How is it, Hester? Doth thy sentence bind thee to wear the token in thy sleep? Art thou not afraid of nightmares and hideous dreams?" (p. 55). Hester took offence to his meaningful smile and felt more disgusted than she ever did: "Art thou like the Black Man that haunts the forest round about us? Hast thou enticed me into a bond that will prove the ruin of my soul?" (*ibid.*).

Hester's history of long seven years is a long-drawn tiringly eventful history, in the Puritan settlement of New England under the Pastorship of Dimmesdale, a learned young Minister, after the discovery of her husband Roser Chillingworth in the crowd and irritating interview with him in the prison, eventually turned still more agonizing. Her release from prison term and his from Indian captivity offered them freedom to meet if wished, if did not, Chillingworth now at large to execute his secret plan of finding out the partner of her sin, extra advantage too offered ironically by the strong recommendation of the Administration for a medical expert like Chillingworth to attend as Dimmesdale's personal Physician to restore his sinking vigour to proper health.

In close company with Dimmesdale Chillingworth began to pursue his secret plan, that's his Black Man role; Hester could not but be worried. Dimmesdale's safety remained her undeclared obligation. Dimmesdale sermons she alone could make the meaning of, one piece is here:

"Hester Prynne," said he, leaning over the balcony, and looking down steadfastly into her eyes, "thou hearest what this good man says, and seest the accountability under which I labor. If thou feelest it to be for thy soul's peace, and thy earthly punishment will thereby be made more effectual to salvation, I charge thee to speak out the name of thy fellow-sinner and fellow-sufferer! Be not silent from any mistaken pity and tenderness for him; for, believe me, Hester, though he were to step down from a high place, and stand there beside thee, on thy pedestal of shame, yet better were it so, than to hide a guilty heart through life. What can thy silence do for him, except it tempt him—yea, compel him, as it were—to add hypocrisy to sin?..." (p. 48).

The irony is neither the senior priest Wilson nor the governor Bellingham had the head to detect who the fellow-sinner could be; more ironical yet the sinner offered himself to Hester to share her shame if she so chose, if did not, yet he shared the pain at heart none the less! All their solemn erudition and powerful persuasion failed, Hester lent all the might of her conviction, and commitment to an answer irrevocable by nature to their utter surprise: "Never! It is too deeply branded. You cannot take it off. And would that I might endure his agony, as well as mine!" (p. 49). When they further urged, "Speak; and give your child a father!" Her determination wilted not a whit yet: "I will not speak! And my child must seek a heavenly Father; she shall never know an earthly one!" (*ibid.*).

Hester is not Faulkner's Candance (Caddy), neither is Pearl Miss Quentin. She did not wreck a family's peace, she did only what at that early stage (around 1630) society was overburdened with affected purity cult and concealed underneath many a secret sin, which yet under purity-pretension passed for dignity and honour. Hester was a revolutionary. Her scarlet Letter struck up in many a soul secret worries, Hawthorne a Victorian due to delve beneath a lot of sham. A long passage in snippet here:

> She shuddered to believe, yet could not help believing, that it gave her a sympathetic knowledge of the hidden sin in other hearts. She was terror-stricken by the revelations that were thus made. What were they? Could they be other than the insidious whispers of

> the bad angel, who would fain have persuaded the struggling woman, as yet only half his victim, that the outward guise purity was but a lie, and that, if truth were everywhere to be shown a scarlet letter would blaze forth on many a bosom besides Hester Prynne's? Or, must she receive those intimations—so obscure, yet so distinct—as truth? In all her miserable experiences, there was nothing else so awful and so loathsome as this sense. It perplexed, as well as shocked her, by the irreverent in opportuneness of the occasions that brought into vivid action. Sometimes, the red infamy upon her breast would give a sympathetic throb, as she passed near a venerable minister or magistrate, the model of piety and justice, whom the age of antique reverence looked up, as to a mortal man in fellowship with angels.... (p. 61)

Hawthorne's irony is self-inflicting. If the passage above leaves any doubt, note Dimmesdale's role and responses as a sinner concealing his sin with persistent pain on the same spot where Hester wore the brand of justice, her shame and sin acknowledged; Dimmesdale's was unbranded burning in his breast, yet he had to deliver justice, his sermon is a piece of poetry like Coleridge's was, poetry out of the depth of his intensest feeling. Wilson a dead wood, Bellingham a hard faggot. Hester's sin is a travesty of Puritan rigidity which seeks man to conform to an enforced pattern, however unnatural that may be. Hers was a mismatched unloved marriage, her sin is practically a love-sin. Chillingworth was for her a chilling partner, unloved; his long absence, untraced existence left her youth blooming, no Puritan cult could arrest it, temptation for satisfaction of natural craving cannot be rigidly prohibited unless by a suitable marriage. Hester is a wronged woman from the very beginning. Puritan Justice is an artificial, unrealistic imposing structure, life sought to accommodate to the code, richness of life and its endless varieties and possibilities outright rejected. Young Pastor Dimmesdale felt, life is more powerful than any cult. He and Hester, he from inside and she from outside, fell victims to the artificial imposition of law. They wanted life to follow law, but the fact remains law to follow life, to make it worth living.

Being a Pastor Dimmesdale was a law-executive, learnt it by his own life. Hawthorne saw Puritans hold up an artificial standard of excellence which excluded all other human qualities, all other values than what barely conformed to this rigid standard. Hester and Pearl remained outside that standard perfection entire, Dimmesdale partly. This caused a difference between Wilson and Dimmesdale. Pearl a product of their secret union, born a catching beauty but more akin to nature than human society and its standard of judgement. Beside her other children of the Puritan settlement formed to fit into their cult-code. Hawthorne describes their usual sports:

> She saw the children of the settlement, on the grassy margin of the street, or at the domestic thresholds, disporting themselves in such grim fashion as the Puritanic nature would permit; playing at going to church, perchance; or at scourging Quakers; or taking scalps in a sham-fight with the Indians; or searing one another with freaks of imitative witchcraft.... (p. 65)

Their life, mother and daughter, isolated from the Puritan settlement, yet not far distant, a deserted hut, one side forest the other side the sea-basin, nature their daily neighbour, needle-work-skill means of livelihood. They are of the settlement, but away from it, they are more of nature than of the purity-ridden town. Still they are within its rule, moreover her support, financial and otherwise, a colonial collective life. The position itself crippling to her free spirit. In this position more complex a character than Joan, two centuries ahead of her time, no voice to guide her save her natural urge and spirit, no leading role in a state of political debacle. Here her personal life in sharp conflict with religious rigidity, she is more human than religious, her society more religious than human. Dimmesdale equally religious and human. Pearl is not at all that Medieval symbol of salvation, all her good qualities are in a disorderly order under an irresistible force of will at that early age, about four then. An age that could stigmatize Martin Luther as 'demon brat' could call a child with a little wildness 'demon offspring'.

Pearl inherited all her mother's beauty, rather a little more glowing, in her mother-designed tunic seemed a fairy on earth may be any moment on her wing. Yet sometime she saw "not her own miniature portrait, but another face in the small mirror of Pearl's eye. It was a face, fiend-like, full of smiling malice, yet bearing the semblance of features that she had known full well, though seldom with a smile, and never with malice, in them..." (p. 67). This Pearl, not like the Pearl of that Mediaeval allegory, is her own salvation nor her mother's. But reminds one of Tennyson's poems: 'Home they Brought Her Warrior Dead'.

Hester's meeting with Ministers and Magistrates together at Bellingham's residence offers an opportunity to expose narrow ethical approach to life against life realistically as it is: should life adjust to ethics or ethics to life? Pearl's presence before the religio-temporal authorities of the time exposes both the sides, which suggests the author's stand clearly, in which Irony is the best-serving device adopted all too frequently in the story. Wilson, Dimmesdale, Bellingham, their guest Chillingworth a leech, all together to face a woman they call sinner, her child Pearl a cunning beauty, apart from her mother an attractive child, when attached to mother she appears to them a scandalous oddity, instantly their judgement changes. In addition to that, one of them is a partner of her sin, the other a devilish deceiver, now turned traitor. The remaining two mere form.

Hester is an open shame, she has nothing to hide, her personality, richness of her mental capacity, a cultivated taste and power of edurance, a loving sympathetic heart, could anywhere recommend her to a respectable position, out of this Puritan rigidity, far more than any woman of this settlement of acknowledged purity. Hester's sin-born daughter is out of the set pattern, which immediately identify her as an ominous oddity. They should have appreciated a three-year old child's so exceptional a flourish of imagination in answer to an item of well-patterned Westminster Catechism; "Who made thee" Her answer was—"she had not been made at all, but had been plucked by her mother off the bush of wild roses, that grew by the prison door" (p. 77). They expected the coded answer: The

Heavenly Father made me. Every child learnt it from the Puritan Primer, but she made an unlearnt answer of her own invention, nowhere coded. She knew she was her 'mother's child', it was not taught, but was her realistic knowledge.

The child is guided by her own knowledge, they wanted to impose what they had learnt from books, hardly ever realized; an artificial mechanism like this can only produce an artificial automaton. Hester held her whole weight against such a plan of their upbringing a child, they would make her a speaking doll, or a cased bird made to talk what it does not know the meaning of. Hester did not tell them this stark truth, neither could Dimmesdale tell his colleagues so; both made a plea of defence on a line of Hester's present position, which requires best the child with her. Irony lies in Dimmesdale, of all people, pleading on her side. Once you forget his position he appears to have told the bare truth, and nobly. Hester's personal appeal to him to plead for her another irony. She spoke frankly, and without fear: "Speak thou for me! Thou wast my pastor, and hadst charge of my soul, and knowest me better than these men can. I will not lose the child: Speak for me! Thou knowest, —for thou hast sympathies which these men lack!—thou knowest what is in my heart, and what are a mother's rights, and how much the stronger they are; when that mother has but her child and the scarlet letter! Look thou to it! I will not lose the child! Look to it!" (p. 78).

Hester's appeal to Dimmesdale a concealed irony, more effective every way for its concealment, further effective because Hester did not mean to hurt, but meant, in her desperate situation, help which, she knew, he would not fail to extend. Naturally Dimmesdale rose with his inflamed self-reproach and with that equal degree of his power of soul-soothing language and the power of reasoning born of it: he began with a voice sweet, tremulous, but powerful, insomuch that the hall reechoed, and the hollow armour rang with it— "truth is what Hester says, and in the feelings which inspires her! God gave her the child, and gave her, too, an instinctive knowledge of its nature and requirements—both seemingly so peculiar—which no other mortal being can possess..." (p. 79).

Interrupted by the Governor and the senior clergyman Mr Wilson, Dimmesdale elaborated, the main point of which is: God sent the child to the lady, He knew best whom where to send to what purpose to serve, it is better to leave it to Providence, maybe Providence's is a cleansing as well as retributive course. Chillingworth, true to his sole intent, suggested how one, gifted with philosophical insight, could read the child to reach back to its unknown father. Reverend Mr Wilson taught him a noble lesson in the true spirit of Christianity: "leave the mystery as we find it, unless Providence reveal it of its own accord. Thereby, every good Christian man hath a little to show a father's kindness towards the poor, deserted babe" (p. 80).

[4]

Chillingworth had more reason to do, his married wife's babe, though he was not the father. But he is not the man to be guided by this catholicity of conduct. Like a serpent he crawled into Reverend Dimmesdale's intimacies, modern serpent only in Leech's cloak, slough only shed for a new cover. There is Eve here to seduce so easily, so he began to tempt Adam himself in a modern method. A close association between these two scholars of two different orders reveals both in their essential elements, only the author's interpretation waiting. The interpretation itself is highly psychological and equally metaphoric in expression, a fragment here:

> In Arthur Dimmesdale, thought and imagination were so active, and sensibility so intense, that the bodily infirmity would be likely to have its groundwork there. So Roser Chillingworth—the man of skill, the kind of friendly physician—strove to go deep into his patient's bosom, delving among the principles, prying into the recollections, and probing everything with a cautious touch, like a treasure-seeker in a dark cavern. Few secrets can escape an investigator, who has opportunity and license to undertake such a quest, and skill to follow it up. A man burdened with a secret should especially avoid the intimacy of his

> physician. If the latter possess native sagacity, and a nameless something more,—let us call it intuition; if he show no intrusive egotism, nor disagreeably prominent characteristics of his own; if he have the power, which must be born with him, to bring his mind into such affinity with his patients, that this last shall unawares have spoken what he imagines himself only to have thought; if such revelations received without tumult, and acknowledged not so often by an uttered sympathy, as by silence, an inarticulate breath, and here and there a word, to indicate that all is understood. (p. 86)

These are the expected attributes, most likely Chillingworth possessed, with all the subtleties in addition to conceal that he had. A. Dimmesdale 'had yet never fairly revealed to him'. 'It was a strange reserve'. By the very 'strong recommendation of his well-wishers his physician was allowed to live in the same house with him under his constant observation. The duo, in sharp contrast in character, represent a tussle between open piety and hefty secret sin, the physician in secret collusion with the prince of hell, against so noble a soul. To easy-believing innocent eyes it appeared an ideal arrangement for the recovery of the Reverend Pastor's health, they took it as a heaven-sent boon. None ironically saw the truth, neither of the disease nor of the leech's motive. They are more ironically deceived than Shakespeare's Macbeth. They are caught in an irony more completely. To an apparent view the story is a simple one, a story of double sin, one regarded the other, under a rigid Puritan judgement, the sinner too cruelly punished. But when critically viewed the characters involved, it becomes very complex, particularly two characters; in spite of wide knowledge of cures, in conventional system of medical science and Indian system of necromancy and herbal remedies, he is all but a perpetrator of evil and vindictive, wily like the Serpent, no love for the woman he married, neither mercy and tenderness of feeling for the unlucky child. He describes Pearl to Dimmesdale:

> "There is no law, nor reverence for authority, no regard for human ordinances or opinions, right or

> wrong, mixed up with that child's composition", remarked he, as much to himself as to his companion. "I saw her, the other day, bespatter the Governor himself with water, at the cattle trough in Spring Lane. What, in Heaven's name, is she? Is the imp altogether evil? Hath she affections? Hath she any discoverable principle of being?" (p. 92)

The child hit back, her intuitive response: "Come away, mother; Come away, or yonder old Black Man will catch you! He hath got hold of the minister already. Come away, mother, or he will catch you! But he cannot catch little Pearl" (p. 93).

The attributed precocity to Pearl is a way of offering intuitive free criticism, if irresponsible, impartial not at all. Sometimes she is a voice of nature that does not discriminate high and low, rank and position; if wildness, that too natural like unchecked overgrowth. Artificial refinement is not her lesson, nothing added but evolved out of itself. She is a misfit in a realm of theocratic protectionism.

Mr Dimmesdale's present life is that of a repentant pious priest with one slip in life, in those days among Puritan zealots a sinner, by Puritan standard other rare human qualities are of no moment. Ironically Chillingworth found nothing in this man, instinctively envied, to appreciate, his envy beclouded his vision, and in frantic search of something in him to build up an image worthy of his hate, unless he finds it he seems to be in a suffocating situation. With such a dark soul he failed to love Hester's beauty, her other qualities, he lacked, failed to cherish a kind of fondness for so nice a child like Pearl, set a standard by which he could at least hate the child, a mind like Iago's. Hawthorne calls him 'Satan's emissary'. Just in pursuit of stinking rot in Dimmesdale's soul he spent his resources over seven years.

Dimmesdale long took him for a pursuer of knowledge in his own field. Pearl intuited aright. But it is not a judgement, one need not be guided by it. He could sense only when his patient should disclose his heart, something was there to enfeeble his body, body was for him symptoms, disease seated deep in the soul. With Urea Heep like humility he pointed his fore finger and said: "You, Sir, of all men whom I have known, are he whose body is the closest conjoined, and imbued, and identified, so to speak, with the spirit whereof it is the instrument" (p. 94).

Dimmesdale's sharp answer reveals him as much as the questioner reveals himself by the question. One wants to know the secret and the other to avoid it, so in a fit of impatience: "Then I need ask no further", said the clergyman, somewhat hastily rising from his chair, "You deal not, I take it, in medicine for the soul!" Both embodied irony. One not cure but cruel, the other not solemn but simulation, Chillingworth in Hawthorne's word: "Calm, gentle, passionless, as he appeared, there was yet, we fear, a quiet depth of malice, hitherto latent, but active now, in this unfortunate old man, which led him to imagine a more intimate revenge than any mortal had ever wreaked upon an enemy..." (p. 96). Not an Othello's ensign Iago but more subtle intellectually, more advanced a version of Iago.

Dimmesdale too meant one thing did another, wanted to cleanse himself from what he thought soiled his soul, burdened his mind and wrecked even his body, but what he did and continued to do entangled him in a mesh, which made it more and more difficult to undo. He is more inextricably a Hamlet, with no prospect of having done an Othello's part which Hester suggested and arranged. Hawthorne's projection is elaborate, only a fragment here: "He had striven to put a cheat upon himself by making the avowal of a guilty conscience, but had gained only one other sin, and also a self-acknowledged shame, without the momentary relief of being self-deceived. He had spoken the very truth, and transformed into the veriest falsehood. Yet by the construction of his nature, he loved the truth, and loathed the lie, as few men ever did. Therefore, above all things else, he loathed his miserable self" (p. 99).

Chillingworth is a conflict-free brutality of purpose, where Mr Dimmesdale a quivering tenderness of feeling urge, fallen with a beauty, then unending self-reproach, detestable to himself, no easy way of exculpation, his high position as a preacher barred the way to confession immediate, which made the lady's position more miserable, child's position more obscure, further stab into his conscience more difficult. A man of Hamlet's keen susceptibility, erudition, and prolonged indecision, suffers more miserably than the Prince. Only soliloquies assume the form of sermons, more winning than anything else in this drama. Chillingworth more confidentially cruel than Guildenstern-Rosencrantz. Hawthorne is full of irony, Shakespeare is sparingly, and as much as he is her Hamlet, only from a different background, he repeatedly had appealed in her mind in Hamlet's word: "The fair Ophelia-Nymph, in thy orisons/ Be all my sins remembered" (Act 3, Sc. 1). Hamlet's worried, loveless, love-seeking importunity rebuffed made life more desolate, what remained potent was 'the native hue of resolution siklied over with the pale cast of thought.' This happened to Dimmesdale in a little different situation. Here Hester loves him as he too does yet, but instead of one Father to advise her wisdom Hester had too many, and Dimmesdale too had many obstacles to keep them apart. The result is similar with him: 'resolution siklied over with the pale cast of thought'. He thought and could not translate into action, rather got himself inextricably caught in the spyder web of his mind.

Chillingworth himself, antagonistically though, defines Dimmesdale rightly; all the three main characters of the story, though of their time and situation, are far ahead of the time's intellectual power, and more or less ahead of formalism of faith that allowed human consideration, if at all, to serve in an insignificant secondary role to the codified tenets. Chillingworth, intellectually though their equal, had sensitivities blunted and long in disuse atrophied, his detection of his victim essentially true:

> ... He knew, by some spiritual sense,—for the Creator never made another being so sensitive as this—he knew that no friendly hand pulling at his heart-stings, and that an eye was looking curiously into him, which sought only evil, and found it. But knew not that the eye and hand were mine! With the superstition common to his brotherhood, he fancied himself given over to a fiend, to be tortured with frightful dreams, and desperate thought, the sting of

> remorse, and despair of pardon; as a foretaste of what awaits him beyond the grave.... (p. 117)

[5]

Hester Prynne's meeting with Dimmesdale on the same scaffold, a tottering weakling, on his vigil, and she returning from Governor Winthrop's death-bed, flung her into additional worries how to save him from the evil spirit, she thought, Chillingworth embodied and keeping constand company with him those seven years, a wily serpent in disguise. She immediately decided to meet Chillingworth. This meeting reveals the true nature of the problem Hawthorne takes up in the story, so important. Both Chillingworth and Hester plainly argue their present position and past, and locate the seed of the whole problem. To avoid a long quote, one need only know, Chillingworth was never a warm lover in his "late autumn" of life, an intellectual in search of knowledge, not religious by temperament,—here his difference from Dr Casaubon—but harmlessly upright. Their marriage was ill-assorted, the scholar needed a warm fireside at home, and the warming smile of a young beauty in return for honest unreserved affection. The young lady detected quite late: "Yes, I hate him!" repeated Hester, more bitterly than before, "He betrayed me! He has done me worse wrong than I did him" (p. 120).

The author lends her his support on the same page above: "...she thought of those long past days, in a distant land, when he used to emerge at eventide from the seclusion of his study, and sit down in the firelight of her nuptial smile. He needed to bask himself in that smile, he said, in order that the chill of so many lonely hours among his books might be taken off the scholar's heart. Such scenes had once appeared not otherwise than happy, but now, as viewed from the dismal medium of subsequent life, they classed themselves among her ugliest remembrances. She marvelled how such scenes could have been! She marvelled how she could ever have been wrought upon to marry him!... And it seemed a fouler offence committed by Roger Chillingworth, than any which had since been done her, that, in the time when her heart knew no better, he had persuaded her to fancy herself happy by his side."

Chillingworth too now could realize: "Peradventure, hadst thou met earlier a better love than mine, this evil had not been, I pity thee, for the good that has been wasted in thy nature!" (p. 118). Hester too pitied him, "for the hatred that has transformed a wise and just man to a fiend!" (pp. 118-19), and in spite of God's one special gift to woman her blooming beauty and youthfulness and attendant natural privileges, her judgement has not been beclouded, which is an additional grace of this character, had she been born in a later time she could have been Mary Wollistone craft; she nobly suggested to her wronged husband how he could still fare better than the wrongers: "There might be good for thee, and thee alone, since thou hast been deeply wronged, and hast it at thy will to pardon, Wilt thou give up that only privilege? Wilt thou reject that priceless benefit?" (p. 119).

From a different angle Chillingworth views the other side of the truth, an inevitability in the creed-crippled society of those days, which knew no modern adjustment, no recognition of natural human urge and involvement: "It is not granted me to pardon. I have no such power as thou tellesh me of. My old faith, long forgotten, comes back to me, and explains all that we do, and all we suffer. By thy first step awry, thou didst plant the germ of evil; but since that moment, it has all been a dark necessity. Ye that have wronged me are not sinful, save in a kind of typical illusion; neither am I fiend-like, who have snatched a fiend's office from his hands. It is our fate. Let the black flower blossom as it may! Now go thy ways, and deal as thou wilt with yonder man" (*ibid.*).

This meeting is one kind of revelation, one side of the truth, another meeting of Hester with another person related to her life as Chillingworth was, is a different kind of revelation, the other side of the same truth. Hester's role is the measure yard of judgement. When a woman cannot love a man as her own, no bond of marriage can keep them together unless forced by circumstances or otherwise. Though Chillingworth intellectually understands it he cannot really spare Hester and grant her freedom even for her own happiness. His revenge is Satanic, wreaked upon the object of love, the man whom Hester loved. He assumed Satanic subtlety of revenge. Hester's meeting with Dimmesdale in the forest attains a rare sweetness of two estranged lovers, to which even mute nature lent its sympathetic support:

> They sat down again side by side, and clasped in hand, on the mossy trunk of the fallen tree. Life had never brought them a gloomier hour; it was the point whither their pathway had so long being tending, and darkening ever, as it stole along;—and yet it enclosed a charm that let linger upon it, and claim another, and another, and, after all, another moment. The forest was obscure around them, and creaked with a blast that was passing through it. The boughs were tossing heavily above their heads; while one solemn old tree groaned dolefully to another as if telling the sad story of the pair that sat beneath, or constrained to forebode evil to come. (p. 133)

Here they meet, not as pastor and parishioner, but as humans, Adam and Eve in Eden, in spite of their sin as in Eden; only she did not fail to detect the seducer and could early warn her Adam against the serpent she knew better. Role reversed. Hester led Dimmesdale still sinking under the burden of sin, she corrected: "What we did had a consecration of its own. We felt it so! We said so to each other! Hast thou forgotten it" (*ibid.*). He did not. She suggested a self-ambraced expulsion, so seemed not like expulsion. They were literally in the forest, like Primitive Eden, Pearl a little way off. Hester taught him how to lift himself from this morass of morbidity: "Doth the universe lie within the compass of yonder town, which only a little time ago was but a leaf-strewn desert, as lonely as around us? Whither leads yonder forest track? Backward to the settlement, thou sayest! Yes; but onward, too! Deeper it goes, and deeper into the wilderness, less plainly to be seen at every step; until, some few miles, hence, the yellow leaves will show no vestige of the white man's tread. There, thou art free! So brief a journey would bring thee from a world where thou hast been most wretched, to one where thou mayest still be happy! Is there not shade enough in all this boundless forest to hide thy heart from the gaze of Roger Chillingsworth?" (p. 134).

This is the least he can do. There is yet a promising prospect for a man who is ready to buy his liberty at a simple cost of crossing the sea again from 'the iron men' and 'their opinions'. He was not yet assured, caught in a sin-syndrome. One breach of custom to hide invited too many real sins, and suffered from joint of all of them, and was sinking in bitter self-reproach, especially under the penetrating evil eye of the physician, in disguise the serpent in their Eden. Whatever Hester may have said encouraging, he lost all faith in himself: "There is not the strength or courage left me to venture into the wide, strange, difficult world, alone!" Hester had no other alternative but one, final and decisive, to assure: "Thou shalt not go alone!" (p. 135).

Hawthorne concentrates on the three characters, and their evolved complexities of relationship added to the already existing fractured relationship. Originally Hester's mis-match marriage, unloved too, against a passionate fulfilment of love-relationship, got later intrigued in a wider perspective of blunt laws, and loss of personal purity felt acutely by one not by the other of the love-pair, and the unloved husband turned unforgiving cold enemy always nagging like a blood-sucking fiend. Under the circumstances "the clergyman resolved to flee, and not alone" (p. 137). So long suppressed basic human urge overtook him, he immediately declared to himself "if this be the path to a better life, as Hester would persuade me, I surely give no fairer prospect by pursuing it! Neither can I any longer live without her companionship; so powerful is she to sustain, so tender to soothe! O thou to whom I dare not lift mine eyes, wilt Thou yet pardon me!"

In the forest scene, in close neighbourliness with nature, Hester and Dimmesdale together, could have granted them an Eden intimacy, if only there had not been Pearl. Pearl is an irony in Eden, as she ever was in the story. She is a living irony in their life, both joy and misery in one. When they are together, and make it their Eden, Pearl on the other side of the brook, hesitates to cross, Medieval Pearl did not cross. The Pearl of this story would cross only on condition, mother wear the badge of her shame! A bitter concealed irony, as everywhere her role is. The irony continues when she would not oblige the clergyman beside her mother, nor would she wear the smear of his loving caress on her forehead long. A child of seven years only passes judgement, without knowing she did:

> What strange, sad man is he!" said the child, as if speaking to herself. "In the dark night-time, he calls us to him, and holds thy hand and mine, as when we stood with him on scaffold yonder! And in the deep forest, where only the old trees can hear, and the strip of sky see it, he talks with thee, sitting on a heap of moss! And he kisses my forehead, too, so that the little brook would hardly wash it off! But here in the sunny day, and among all the people, he knows us not; nor must we know him!... (p. 155)

Hawthorne depicts life with its natural urge, its excellences and limitations, as against cultist artificiality mismatched with life, as if life is not life if not conformable to it. It does not suit Hester, nor Dimmesdale. Hester asserts, Dimmesdale cannot, he wants Hester's help, Pearl his innocuous critic. Chillingworth belongs to a different class, Biblical knowledge his skill, that made him exceptionally shrewd and crafty. If greatness, definitely at the cost of goodness. His love is selfish, self-comfort only, not loving, a moral defeat, serpent's defeat, Paradise regained, and role-play exposed, here to Hester, then to her Adam.

Serpent does not move straight, Chillingworth does not. He is the serpent in the story. Seduction is in his nature. Hawthorne paints preconceived modalities of a Faith, artificial, lifeless formalities, so preconceived is a different mode in Chillingworth, all his own, shared with none. Miltonic Satan could boast of a large following of fallen angels, he is a born leader of evil, Prince of Hell. Chillingworth has no personal glamour, no leading power. In and out a lonely fellow. His intellect stiffened his ego, otherwise crippled in everything. A voyage upon life requires many other qualities which he lacked. He miscalculated, more grievously than Casaubon, that his intellect could buy a beauty who would bask in the sunshine of his wisdom unquestioning. His wisdom misfired. The settlement itself an uprooted horde resettled, their law, religion and custom—all assumed a weird shape—home away from home, society away from society, uprooted saplings replanted, soil different, climate too, struggle added, kind quality different. Law and religion shaped anew, extra caution incorporated unusual astringency. The whole system in the new land withheld original Elizabethan flavour of 'Merry England', religion reshaped itself under Puritan rigidity, open air agility controlled by cautioned performance.

The grand ceremony of inauguration more attuned to solemn seriousness than Merry England's robust ribaldry. They planted forest in the old land for hunting, but in the new colony they cleaned forest for cultivable land and settlement. This trend in their new home set the tone of their entire life to an unusual seriousness. The inauguration ceremony the new Governor's administration, exposed the pattern: "Had they followed the hereditary taste, the New England settlers would have illustrated all events of public importance by bonfires, banquets, pageantries, and processions. Nor would it have been impracticable, in the observance of majestic ceremonies, to combine mirthful recreation with solemnity, and give, as it were, a grotesque and brilliant embroidery to the grave robe of state..." (p. 156).

The solemnity of the celebrations had a fringe of ribald relief. The medley of Indian visitors of particoloured grotesqueness, and more unsettling the sailors of the Spanish Main in their professional costumes with licence of their tongue and drink from their waist-band flasks, and curious Mistress Hibbins's witchy entry, added a contrasted colour to the sober atmosphere of the ceremony. Pearl finally a little imp, a free spirit of carping contrast among them. Mistress Hibbins declared 'Thou art the lineage of the Prince of the Air'. A great part of the multitude formed a ring around her, the 'centripetal force of attraction; the undrained full vitality and unrepressed bloom made her so lively and handsome! No Puritan discipline could spoil her natural gifts.

Christ preached a realistic religion, of Faith and Love, everyday things, with which life is equivalent to Peace; Puritans made it one of hate, gave man knowledge of sin, what to hate; when they made knowledge of sin more prominent, that knowledge took the mind entire hardly leaving any room for virtue to pervade, the soil is invaded by sin-weeds already, seeds of virtue, when sown, are likely to meet early suffocation-death. Even a gifted priest like Dimmesdale met with virtually such a suffocation-death. His mortal body died with all inherent virtues choked in seven years long nursed bed of 'tares'.

Hester and her daughter Pearl never shared this constant sin-sermon, she is essentially a rebel against the constant gossip of sin, her Scarlet Letter, she is better outside this society, close to the forest and the vast sheet of water, akin to her nature, and with their mute sympathy rather more lively than anyone in the New England town, undoubtedly than Dimmesdale who spent all his vital energies in constant sin-contemplation, which momently sought release in his memorable sermons, all Hamlet's soliloquies.

[6]

Dimmesdale's Election sermon, the last sermon of his life, and the best, the text of the sermon is withheld, instead the whole response-pitch, irrespective of different levels and kinds, of the audience is made to speak for itself:

> In the open air their rapture broke into speech. The street and the market-place absolutely babbled, from side to side, with applauses of the ministers. His hearers could not until they had told one another of what each knew better than he could tell or hear. According to their united testimony, never had man spoken in so wise, so high, and in so holy a spirit, as he that spoke this day; nor had inspiration ever breathed through mortal lips more evidently than it did through his. (pp. 167-68)

Even the speaker himself felt its hallowed impact, as if he were one of his audience to respond: "Its influence could be seen, as it were, descending upon him, and possessing him, and continually lifting him out of the written discourse that lay before him, and filling him with ideas that must have been as marvelous to himself as to his audience..." (p. 168).

Almost the same situation with Hamlet: innocent love held out of his reach, betrayal close by secretly active, friends no friend, the ghost prompts him to revenge. Dimmesdale a forlorn soul urged by the ghost of repentance to declare and reach out to his love, held out by the paternal authority of the priests and protectors of the State. Hamlet is better placed than Dimmesdale, he had not at least priestly protection; Dimmesdale's conscience crippled him, only suppressed agony lent extra force to his language and release in its vibrations a charming undulation to his voice. Like Hamlet's declaration of his love for Ophelia in the grave yard, his takes a different form of declaration at a similar place and in a different mode of expression when Dimmesdale ascended the scaffold where once Hester, his agreeable Ophelia, displayed her badge of shame to the public, and acknowledged his share of sin, and in the open view of the public, just like a rebel, broke away from the discipline of life, position in the ceremonial procession, declined help from a brother priest and the governor, sought help from Hester and her child to support him on to the scaffold, and asked the child to kiss him for everyone to see.

It is not only an atonement but also a fulfilment of a suppressed dream, once for all; Hester helped him with her loving arms, so did little Pearl with her small hands clasping his legs, her wildness gone. The clergyman asked Pearl, "dear little Pearl, wilt thou kiss me now? Thou wouldst not yonder, in the forest! But now thou wilt?" (p. 173). Yes, Pearl will. She is changed. All their formal catechisms could not convert her, but true love could. She kissed, 'her tears fell upon her father's cheek', she turned to her mother, this time not for the Scarlet Letter, but with a weeping assurance, a pledge, that was love. Both the parents felt she was their love-link, a bond inseparable! The Minister's last word for them—Hester and

Pearl—the finest ever he uttered in sermons: "Praised be his name! His will be done! Farewell!", which welled up from his purest of moments of resignation and peace, more valid, more enlightened than St. Francis's 'Death, my little sister, who hath no sister', more philosophic than surrendered solace.

Here Dimmesdale is true, true to himself and to the world. Perhaps this last scene bears out Hawthorne's suggestion 'Be true! Be true! Be true!' (p. 175). The Puritan Patricians looked for sins and seems to have forgotten everything else, valued only a sin-free life, the cruelest possible punishment for a witch, burning alive, stirred the heart of many Christians even in those days. God-realization from a well-laid human basis is an upstream appealing progression. Those who are entrusted with this mission must be loving, sympathetic, and not rude and unsympathetic even to a sinner. This is real Catholicity. Purification is better than punishment, love more effective, hate is not. Hate is a loss, love is a gain. They lost Hester, Pearl, then finally Dimmesdale. He knew he would have no sympathy, was afraid of ignominy, even hate. His love for a woman is a breach of discipline, not a grievous unaccommodatable sin. He himself could accommodate it if Chillingworth abjured hostility and took it sympathetically. In modern times it created no problem, even in those days compromise was possible.

Chillingworth is the real sinner, he forgot his original sin, his fresh sin began with Dimmesdale a prey to his ill-conceived revenge pursued with unflagging interest, an embodiment of inveterate evil. Even when he joined Hester, Pearl, her father together on the Scaffold, a crisis moment for them, he could not abjure his evil motive. He thrust himself amongst them and whishpered: "Madam, hold! What is your purpose?" Then to him "Wave back that woman! Cast off this child! All shall be well! Do not blacken your fame, and do not perish in dishonour! I can yet save you! Would bring infamy on your sacred profession?"

Dimmesdale read him well, if we readers fail to, for his apparent well-meaning advice, "Ha, tempter! Methinks thou art too late! Thy power is not what it was! With God's help, I shall escape thee now!" (p. 170).

Chillingworth acknowledges that Biblical term 'tempter' for himself in clear lánguage: "Hadst thou sought the whole earth over, there was no one place so secret—no high place nor lowly place, where thou couldst have escaped me—save on this very scaffold!" (p. 171).

Dimmesdale's is a public confessional on the scaffold, he wasted his last breath on it, Chillingworth witness on the platform; when he finished he collapsed on Hester's arms, his head held against her breast. Chillingworth kneeled on the scaffold beside him, one may think in prayer, no: "Thou hast escaped me!" he repeated more than once. "Thou hast escaped me!" (p. 173). He would have all along him his perpetual victim, and wished him alive rather than dead for this satisfaction. A man like this cannot be Milton's Satan, he is not a hero, but a fiend. He too died within a year with nothing to sustain his revenge-prone pursuit. He planned to pursue them to the other side of the Atlantic, but God spared him further devil's task.

[7]

The authors conclusion to the story is a sort of victory of a defeat, victory of the defeated love; Puritan rigidity, man-invented legality, satanic seduction all at work against love pure and simple that could tie them three in their eternal bond: Hester offered; "Better? Yea; so we may both die, and little Pearl die with us!" (p. 171). To which the clergyman answered before he could tell the world his self-accepted defeat, "So let me make haste to take the shame upon me" and die; but he did not know that he won a decisive victory leaving them upon God's Mercy: "For thee and Pearl, be it as God shall order, and God is Merciful!", the author seems to add to it, 'that they are not'.

The last scene is a pure love-scene, which Milton's serpent envied, as did in the Biblical Eden, and did the serpent here. The love so true that it converted a 'demon child' they called, shedding tears on her father's cheek (p. 173), her jealousy of the priest's share in her mother's love in the forest is converted to love. The three together are here tied in a fresh inseverable bond of love. The Angels of heaven said 'Amen!' For a moment the fiend too 'knelt down', a conversion, though he may not know! Roser Chillingworth bequeathed "a very considerable amount of property, both here and in England, to little Pearl, the daughter of Hester Prynne" (p. 176). The author did not account for what prompted him to do it. To say all is not art, it is a conversion-grace, durable or not, no doubt, converted to love. They paid enough for guilty love; now love alone remains, guilt expiated by seven years of suffering in mind and body. Hester is a different woman. Pearl too a loving daughter to her mother, well-married and rich; yet Hester returns again to her old cottage still with that Scarlet Letter on her breast, no one imposed, but self-adopted, not as a badge of shame, but as a memory of love, just a Hindu emblem of widowhood.

Every moment you know a change is there, in your appearance, your dress and in everything in your life, a loss you recall, and recall endless story of your happiness with that lost entity, your whole existence is filled with love, no absence but presence in innumerable forms. This is Hindu widowhood, where there is deep love it assumes this character. Hester cannot stay away from the place where she found and enjoyed this love, her sufferings were sweet, her sin was sacred, the symbol a sweet reminder every moment. Thus Browning could make a moment 'eternal'. The richness of such a human possibility is one of the greatest gifts of God. No religious or pious code can demolish it. What code can is to adjust it suitably, which is true marriage.

Pearl, according to Pue-investigation, in her early motherhood "mindful of her mother, she would most joyfully have entertained that sad and lonely mother at her fireside" (p. 177); but she would be back to the scene of her love, if sin, love-sin, Milton's 'guilty love'; her return a role-change, not a pitied condemned woman, but a prophetess's seat of consolation and care. Long before Mary Wollstonecraft hoped for "in Heaven's own time, a new truth would be revealed, in order to establish the whole relation between man and woman on a surer ground of mutual happiness" (*ibid.*).

Milton's guilty love could not separate Adam from Eve, innocent love in Eden softened even the seducer serpent's mind, though for a time; even their guilty love cast its spell on the tempter, rather awakened envy and made him more determined in his purpose. Here Chillingworth's role. His seduction failed, Hester clearly told him, she did never love, nor pretended any. On the scaffold they three together isolated him as a dreaded pest, yet clinging there to earn recognition, a rejection no Bradley was there to pity or lament. Only the Puritan law ruled for the clergyman a grave without epitaph, and finally for Hester a grave a little space apart beside it with the semblance of an engraved escutcheon' thereon 'a device of herald's wording' then a 'brief description of our now concluded legend': "On a field of sable, the Letter A, Gules". The brief description is to preempt passing of judgement in blatant disregard of the Divine dispensation. Better the clergyman's version 'God's will be done'. Why can they not yet forget that red letter? They preempt Divine Justice. Hawthorne leaves clear suggestion at the end of the story, the child they called 'demon child' turned humanly dutiful, more pious than they expected one of their children perhaps!

3

Rappaccini's Daughter

[1]

Only four years before in 1846 Hawthorne wrote this story in the collection *Mosses from Old Manse*, it appears deeply related to *The Scarlet Letter*, more than casually an eye can see. So I take it up just after Hawthorne's revolutionary novel. Giovanni's Paduan Professor told him the secret folly of Dr Rappaccini's method of research: "he cares infinitely more for science than for mankind. His patients are interesting to him only as subjects for some new experiment. He would sacrifice human life, his own among the rest, or whatever else was dearest to him, for the sake of anything so much as a grain of a mustard seed to the great heap of his accumulated knowledge" (p. 83).

Why this story is quite relevant to *The Scarlet Letter* is a clue to what Rappaccini daughter laments was her fate, a position of love but no touch; her young lover Giovanni a scholar, living in the upper storey of the same house in another part, Dr Rappaccini's garden only intervenes between them, otherwise very close. She understands he loves her, she too does. But "what a jest is there! No; though I have grown up among these flowers, I know no more of them than their hues and perfume; and sometimes methinks I would fain rid myself of even that small knowledge. There are many flowers here, and those not the least brilliant, but shock and offend me when they meet my eye. But pray, signor, do not believe these stories about my science. Believe nothing of me save what you see with your own eyes" (p. 91).

Then follows a true love scene, restrained yet, a distance maintained; a caution intervening. She understood when Giovanni said "Bid me believe nothing save what comes from your own lips" 'There came a deep flush to her cheek'. She responded to his gaze of uneasy suspicion with a queen like haughtiness: "I do so bid you, signor. Forget whatever you may have fancied in regard to me. If true to the outward senses, still it may be false in its essence, but the words of Beatrice Rappaccini's lips are true from the depths of the heart outward. Those you may believe" (pp. 91-92).

To the fresh lover it may appear a riddle, but the key phrase is 'from the depths of the heart'. Instead of 'femme' she is a fleur fatale in her father's garden, well-tended within, segregated completely from the outside world. Almost Prospero's daughter Miranda, Giovanni her Ferdinand; unlike Miranda she a grown-up complex character, her father's science-craze victim. Arrested love at the centre of the plot. Love violated by another love, Dr Rappaccini's love for his science which another Professor of Medicine Baglioni rightly explains against humanity, and Beatrice learnt with her life how a fatal blunder her father had made. Prospero's magic and Rappaccini's science are totally two different kinds of power, one benign the other malign. Their security sense of their daughters is also different; though both loving fathers, daughter their well-taken care of cherry, their methods different: Prospero repulsed a beastly creature to secure a loving worthy match for her with no harm to anybody else in the whole world; but Rappaccini was up to the extreme harm to the world to secure his daughter's love-match, their withdrawal from natural human perspective, artificially contrived, fatally repulsive, criminally perilous, exclusively in their own protected Eden; the Primeval pair's condition, miserably God substituted by a fragile father who created only more venomous versions of original poison in plants and shrubs and populated an Eden more to be dreaded than endeared.

Dr Rappaccini's plan for his daughter's happiness is inhuman, love to be realized in complete seclusion in a sort of poison-protected Eden, only . Giovanni required the pair converted to a progenitor of a poisoned progeny, the progenitor of a poison-race. Both Beatrice and Giovanni hated it:

> "He is a man fearfully acquainted with the secrets of nature", replied Beatrice; "and, at the hour, when I first drew breath, this plant sprang from the soil, the offspring of his science, of his intellect, while I was but his earthly child. Approach it not!" continued she, observing with terror that Giovanni was drawing nearer to the shrub. "It has qualities that you little dream of. But I, dearest Giovanni—I grew up and blossomed with the plant and was nourished with its breath. It was my sister, and I loved it with a human affection, for, alas!—hast thou not suspected it?—there was an awful doom." (p. 99)

Then explaining this doom she further added: "There was an awful doom, the effect of my father's fatal love of science, which estranged me from all society of any kind. Until Heaven sent thee, dearest Giovanni, oh, how lonely was thy poor Beatrice!" (pp. 99-100).

Dr Rappaccini practically bartered his soul to knowledge as did Marlowe's Doctor Faustus, he knew it was his knowledge, Hawthorne's Chillingworth did; all the three escaped notice of other valued, and inescapable, side of humanity. In the Biblical myth this problem of knowledge is highlighted, and raised to its inevitable crisis in the spiritual level. Life is far more insistent than knowledge. Biblical Eden provided more important a place for the Tree of Life. All the three made the wrong choice of knowledge, not knowledge for Life. This is essentially Baglioni's point of contention. Rappaccini's offered solution to his daughter's crisis in life, and in her love, is a damnable solution, the solution of a cursed race in the nearest future, a threat to humanity. Their Eden is sure to demit its status to a concentration camp. Immediately Giovanni, in spite of his deep love for Beatrice, momently felt repugnant. It is more terrible a barrier than Rushdie's Ophelia in 'Yorick' had for her protection of a beauty's body by an ignobly offending smell. Beatrice's body is poison, Ophelia's offensively odorous, which could keep Hamlet at bay sometime, but, for Giovanni it was a death-trap.

[2]

It is a four character-story, two young lovers and two men of medical science, these two men in sharp contrast in their approach to science, Baglioni's discovery curative. He saves the two lovers' life and their love—a thing that Scarlet Letter—patricians never could think of. They were not scientists like Baglioni, but they could have been at least inspired by a human sense which really guided the scientist Doctor to help the two lovers' sincere love and life too. They were like Rappaccini guided by their cherished faith and lost all sense of humanity, Hester's *Scarlet Letter* badge is a mechanism of complete isolation from possible human contact, Beatrice's isolation enforced by poison only instead of a blazoning badge, to prohibit contamination. The Letter of a deadly poison to the wearer, every moment reminding her of segregated security. If Beatrice could give birth to a child it would have been fated to a position of Pearl, forsaken by all the children for fear of contamination. If Rappaccini's plan succeeded it would have been a family without society, even their birth would have been their own stake, none could help them even if any wished to. A miserable incarcerated existence.

Such a life was imposed on Hester's family for one love-fault, she could not join her Giovanni, already her body poisoned by one trick of nature, her blooming womanhood, Beatrice-beauty, attracted her Giovanni, finally for death release, one touch alone sealed their fate. In *Scarlet Letter* this happened on the scaffold for a public show. No Baglioni was there to save their life, their love, Dimmesdale fell a victim, Giovanni escaped that fate only because there was a Baglioni to cleanse Beatrice of all her poison, Here in *Scarlet Letter* none came forward with similar cleansing power. Chillingworth is a chilling anti-type of Baglioni in the earlier story, so a step closer to Rappaccini, only more vicious and vindictive. In the earlier story it is science that ignores human values, in the later novel it is religious cult that does it, with the same possible harm. Hawthorne's position inclines towards a human adjustment. Humanity for any kind of human society is a basic stake.

Everyone in Padua, particularly the younger section, fell in love with Beatrice, but dreaded to close in, even dreaded her father's garden; only a little realistically revised in the novel, the people of the Christian settlement all secretly adored Hester and her daughter, but never ventured to be intimate, they taught themselves to hate her, which alone could serve them as their watch-dog to protect their purity, purity of a barren kind. Hate-barrier of any religious community does not make them more pious and closer to God, rather their confined self-aggrandized self-cherishing drags them further down the scale of humanity. Law is for keeping humanity safe, peace undisturbed, and progress in any form unhindered. What the guardians took into account was sin and its due punishment, as if punishment, alone could preserve humanity from sin's poison-contamination. Never did they think like Baglioni, to accommodate humanly, they read Pearl wrong, Hester too, had Dimmesdale been alive, him too wrong! Pearl was not a demon child, neither Hester a confirmed sinner, if sin they call it; when out of their mechanical artificial purity cult they normally developed in their own natural way a form of unenforced purity, which is their own. A true critique of their prescriptive purity, as the author's whole story is, viewed from outside!

Whatever his artistic manoeuvres he is a serious writer from the very beginning, critically sober, no 'sound and fury' for a dramatic display, he did not allot any major role to Mistress Hibbins, which could introduce a high drama of its kind, of cheap fun and bemused orgies of its kind, if not her execution immediately. Hawthorne evidently wanted to insist upon something of basic humanity a layer below the recognized moral, ethical, even religious, codes. If religion does not enrich human life and blossom into values it may feel like shackles. Hawthorne's story is allowed to speak for itself.

4

Tom Sawyer

[1]

Mark Twain (real name Samuel Langhorne Clemens), born in Florida, Missouri, shifted with his family at the age of four, to the Mississippi river town Hannibal. The river seemed to enter into his blood and gave a romantic turn to his sense of life. Tom Sawyer is born perhaps with this life-sense which further developed in Huck. Neither Tom nor Huck was ever a part of the civilized life of their time, nor aspired to be. Their life-sense was exotic adventure for itself, so no chivalric cult, just a way of life best suited to adolescent irresponsibility. If wickedness it is not of Faulkner's Compson children's kind; they rather recall Robin Hood, only not regimented banditry. Not for personal benefit of anybody, even not for themselves, it is a mere play of their childhood fancies, inventiveness and love of carefree life. A class by itself.

If these stories are retold in simple English they can provide good reading for children. For the intellectual grown-up section of mid-nineteenth century, highly modernized America had still exotic areas for a graceful relief; Faulkner's Sound and Fury in the early twentieth century a further ahead graceless anathema; Hawthorne's *Scarlet Letter* is a variation, a far back picture of early immigration unreality, combative protectionism. Tom is nature's free-born, free-booter, abhorrent of artificial second-hand acquisition. Tom is an orphan, his mother's sister's protégé, not alone but along with his brother Sid. Both the same mother's sons but difference a gulf. Sid is almost a smudge, colourless commonplace, Tom absorbs the whole attention, sometime alone his own guide; when Huckleberry joined kinship struck easily.

Pre-Huckleberry period of Tom's life was truant-type adventurous, unmindful to school lesson and discipline, outward inventiveness kept him busy outside home, Sid by contrast a home-keeping obedient child, Aunt Polly's pet; all troubles of her peaceful life were due to Tom. At school Mr Dobbin's bad boy, punishment to his liking, sitting in the girls' row instead of boys', an object of ridicule to other boys of the class, yet he tricked it to deserve, to sit beside his chosen girl. At home he constantly Aunt Polly's worries, once he stole jam from the kitchen cupboard, when she suspiciously questioned with a stick in hand he played a trick upon her, 'Aunt look behind' she fell back to look and by the time he ran out of the door and made his escape! Attended school late, came away early, occasionally did not attend at all, rather spent the whole school hours swimming and playing with naughty boys of the village. Already Tom earned the reputation of notoriety. Protective families in the village asked their children to shun his company.

He could yet find other stray boys, one such boy, just his contrast, well-dressed, well-groomed boy, a stranger, he thought to impress him with his superiority, he picked a quarrel and engaged in a trial of strength. They fought with feline ferocity. Tom won, but when back home Polly saw his shirt and trousers all covered with dust and knew he was again fighting. She decided punishment, next day Sunday, he must work, no swimming, no play! She engaged him the whole day to white wash the fences! He befooled other boys into doing it for him by a pretended pleasure of doing it, and boys had to pay the price of this pleasure, someone his apple, some other their marbles or other juvenile treasures, all available village fripperies. Aunt Polly is a type of character, easy-believing fickle, malice never consolidated, ill-feeling never durable, trick is a thing never known to her, her intolerance of evil out of her essential goodness, so easily back home to goodness for his ease.

Tom exploited this plain simplicity of this woman, the purity of her soul. Tom and Sid enjoyed pilferages of delicacies from the cupboard, when Sid reported to their Aunt, Tom was always to face the furies, Aunt accused him and punished. Once she made the mistake, Sid took out the sugar-pot for a small quantity, the pot slipped out of his hand and broke into pieces. Aunt Polly hit Tom in spite of his innocence this time. Tom felt terribly hurt at heart, wanted to punish Polly, he would die and Aunt then had to lament his loss. Just a juvenile method of punishing the elders. To avert death-toll Tom sought immediate engagement, one his new found girl who threw him a red rose, Amy Lawrence supplanted by a superior beauty Becky Thatcher. Another playmate Joe Harper whom he did not find. Becky's heart not known, he knew only his. He reached that house, waited long for Becky to appear. Nowhere Becky could be seen, he crossed the wall, came up to below a window, from an upper window someone poured a potful of water, and he was washed all over in the early darkness of the night.

[2]

Sunday over, now Monday, Tom knew Aunt Polly would prescribe medicine from her medical books for every disease he might pretend; the whole night he writhed and groaned, Sid his witness to his aches; but all tricks failed, Polly knew it was School, then a loose tooth, from toe to teeth—clever shift; she prescribes immediate remedy, applied village method to pull it out. No help! School was never his interest, now only Becky's presence there warmed up an attraction, but school discipline and book-knowledge still remained an abhorrence. Aunt Polly knew very little of Tom's outside adventures. His chance meeting with Huckleberry Finn confirmed him in further advance. Monday he had reason to be late at school, Aunt Polly managed the matters and sent him to school against his wish. But he had a secret plan to explain his lateness to his teacher, he met Huck on the way, perhaps invented; Huck a detested bad company, Mr Dobbin caned him for that and in addition asked him to sit with the girls, he obeyed with pleasure. His hushed intimacies with the girl provoked Mr Dobbin immediately to revoke his order and withdraw him seizing him by the ear.

Huck a brutalized child of a boozy untraced father, never went to school, never knew decency, no home for him, is now Tom's friend, friendship with an estranged child, hated by everyone. Immediately Huck took Tom to Horse William's grave in the dead of night. This nocturnal visit is their first joint adventure, and a major event in the story. They saw the coffin exhumed from the grave by the instruction of a doctor, hands engaged were Muff Patter and Red Joe, then followed scuffle between the doctor and the two grave-diggers over a claim of extra money over the settled amount and the doctor's stiff refusal. The doctor gave a stunning blow to Potter with a slab of gravestone and the doctor was stabbed by Red Joe to death. The dagger was Potter's and managed by Red Joe to incriminate Muff, the dagger stuffed into his right hand; but Muff revived and saw the doctor dead. In his fuddled state Muff Potter had no clear memory of what he had done even before his stunned state.

Red Joe convinced him that it was he who did it. They fled leaving the dead body, Tom and Huck, who saw everything from behind a tree in Moon light, also fled in fright, spent some portion of the night in a deserted barn, then left it, Tom for home and Huck for a tree-shelter or anything else. On their way back saw Muff Potter sleeping and his dog stood guard by. Huck and Tom took an oath and signed not to tell anybody anything about it. They were afraid of Red Joe. Sid at home knew Tom was away at night and reported to Aunt who only modestly told Tom he was getting more troublesome than ever before. Tom mentally getting worried, he formed a web of fear around him, Joe a horror in sleep, dream splash of blood, wakeful thought of Becky made him disappointed and angry, Muff in prison could be also hanged! He fell physically ill. Aunt Polly initiated home treatment, first cold wash, then hot bath, then finally a liquid like fire to taste which Aunt herself stopped when saw a cat too got crazy swallowing a little of it!

Tom's recovery brought no relief, at school Mr Dobbins was angry, Becky was absent, when back to school she behaved like disinterested, at home Aunt not happy with him. He decided to teach all by straying away from them all, he would be a pirate, and dreamed to be a rich man. Readily found Joe Harper to accompany him, a boy who could not convince his mother that he did not steal cream from the kitchen cupboard. Tom knew Huck would be happy to join them. The three boys from a Mississippi-coast village left home with some days' provision on a raft, best place for them, as for the pirates in general, was Jackson Island. The author of the story has not conceived any prosecution threat to anybody, no such 'motive' in it, the story of adventure is really a fair document of healthy village life once America enjoyed, everyone for everyone in their joy and misery, their closeness to nature added idyllic grace to this life and to that extent an envied simplicity of their happiness—a thing altogether missed in the modern world anywhere.

The three boys left the village, untraced, they amongst themselves on the island quite happy, free to do whatever they liked, fishing, swimming, playing, a crude camp under a tree-shade for shelter, cooking their own job, menu their own choice, no school, no family protection or guidance, they are their own guide! But a life like that, though seemed ideal, their Arcadia, soon showed its limitation. It could have been a treat like a picnic or a day's outing, permanent life out of society's protection, its love and affection, if reproach and restrictions, that too a part of love, love's exercise of authority and expected claim! This side they left out altogether. They wanted adventure, they forgot the whole civilization was a regulated adventure, which is evolution out of too many mistaken false steps as theirs' now! So, soon they felt home-sick, everyone in his secret heart! The Author of *The Jumping Frog* knew their forefathers, like these boys, made a frog-jump across the Atlantic determined to build up a new society abroad, and they did, no less adventurous than Huck and Tom. Now they enjoy the fruits of their adventure, a settled social order.

Their piracy-plan failed, ended sport-like, their forefathers targetted a settlement in New England, an organized society, adventure for them realistically a part of this plan, not free-booting or child's play, they inherited that seventeenth century spirit, which was a sort of Quixotic Romance, which sent abroad several navigators in search of new lands, their El Dorado, amongst them Sir Ralaigh. Their community feeling in New England was a simple surviving truth, glowing in several widows' eager benevolence, a shared sentiment, a part of their faith. Christianity was more realistic than institutional. They could have been naturally nationalistic, a nation in the making, integrating force not entirely Faith, but more the inherited blood of their forefathers who led the unsettled émigrés into an organized community. Faith to some extent failed in Hawthorne's *Scarlet Letter*. Mark twain's heroes are not faithful, averse to School education and discipline, but they are not really bad boys, British navigators were not by nature cruel, unless compelled to cruelties, they ethically chivalric, not unethically heroic. They continued the Medieval Chivalric Cult.

Tom is the first of this generation in his adolescence, then follows Huck. Mr Jones in his old age of their lot, so he could appreciate Tom and Huck properly. Mr Jones's is a self-embraced Knight's duty to the community. When Huck reported to Mr Jones in the dead of night what was going to happen in Widow Douglas's house he immediately rushed towards Widow Douglas's house with his gun and his two strong sons. The Spaniard, a pirate, Red Joe's partner, attempted, if not to kill, at least to deform her to look ugly to retaliate her husband's sin upon her. Tom had troubles enough, one was his love for Becky who appeared to him siding with another boy of his class Alfred Temple. This love, not a common adolescent love, is unreserved sincerity-supported. Becky, of course plays some tricks, to wean him away from Amy Lawrence, and intensify his eagerness, if at all, by a fake show of intimacy, and by omitting him to join her party, though she was asking Mary Austin to join in his presence; Tom too tried to play the same kind of trick to test her love, when he became more important a fellow after his short pirate career back home in the midst a funeral service going on in the church for their supposed death in the river. He pretended disinterest. They are not 'Araby's' boy lover, his consistent 'vivid waiting' not theirs, they know how to trick and test.

Mr Dobbins Tom's another problem, he is unmindful at school, he failed on the Prize day to recite the full poem, stammered and dropped, now his worst show, his lesson-page of his book smeared with black ink, secretly done by Alfred, himself declared the culprit in presence of all, then Dobbin found his book torn at a page, the whole class was shown who did it, it was done by Becky inadvertently while handling it in a hurry to restore it to the teacher's desk, but she would not acknowledge it to avoid infamous embarrassment and punishment. Tom bravely acknowledged the crime and embraced the punishment for Becky, finally to win her heart. These are all childish game. Tom felt no shame, he is in his childish way chivalric. He perhaps sensed it was Becky and took the blame upon himself in the traditional chivalric spirit for a woman's honour. Alfred is childishly wicked, exposed to Becky who saw him do the mischief, soiling Tom's book slyly.

Mark Twain paints adolescent love which agrees well with the adventure story. Becky is not grown up to claim Maid Maria's position in Robin Hood's band of outlaws. Becky's picnic party on the Jackson island was an adventure in which Becky and Tom were thrown exclusively together and lost in the dark cave, which required Becky's judge father to lead a search party of two hundred strong villagers on the island. It is a full-scale adventure, more than the three boy-pirates' several days life on the island, storm-blasted helplessness and return home on the day of their funeral service.

[3]

Tom is all along a leader, he and Huck signed agreement not to disclose who murdered the doctor, they feared Red Joe might retaliate; but when they saw Muff Potter was in prison and thought for their not disclosing the truth an innocent man could be hanged they took pity on Muff, and often visited him in prison with cigarettes and sweets. The trial proceedings were going on. Tom felt sorry for Muff, and began to see in dreams horrors of every kind, had a talk with Huck, he too was sad. Then he met Muff's lawyer and told him the real story. On the last day of the trial Tom told the court what he saw, Red Joe killed the doctor with Potter's knife. Red Joe fled from the court breaking through a window. Tom was afraid Red Joe might appear in the village to kill him, but soon he forgot his fear. He kept himself busy in other engagements. His pirate career with Joe Harper and Huck, foiled. Tom paid a secret visit to Aunt Polly's house, hid himself in Polly's own bed room and learnt everything they were doing, they finally listed them as lost and fixed next Sunday a funeral Service for them in the Church. They decided to appear on that day in their midst in the Church, another grand adventure.

They were enthusiastically received with great relief. Tom made out of his earlier secret visit a fascinating story of a dream and narrated to his Aunt to her enormous joy and further extended endearment; but the Aunt's unscheduled visit to Mrs Harper's house revealed it was not a dream but real experiences only formed into a dream to befool Tom's Aunt, an easy-believing lady. Joe Harper told her. Tom managed it by his utmost sincerity of a really confession. The sorrowed Aunt now quite happy that Tom really kissed her in her sleep. The Adventure story exudes only a happy earlier unsettled life in its settled state of mutual help, each-for-all kind: The next adventure also testifies this affinity that hold the settled community in peace and mutual love. In their pursuit of wealth of Red Joe and his Spanish accomplice Huck could know that the Spaniard was hell bent upon vengeance to his Widow Douglas—her husband's due visited upon her. Huck immediately called the service of chivalrous Mr Jones.

Tom and Huck in their joint venture closely followed Red Joe and his accomplice Spaniard to locate where they could have stocked their treasure they had heard them talking, stored at 'No. 2 under the cross'. The search only took them through one adventure after another. It is a stage in New England life, a little advanced from Hawthorne's stage of early settlement when their first batch of settlers came with a sword in one hand and a Bible in another hand; Mark Twain follows the adventure-streak and paints their faith, not in external exaggeration, but in their everyday life and character and a community life of cooperation and shared risk. Huck fell ill, his worries to save Mrs Douglas's life and property so exhausted him that Mr Jones had to arrange his stay at his home as good as an inmate and taken proper care for his recovery; Mrs Douglas was no relation neither Mr Jones, yet Huck enjoyed hospitality at Mr Jones's house and found a permanent shelter in the widow's establishment. Huck's was an unregistered adoption, it required no legal sanction. It was a social culture then, more valid than any religious ethics, which was early settlers' only support they thought, as in Hawthorne's *Scarlet Letter*, a badge of religious rendition.

Becky and Tom lost to the whole settlement in the cave for several days, a loss shared by the whole community, rescue operation by 200 people, all able-bodied persons joined, eager waiting for all; Tom of course took under his charge the safety of the girl not simply because he loved her, but because it was his chivalric duty imposed on him then. They managed to reach a point of open riverine course out of the dark cave, beaconed a passing boat for rescue, when rode together into the settlement, it was a solemn relief for all, Tom turned a hero, no question of ethics and etiquettes, the Judge father took Tom for a holy rescuer of his lost child. Tom saw in the dark a hand, recognized Red Joe's, an extra risk of their life, a violent bat-attack another, he took particular care that no harm done to his protégée!

Now out of danger Tom could plan afresh the recovery of Red Joe's hidden treasure. He took Huck, as he did before, for a further search inside the cave. Becky's father Judge Thatcher told him he had closed the mouth of the cave with an iron door. Tom knew Joe was there inside locked to die of starvation, the Judge found him dead; they entered it, with their digging implements and sacks and candles enough, followed his footprints up a place where dug up the heavy box filled with gold coins. They carried their loot in their bags and rowed ashore both rich men.

[4]

Tom won one victory, he saved Becky's life under his conduct home, still Huck was in Mr Jones's house recovering. He met Huck there and reported the Spaniard was dead, they found his dead body floating in the river, perhaps killed by Red Joe. Now learnt from Judge Mr Thatcher that Joe too was dead. They could then look for Joe's treasure in the cave. Huck agreed to join him in this venture. The venture was their possession of Joe's treasure-trough entire. Their long-awaited wind-fall in their possession, they joined Widow Douglas's party in a treasure-sacks loaded cart just outside the house. Widow Douglas assured Huck of her constant care of a mother, her declared heir in presence of her guests. Tom surprised them declaring Huck was already a rich man, he did not require anybody's wealth. The two sacks were brought inside and unloaded on the table, all gold coins.

The end of the story is really with a responsible management, the whole community joined to help these two Medieval unaccoladed real Knights in their midst. They began to cherish them like that. Judge Mr Thatcher began to like Tom, he put their wealth into a bank for safety and wished Tom to be their crusader, which they needed at the promising stage of New England colony, still to be an organised secure society. All the virtues of Medieval Chivalry now needed more than in the Medieval context. Ashbey Tournament was a Chivalric sport, now it was a serious social duty. Tom was at the end changed in his view. He advised Huck what it was for him to do, to be with him and in his band: to avoid a long passage the sum:

> Tom cannot accommodate a rough and uncultured unschooled fellow in his band, the Robin Hood days are gone, now boys are needed to go to school, to be civilized, live in homes; only like Robin Hood they will take from the rich and give away to the poor. Huck to be civilized and live like civilized people with a humanitarian pledge to be of help to who may need it. This is how Tom is converted to a chivalric vow. Mark Twain's story depicts an early stage of a nation in the making. The next story is only expected to continue the process of development in spite of other many changes.

5

Tom's Heir Huck

[1]

Tom Sawyer initiates adventures Huckleberry Finn continues, as heir to Tom. Tom appeared in 1876, after a long gap of eight years Huck, Tom's street friend originally, banded with him in the earlier story, continues a more complex, more intriguing series of adventures dialoguing as many as six varieties of regional speech of the same language at the least. The author meaningfully with a warning: motive, moral and plot, need not be made the standard of literary judgement. He is right from his point of view. His point is, beside those three, real judgement of a literary creation, which is enjoyment, both ways, author and audience, in a sharing principle of enjoyment closely engaged.

The question inevitably is what do they enjoy? The same thing can be enjoyable to different people for different reasons of their own. Adventure stories are most relished by children, but grown-up people are equally interested, if they are, they find something which children are likely to miss; their something varies in a sort of critical response. It is not definitely Lewis Carroll's Kind of Wonderland, published in England a little earlier 1865, a phantasy, Tom and Huck's *Adventures* are real-world accounts, Mississippi is their Congo, the river itself a story, life on either side and on big and small islands in it inseparable from its mysterious history. Before the European emigration America as a whole remained more or less an African Congo, emigration was a boon to America, emigrants by their tireless endeavour and acumen made the land fruitful and gave it a civilization against great odds. Theirs was not a failed El Dorado exploration, because they were not after Alice Wonderland, they were realistic, forsook all dreams of a mountain of gold, Tom and Huck are their progeny, if gold, they knew where it could be found and how. Their adventure realistic.

The whole American civilization was built up by the further refined realistic adventurism, which required witty utilization of available means to an overall success; this success story required an honesty of purpose which was ultimately the essence of Christianity, love and faith. Tom and Huck were never a bloody killers, their women Aunt Polly, Sally, Douglas and Watson imbibed best of honest simplicity, ready to forgive, easy to forget, finally to love. It is they who alone could rescue a bonded nigger even at the cost of their own comfort, even their own security. The first voice of protest was raised against slave trade by one of their forefathers, noble Dr Johnson. Further remote Pope Gregory I the Great pitied the fate of fine boys for sale in the slave market of Rome and decided to send missionaries like St. Augustine to eradicate this inhuman evil by a message of love.

Emigrant Christians from their original home land held out their faith in life, not as a mere faith, the widows are devoted Christians, but Tom and Huck are not church-goers, they are selfless perpetrators of good, even through apparently evil means, they inherit the spirit of Robin Hood. But they have not acquired strength enough to materialize it, the spirit is inherited, materializing maturity yet to wait. American civilization is now built up by materializing this waiting spirit. Tom Sawyer is their band leader, he has gone through all those in adventure literature, Robin Hood down to Robinson, all raw stuff inflamed his fancy, all the other boys, Huck most, formed a circle around him, and turned his juvenile critics. He found in those records a captivating term 'ranson' whose meaning he did not know and could not finally explain. He is Cervantes's Don Quixote, only juvenile in nature, in American context not satiric.

He alerts his friends to ambush a Spaniard-Arab party of merchants, their elephants and camels loaded with treasures like diamonds and gold, four hundred soldiers on guard armed with guns, his description of elaborate plan of a surprise armed attack and easy plunder watering their mouth, but they recalled; "He never could go after even a turnip cart but he must have the swords and guns all scoured up for it; though they was only lath and broom-sticks, and you might scour at them till you rotted and they wasn't worth a mouthful of ashes more than what they was before" (pp. 13-14). Huck ready 'on hand' in the ambuscade simply because he would see elephant and camel. What they found was a sunday-school picnic. Like a wind-mill charge they chased the childred away, and grabbed their 'doughnuts and jam', Ben Roger 'got a rag doll and Joe Harper a hymn book', 'then they charged in and made us drop everything and cut'. It is child's play, so one cannot take it for a satire.

Tom's explanation in the story removes the shred of satire, if his elders conceived it so at all, he told Huck everything, camel elephant and all, he could know if he only read *Don Quixote*, it is beyond his etches of neglected schooling, it was 'enchantment'. Huck and Tom then engaged in a sort of debate, Tom sought support from Arabian Night's Tales, Huck would not go beyond common everyday realities, Huck too forgot he was also unrealistic; within a month of their adventure they all felt they should return home, only Tommy Barnes spoke clearly, then Huck, the narrator of the story, spoke for all: "We played robber now and then about a month, then I resigned. All the boys did. We hadn't robbed nobody, we hadn't killed any people, only just pretended" (p. 13).

[2]

This could terminate the story. It is art. Their joint venture can so terminate, but a nation built up by a joint venture, when allows everyone his right to decide his destiny, cannot so stop short, everyone should exert himself, and must not expect Aladin's lamp to build his palace. So Huck is left alone to face the music, cultivate his mind, exert his efforts in whichever way needed and chosen. Back home to Miss Watson, three or four months Huck was a regular school-going boy, trying to accommodate himself to civilized ways, Miss Watson too satisfied, though progress slow; in Huck's language: "could say the multiplication table up to six times seven is thirty five" (p. 16). Civilization could yet conceal under ceremonial cover many a superstitious shred. He turned over the salt-cellar at breakfast, ominous, remedial ritual observed by the widow, yet Huck to be over-sure had his fortune read by Jim's hair-ball witch. Jim, Miss Watson's nigger, told, rather foretold, what was awaiting him. Huck met Judge Thatcher, sold his money to the judge, indeed to escape father's apprehended exploitation, the Judge too appreciated. Now soon after father's ghost appeared, caught him in his safe den, a living trouble, in short Huck's life took an adverse turn, led him into a single-handed adventure, bereft of Tom's imaginary self-created adventure drama, Huck's is all real, a difference that can be made between the European El Dorado expedition and American emigrant adventure of a later period.

Over a year untraced father, considered then dead, a floating dead body some identified as Huck's pap, Huck doubted, all on a sudden appeared in Miss Watson's house, broke into Huck's peace, ugly dirty boozy, for money and to teach him their traditional manners, unschooled adventurous savage life, more of the Injun adventurous life in the open. A representation of the lower section of the migrants. Huck too inherits this kind of taste, so in sharp contrast with Tom and his ilk. He knew it and acknowledged. In the earlier story Huck was a hated Pariah, no parents allowed their children to mix up with him, he had no fixed place to stay up, no fixed schedule to follow, a carefree open air life was after his liking. If he continued like that most likely he would have been his father's faggot. Only one virtue endeared him to a class above him, mostly childless pious widows; his unreserved openness, and to be of help to others associated with it made every good heart easily respond, it did Mrs Douglas', and two stranger young girls' in their families.

The entire American civilization and achievement is a long-trudged adventure story of a people who knew the ethics of self-help, the tradition of monarchy left behind, cherished a system of government of Uncle Sam, the guardian of the same family, first among equals, a nation thus formed rose easily to the peak of power. The story shows people of this temperament, independent every one, yet united, not afraid of risk, even danger, not in a mood to shy away, rather to face with confidence and inventive acumen, individually and unitedly, never made religion a sort of idle opium dose, which true religion is not. True religion makes brain fertile, body competent, mind clear and pure, heart compassionate, loving. Without these qualities in the wake any system, however apparently attractive, mechanical routine, less of help to human good.

Hawthorne's *Scarlet Letter* represents an earlier faulty stage of these people who made religion their mode of adventure, religion an artificial form of rigidity. Mark Twain's the further developed stage of adventure, where human values in their simplest possible form adjust themselves. Life itself represents a pattern. Huck's pap a rough and rude person, a roguish fellow, in his family he boasts none learnt letters, none cared for religion, but they were free and independent, earned their own bread and ate their own meal. This spirit is a shared spirit. He did not like Huck to be in Miss Watson's charity, rather he should be his family and free in his own way; Huck wanted himself free from the widow and father, both. All that he did, did to undo what his father had done already, locked him in a log house to keep him as father's property including his possessed wealth; he was to release himself from father's captivity, to get fresh freedom. Father took him from one kind of comfortable captivity, Huck himself from another kind of physical captivity. All that he and his father did was no fancy but practical adventure story.

The Mississippi in all their life plays a vital role more intimately than the Congo in *Heart of Darkness*; the Congo led them, Kurtz and all, into the heart of darkness; but the American Colonists in no way lost themselves in the mystery of any such darkness as Kurtz did, a civilized man turned savage. They created a new civilization, to them the river disclosed the mystery, Jackson island their Jericho where Huck secured his liberty, Jim too found a Good Samaritan in him, no shred of Kurtz's cruelty shrouded his humanity. Huck and Tom acted the part of a rescuer of the savage more successfully than Captain Lingard. They are not of the kind of Kurtz or his cousin Picton (in Naipaul's El Dorado) with his Savage Sweetheart Mrs Smith, they are the true descendants of the Medieval Chivalry in their boyish way.

[3]

Huck's father stole Huck to a new captivity and filed a suit against Judge Thatcher and Widow Watson, he created trouble in the town and was several times imprisoned, Judge Thatcher made a plea to the trying Judge to place Huck in his personal Custody and safe from his father's tyranny. On moral ground he could not agree to do it, to separate a son from father. He did the other noble alternative, he took the father home to civilize the savage, he behaved quite well, but fled when his true nature got the better of civilized regulation. Huck's is a little reformed stage of his father's adventurous life. Tom's is a further developed stage, he adds style to adventure, even fancy and vision, which gave him all along a leading role. Tom helped the run away Nigger Jim, saw him cross over the hill, Huck was then in father's captivity, and managed to get his freedom, leaving misleading signs of his murder in pap's absence, trails of hog's blood and corn flour did the hoax.

He meets Jim on Jackson island and learns all about his flight for fear of being sold, a slave dealer was then around pressing the widow to do at a price, eight hundred apiece. He did not wait for the last word of the bargain. Jim too got everything about Huck's adventure. From then on they were each other's company and accomplice in adventure. Jim's inherited fear of witches, for a Negro the world is witch-infested, nothing is, weal or ill, achieved but by the grace or curse of the witch; when he first saw Huck in the dun shadow of the forest 'he drops down on his knees and says':

> Doan hurt me—don't! I hain't ever done no harm to a ghos' I awluz like bad people en done all I could for 'em.... (p. 39)

He thought the witch sent him a dead man's ghost to harm him. It was already circulated in the town by Huck's father that he was dead, killed by some pirate and his stock taken. His stratagem gained ground. Clear-sighted Huck and witch-besmirched Jim, a white man and black negro, henceforth formed a free adventure-band. The difference between them is very great, not of colour alone, but of a culture, theirs a world of 'signs', mostly of evil, all their faith formed by a tradition of unexperimented belief generation after generation, unreasoned too; when Huck would have none of it unless rationally experimentally proved sound and acceptable. Unconfirmed conviction is not faith. Confirmation is conviction, which evokes trust, call faith. The whole Western world is guided by it, Eastern idea is further deepened to conviction equivalent to 'breath of life' (Sans. Biswas), so true and inescapable.

Cultural difference is not marked out by the colour of the body but by the quality of faith. Huck Tom ignore colour, ignore formal religion, but deep in their faith, which Huck's father lacked, he blamed the government who could not sell out a mulatto professor. Huck wanted Jim a free man, free from all those untenable traditional belief, but did not blame him for his incapacity to shed all those long cherished beliefs of his community, rather appreciated his human qualities. Jim learnt from experiences the net truth, only in a different sense than he knew:

> 'Yes—en I's rich now, come to look at it, I owns myself, en I's wuth eight hund'd dollars' (p. 44). Any self-helping American, including Huck, could appreciate it, but not the other: 'I wisht I had de money, I wouldes' want no mo'.

Huck would have none of it, he cannot sell himself, his self in his own possession. This is the spirit behind all his adventures. He is not even in his father's possession, he duped his father, Jackson island made his home, got a cave for shelter, thought it safe, got a skiff, a raft, all hidden there amongst the willows his present possession, filled his store with whatever he found in a two-story abandoned raft, the raft itself a story of the great river, a family ill-fated. Then trouble in their cave-home, first inside Jim snake-bitten—a rattle snake he got dead home for fun, but the dead's mate retaliated at night. Jim her unluky victim. Four days required for Jim's recovery—a negro method of recovery prescribed by Jim. But soon they required to shift. Another adventure. Huck dressed as a girl made a secret visit to a village at night on Illinois side of the river, learnt from a lady in a solitary shack he visited when he found none other near-by. It was the lady's temporary shelter, her husband then out for a company in the other end of the small town St. Petersburg. This lady disclosed to him all that he had already known—a search for his dead body, his murder—and something in addition he did not know: her husband out for a boat and a man to search on the island for the fugitive nigger for the reward of three hundred dollars (he is suspected to have killed Huck), another reward of two hundred dollars for Huck's father, another suspect. Her husband a poor man, need that money so the search would be on at midnight.

The visit to the young lady (forty years old) all a fun, how Huck was detected, he was in no way a girl, but maybe a runaway 'prentice', of course not his exact identity, she assured him of her help as a true Christian, though in a sweet turn of humour; "Now trot along to your uncle, Sarah Mary Williams George Eleczander Peters, and if you get into trouble you send word to Mrs Judith Loftus, which is me, and I'll do what I can to get you out of it" (p. 57). Huck is a person to depend on himself to 'get out of it', if there is any. She only helped him by timely information to shift within an hour, it was then eleven at night. To elude the search party Huck built, a big fire at the place where he found Jim and quickly left the island in their skiff and raft. In spite of Jim's witch-wisdom nowhere in the adventure story Jim could suggest any concrete course of action except by 'signs' of weather and impending evil traditionally known to them. It is Huck's inventiveness and initiative that account for the entire success, including Jim's safety. Jim could put in his physical labour and faithful company. A brain and body combination, natural division of labour the East knew better in their ancient era of civilization.

Huck is not formally educated, Jim a negro is not; but education is not the only source of knowledge, though human civilization evolved out of knowledge for life to live. Huck is a close ally to Jim so far as formal education is concerned. Their knowledge of Biblical Solomon is poor, still their difference of understanding of Solomon's wisdom in the episode of two quarrelling women over a baby's parental claim. Huck could appreciate a little complex method of detection of true parental love, but Jim would take it straight. Huck understood he could not teach otherwise: "I never see such a nigger. If he got a notion in his head once, there wasn't getting it out again" (p. 73). He does not understand a French King speaks a different language, man anywhere speaks the same language, as a cat or dog anywhere does. He would not count other factors that make the difference inevitable. Knowledge is a distinguishing and synthesizing principle, a level above is realization which is wisdom. When it is human feelings difference of language or knowledge makes hardly any difference at bottom, unless otherwise distorted. Culture is cultivation of a mechanism of distortion management, education is a part of it, essential, if true.

[4]

Huck is nature-educated, his adventure is a projection of this education. He fled from Jackson island to his next adventure down at a wrecked steam boat a little below St. Louis. He robbed the robbers' and lost raft in the operation. He left the three robbers quarrelling amongst themselves, maybe over their share of the plunder, one roped and laid upon the deck and threatened to fire for a sort of betrayal. Huck felt a kind of compassion for them, stranded there, and likely to be starved dead. Their skiff too stolen loaded with their loot. He would keep the plunder safe and make a yarn for their rescue, at least they must not starve dead! He did, met the steam-boat ferry watchman in the dead of night, persuaded him to the rescue operation, then left everything to chance, course of justice and all!

Huck always remembers Tom, appreciates his style of adventure, he is only a raw version of Tom's kind, a step closer to nature, his natural humanity unbeclouded. He knew Jim was Widow Watson's renegade negro, he never encouraged him to runaway, but now he was his protector, a nigro seeking his freedom, his wife's and even his two children's; it touched his heart as much as did his love for the honest widow who gave him shelter, tried to civilize him and make him comfortable in life. Here is a conscience clean:

> What had poor Miss Watson done to you, that you could see her nigger go off right under your eyes and never say one single word? What did that poor old woman do to you; that you could treat her so mean? Why, she tried to learn you your book, she tried to learn you your manners, she tried to be good to you every way she knowed how. That's what she done. (p. 82)

Jim in his simple way defined a sharp difference from European culture here in America: "Dat's good! But he'll be pooty lonesome—dey ain' no Kings here, is dey, Huck?" (p. 73).

Huck was speaking of the executed Louis XVI's son the Dauphin Philippe who fled from France during the Revolution and sought political asylum in America. Jim reasonably apprehended there was neither any 'dolphin' nor King in America, so 'no situation' for him. Uncle Sam set no rule for avuncular patronage! America can tolerate, even indulge, a Tom or Huck who believes in his own resources. These people laid the foundation of true Democracy. The individual is the final source of all resources. The State only to utilize it. Only a Ministry of Human Resources cannot make a nation Democratic. It requires a change of attitude, if it did not have it, or lost it, the last explains Naipaul's title, *India: A Wounded Civilization*, when India is concerned. America was born with the character that made them normally Democratic.

In his raw style self-responsibility unshared, unshifted, a nigro slave his protégé, his freedom his responsibility, though he feels he has no reason to be ungrateful to the widow, and cannot be indifferent to her undeserved injury. He loves his own liberty, so, cannot condemn, another fellow-man's share, if he can help it. So Huck now sails towards the Ohio state, to reach first Cairo, but he was misled to a creek or head of a bend mistaken for Cairo, light on shore got them think so. Two men, one with a gun, appeared in the dark in a skiff, in search of five runaway nigroes. They would search Huck's raft a little way below, Jim there. Huck instantly made a story of his whole family: "I wish you would, because it's pap that's there, and maybe you'd help me tow the raft ashore where the light is. He's sick—and so in mam and Mary Ann" (p. 83). He did not say clear, pretended, everyone earlier left him alone none helped him to haul up the raft with those sick people, they were way down towards the raft, one insisted, "what is the matter with your pap? Answer up square, now, and it'll be better for you".

Huck still bit his word, modulated language slow, punctuating different, his earnestness made clear: 'don't leave us, please', then infusing in them some fear if very close, as though to ensure their safety, said: "It's the—the—gentlemen, if you'll only pull ahead, and let me heave you the head-line, you won't have to come a-near the raft please do" (p. 84).

They suspected small-pox, other people could not help him for that, they held, gave Huck twenty dollar on a piece of flat wood and advised him just to float down about twenty miles and find a town on the left hand side where he must not be a fool to say small pox, would rather say Chill and fever. Huck escaped from them and found Jim out of the raft, in water dipped whole body only nose a little above water. Their journey began for another major risk of life, in the deep darkness a speeding steam boat like a dark bank of cloud hit the raft in the middle before the boat stopped engine; Huck and Jim toppled into the water on either side of the giant boat, their destiny. Huck dived thirty feet deep to avoid being crushed by the giant wheel and surfaced on his side to swim safe the treaturous river, long struggle for bare life alone on shore, Jim lost sight of, raft too. On shore a different venture, more particularly important for Twain's story.

Naipaul's to his Oxford audience, while a student, said Defoe cannot expect his audience always under-aged, they must grow up; a significant comment, Mark Twain's Adventure story is for the grown-ups and has a different interest, Huck received by the Grangerfords, as if in a fortress, a defeated prisoner, with all the formalities of surrender, drenched all over like a cat in the storm. Colonel Grangerford was to know whether he was someone from the Sheperdson camp, a constant enemy through generations. Huck once inside at that hour of the night could know the history of the family and their feud with the Sheperdsons. This story reveals an important Chapter of American history, their yet unsettled stage of a growing nation. They inherited a Chivalric culture, the home is reminiscent of that culture, they are merciless to the enemies when they are strong, and can fight them even over ages, no question of life and loss, honour their cult; on this bedrock was built up the plot of all those Heroic Tragedies of seventeenth century British drama on the supplied model of Corneille, author of Le Cid.

The other side of their culture, they are friend to the distressed, Huck's stay there since his distressed entry never made him feel uncomfortable, their youngest child Buck was of his age, his mother at once pointed out to their father: "Why bless you, Saul, the poor thing's as wet as he can be; and don't you reckon it may be he's hungry?" (p. 90). He submitted, the lady at once ordered: "Betsy, you fly around and get him something to eat, as quick as you can, poor thing; and one of you girls go and wake up Buck and tell him—Oh, here he is himself. Buck, take this little stranger and get wet clothes off from him and dress him up in some of yours that's dry".

Nowhere in the story a house is so, thoroughly described, the description itself a stamp of inherited tradition and culture transported from across the Atlantic, which involves an adventure story, a heroic feat. Hawthorne's forefathers crossed the Ocean with a Bible in one hand and a sword in another, and included in their first plan of settlement a prison and a Church. That phase is left behind, now the Bible is replaced by catholicity and sword by gun; at home a commodious culture nursed, outside heroic confrontation with courage and determination.

Among, the children Emmeline the daughter dead at fifteen is the sweetest flower of their garden whose memory is fondly cherished in as many ways as they can. For every death she wrote a dirge even before the undertaker attended. Her feelings rhymed into a piece of verse. She is an unapprenticed born poet. The family's extensive farm lands needed hundred hands to work, hundred pieces to provide, every member in the family was provided with a nigro servant to attend.

The Grangerfords and the Shephedsons enjoyed the same gentleman's status. The cause of their feud so long-drawn and bitter must have been rivalry any way, possibly possession of land initially. Such a rivalry could further extend to other areas of common interest. One of the Grangerford daughters must have ignited it more into a blaze by her unmindful flight from home with her Romeo young Harney Sheperdson. The episode recalls Montague-Capulate family rivalries and secret love-relation. Sophia the younger daughter, only twenty, came to be in love with Harney, how no one knows; only later Huck could know if he could 'read writing'. The young lady sent him to pick up her Bible she left in the Church, in which he found a scrap of paper written only 'Half past two', He later lamented he could save the trouble and loss of life if he only got the paper to the father. Sophia's elopement immediately provoked war between the two families leading to loss of lives on either side, very sad for Huck when he found Buck killed.

Twain has no need to continue the story further, when he felt no need his reason must be honoured. Twain is not writing a tragic play, he seems true to his subject: the kind of people who accommodated their spirit of heroic adventure to the building of a nation, their love of liberty and self-reliance, self-respect and indomitable courage and determination of a crusader, everyone in his own place in his own capacity. Hawthorne depicts Puritan rigidity of the time immediately after the New England settlement around Boston, the Mississippi still far away, Mark Twain depicts a later time hundred years or so after the Independence, farther south the more adventurous zone of the mysterious course of the River, which itself was a major object of conquest that had never been the Congo savage area to the civilized west. The people like Tom and Huck never had to fool about the savage as Kurtz was to, neither were their superiors, the Grangerfords and the Sheperdsons; no sagamores-contact did they need, they were their masters already. Jim predicted a black woman for Huck, he was wrong, Huck had no such tendency; Huck could feel soft-hearted for the first white lady Miss Sophia whom he assured 'he liked her' when she asked him, but could not blame her for all the troubles she caused to the family and lamented that he did not, rather could not, serve the benevolent family in time handing over her scrawled slip of paper to Mr Grangerford:

> I judged that that piece of paper meant that Miss Sophia was to meet Harney somewheres at half-past two and run off; and I judged I ought to told her father about that paper and the curious way she acted, and then maybe he would a locked her up and this awful mess wouldn't ever happened. (p. 106)

[5]

Uncultured Huck is the true keeper of conscience of American culture, his is not a killer's adventure, his adventure is a display of his 'wit' and self-confidence against all adverse circumstances, not at the cost of his humanity which made him win every heart wherever he had been. He left the Grangerfords in great danger, he wished if he could help them. He left the shore with a heavy heart, but leave he must, there was a nigger under his protection. They fled the scene, luck favoured him Jim found the raft, repaired the damage, and waited for him, he saw him enter that house, himself in the woods waiting. Now very soon when they were shoving in through a chute about two hundred yards to reach the main bank, two white men strangers with carpet bag in hand sought shelter for life chased by people behind on horse back with dogs. They said they had done nothing. Huck doubted, yet could not avoid their earnest appeal.

A new chapter of Huck's adventure opened. These two strangers remind me of a late 19th century Bengali novelist Saratchandra, his City-bred Babu and boat man Srikanta, only the Babu is not a fraud like these two strangers, Mark Twain makes them contribute to not only fun but also to a contrast to values Huck stands for. Saratchandra's Babu would appropriate all the comforts to himself even at the cost another's protection against chill, he would ask the poor man to spread his wrapper on the board of the boat deck for his comfortable seating, yet urging him to paddle quick with his bare body exposed to cold wind. These two strangers, stranger also one to the other, claimed one deprived of his rightful title, Duke of Bridgewater, another claimed for himself the Dauphin of France, Louis XVI's and Queen Antonoitte's eldest son, now in exile nobody here. Jim wondered, Huck pretended to accept their claim with due honour. They taught them how to address them, how to attend at dinner, all on a raft, a small boy-naked and a nigger to keep watch and pilot the raft night after night in storm and heavy shower on a river like the Mississippi, their beds in the wigwam occupied by them according to their ranks, that too in America that abolished such ranks already.

By the side of such an inhuman rank-prude Huck's judgement turns fun to a serious subject of true wisdom:

> It didn't take me long to make up my mind that these liars wasn't no kings and dukes, at all, but just low-down humbugs and frauds. But I never said nothing, never let on; kept it to myself; it's the best way; then you don't have no quarrels, and don't get into no trouble. If they wanted us to call them kings and dukes, I hadn't no objections, long as it would keep peace in the family; and it want no use to tell Jim, so I didn't tell him. If I never learnt nothing else out of pap, I learnt that the best way to get along with his kind of people is to let them have their own way. (p. 115)

Now we are faced with two different kinds of adventures: "Tom-Huck adventure and the two-frauds' adventure. One a part of a character that can, if properly adjusted, build up a nation; the other a characterless fraudulent misadventure, idle profiteering; a difference simplified to one between truth and falsehood, protection and plunder. At their first halt the fraud-duo exposed themselves. There was a little one-horse town about three miles down the bend" (p. 119). The Duke and King got there, and Huck took them there in their Canoe, he to collect some coffee. The duke planned some show, Shakespearian tragedy. Richard III or Romeo and Juliet for example, but saw the street deserted, the duke found an unlocked Printing Press, he remained there tinkering. The king and Huck walked to the Camp-meeting 'about two miles back in the woods'. A country fair-like scene. The preachers there to preach the gospel no better than their audience, no Dimmesdale-elevated preaching pattern, rather a scene of preaching in Faulkner's *The Sound and the Fury*. The king managed there to preach his private gospel, all to his purpose. He played out his story of a repentant pirate in the Indian Ocean turned preacher to covert all those pirate infidels to the true faith, he sobbed and mumbled and sighed. The audience drew their breath too. Only a short fragment here:

> ...he was going start right off and work his way back to the Indian Ocean and put in the rest of his life trying to turn the pirates into the true path; for he could do it better than anybody else, being acquainted with all the pirate crews in that Ocean; and though, it would take time to get there, without money, he would get there anyway, and every time he convinced a pirate he would say to him, 'Don't you thank me, don't you give me no credit, it all belongs to them dear people in Pokenville camp-meeting, natural brothers and benefactors of the race—and all that dear preachers there the truest friend a pirate ever had. (p. 121)

He collected 87 dollars 75 cents, while going home collected a three gallon jar of whisky from under a van. The duke made use of the printing press in absence of the owner, printed bills for customers, declaring himself the new owner, and swindled money out of many such clients on concession rates for a new starting and ready cash, proposed publication of a paper, advanced payment on tempting commission etcetera. Only for Jim's day time safe journey printed a Public Notice: A runaway nigger from St. Jacques' Plantation forty miles below New Orleans, below it a reward $200. Jim to be tied with ropes hands and feet.

All the amusing fun excepted, for the grown-ups this is the story. Then a snatch of Jim's comment: 'Huck, does you reckon we gwyne to run acrost any mo' kings on his trip?'

'No', I says, 'I reckon not'

'Well', say he, 'dat's all right, dan, I doan' mine one ar two kings, but dat's enough. Dis one's powerful drunk, en de duke ain' much better' (p. 123).

How meanly troublesome a king of his kind appears even to an unthinking nigger, let alone their majestic moral standard! As a man they (both king and duke) are exposed to Huck, even to Jim. They prostitute their cunningness and exploit innocence of common people, their next halt is a different kind of swindle, the people in Arkansaw are the right kind of people to fall prey to their humbug. Comedy is an art invented in ancient Greece for low class of village people for their recreation. Twain provides it more than Dickens in this novel, but he does not over step the balanced treatment of a nation in the making with transplanted jamboree elements among the chivalric adventurous batches of European, particularly British, emigrants. The entire river course provided woody fertile land, mostly unworked, the riverine ecology required them to keep up adventurous spirit in them or develop it afresh. A section was poor, without moorings, really commoners, no duke dauphin sailed over to the new continent.

Light amusing comedy fills the pages of the novel, riverside village and Huck's 'one horse-towns' are generally inhabited by working class people, pedigreed elements among them makes a sharp contrast, low comedy heightened to a dignity that assumes sometimes the nature of Medieval romance makes poor people's life and enjoyment more gauche, more amusing by contrast. The kind of people in Arkansaw they met could enjoy hog-squeal and dog fight: "and away the sow would go, squealing most horrible, with a dog or two swinging to each ear, and three or four dozen more a-coming: and then you would see all the loafers get up and watch the thing out of sight, and laugh at the fun and took grateful for the noise.

Then they'd settle back, again till there was a dog-fight. There couldn't anything wake them up all over, and make them happy all over, like a dog fight—unless it might be putting turpentine on a stray dog and setting fire to him, or tying a tin pan to his tail and see him run himself to death" (p. 128).

For such an audience the king and duke went through elaborate rehearsal of Romeo and Juliet, Richard III and Hamlet's Soliloquy on the raft itself, their audience then Huck and Jim and the mute open river; Duke of Bridgewater of Somerset and the Dauphin no less than they, they distort Shakespeare merrily, To be and not to be'—soliloquy made into a miserable hotch-potch, an amusing mixed dish of Hamlet and Macbeth, a usual performs for such a lot, a little above the level of the howling ignoramuses Baconian 'wit' their education, otherwise hollow. Cunning misapplication, just a show of wisdom. The composition of this dish is relishingly misleading, I would I could quote it. Duncan and Ophelia at the same dinner, Scotland and Norway banquetting at the same table. When Louis XVI's heir to the throne of France could be considered King of Franks Charlemagne's heir, six-seven hundred years old now, another Methuselah, and Dauphin never said a word, one can see through their bluff and their knowledge of history and the kind of education they had. Mark Twain makes them appear the same category of scum of the emigrants, and the subject of fun.

Amongst them Col. Sherburn is rightly Col. Grangerford's class. He was born and raised in the South and knew the North, knew there people better, his individuality cannot be blurred by the offscourings around. Boggs a heavy drinker, aged about fifty, now tipsy. He met Sherburn in his store, biggest in the town, and began to accuse him that he swindled him and challenged him to come out, called him any names he pleased, cursed him any way be knew. People enjoyed it, crowded around him, it was 'a fun for them. Sherburn only once came out of his store a proud-looking man about fifty five —and he was a heap of the best dressed man in that town, too'. The crowd 'drops back on each side to let him come'. He said 'mighty calm and slow':

> I'm tired of this; but I'll endure it till one o'clock, Till one o'clock, mind no longer. If you open your mouth against me only only once, after that time, you can't travel so far but I will find you. (p. 130)

'The crowd looked mighty sober; nobody stirred, and there wasn't no more laughing'. But Boggs was not restrained, he continued slanging, howling defying as before. People tried to restrain him and even reminded him of one o'clock dead-line. They were serious, some one went to his daughter, if she could. Sherburn came down, calm and silent, and once only called 'Boggs', no more. Cocked his pistol, held it towards the sky. The daughter then coming, sixteen year old beauty, the crowd silent flanked on both sides, pistol barrel lowered and a bullet rang out, then another. Then he silently turned and walked off, leaving the scene to act itself, unworried.

The crowd and only man amongst them a sharp contrast, the next scene heightens the contrast still more sharp. The daughter left to her own agonies, the crowd consolidated under a Cassius, who must have harangued them about their Roman birth right of freedom and then marched towards Sherburn's citadel. A veritable Roman mob, Mark Twain in his usual vein of humour depicts it, a snatch of its kind:

> They swarmed up the street towards Sherburn's house, a-whooping and yelling and raging Injuns, and everything had to clear the way or get run over and tramped to mush, and it was awful to see. Children was heeling it ahead of the mob, screaming and get out of the way; and every window along the road was full of women's heads, and there was nigger boys in every, and bucks and wenches looking over every fence; as soon as the mob would get nearly to them they would break and skaddle back out of reach. Lots of women and girls was crying and taking on, scared most to death. (p. 133)

Then what happened was not like Scott's Porteous Mob or Shakespeare's Roman Mob. Col. Sherburn set off alone the intended assault, and boasted 'lynching' or 'hanging'; he faced them: "on to the roof of his little front porch, with a double barrel gun in his hand, he takes stand, perfectly ca'm and deliberate, not saying a word. The racket stopped, and the wave sucked back" (*ibid.*).

Sherburn delivered a long exordium on true valour, actually the self-taught laws of chivalry, which they lacked; he ridiculed Buck Harkness their leader, 'half a man', perhaps not even that, The pitifulest thing out is a mob; that's what an army is—a mob; they don't fight with courage that's born in them, but with courage that's borrowed from their mass, and from their officers" (p. 134).

Huck everywhere to narrate the story. He embodies adventure, with a different kind of self-help, valour-values inherited, in that, nearest kin to Sherburn, he from a different level of the immigrants in New England, Sherburn from a higher level, the same spirit of different modification. The duke and dauphin only a perverted misfeature. After circus shows, they got for the first night twelve people their audience, eleven left, only one caught asleep. The duke knew then how to draw the audience there, Shakespeare too dull for them; posters, bills hung up for the next show: The King's Camelopard and The Royal Nonesuch—Ladies and Children not Admitted. The grossness of the show thus assumed tempted all the men folk there. The show itself—King's naked body 'ring-streaked and-striped all over' in all sorts of colours, 'splendid as a rainbow'—cheap approach to circus-girls' eye-catching fripperies sprancing up the stage, crawling capering about several times; every time "they roared and clapped and stomed and haw-hawed till he came back and done it over again" (p. 138). They shamed Elizabethan groundlings.

The duke declared the show was closed, they felt cheated, 'sold' they kept silent for the next show there's a kind of reparation, a cowardly act Sherburn stigmatized: "In the South one man, all by himself, has stopped a stage full of men, in the day time, and robbed the lot" (p. 134). Duke counted the sale—465 dollars. Practically he robbed and went scot-free. The subsequent last show. They planned detailed safety the whole day, the foolish people planned their own, they would have everybody cheated like them, so told nobody how they were, rather asked everybody to come. They came with rotten eggs and dead cats, tons of them, Huck detected. Duke a sly person asked Huck to fly as fast as he could, dickens-chased, himself too made off, leaving king to face the music; duke, Huck and Jim shored out of the hiding place into the mainstream, when king form under the wigwam asked, "well, how'd the old thing pan out this time, Duke?" (p. 139).

[6]

Sherburn cannot be among this rabble audience, it is below his dignity, duke and dauphin here are not much above them, their assumed dignity is a cover for the meanness of their mind, frauding trade only denies them freedom of frivolities these people enjoy, everyway the crook. Even between themselves there is no love lost, no openness of heart, no intimacy, nothing common except their professional betrayal. They can neither form nor belong to any growing civilization. If any such civilization growing up they are sure to be ousted or imprisoned.

America was then a growing civilization by the fruits of honest adventure, by the right kind of utilization of adventurous labour. Huck at the lower level their leader, at a little higher level Col. Sherburn and Sheperdsons and Grangerfords. With his facetious wrong information of history —an amusement for the academic world—Huck sets the pattern of American polity. An excellent piece of humour for the intellectual section of readership, for children a gripping story, Huck's lesson to childish unknowing Jim:

> You read about them once—you'll see. Look at Henry the Eight; this'n's a Sunday-School Superintent to him. Look at Charles Second, and Louis Fourteen, and Louis Fifteen, and James Second, and Edward Second, and Richard Third, and forty more; besides all them Saxon heptarchies, that used to rip around so in old times and raise Cain. My, you ought to seen old Henry the Eight when he was in bloom. He was a blossom. He used to mary a new wife everyday, and chop off her head next morning. And he would do it

> just indifferent as if he was ordering up eggs. 'Fetch up Nell Gawynn', he says. They fetch her up. Next morning, 'Chop off her head!' And they chop it off. 'Fetch up Jane Shore,' he says; and up she comes. Next morning, 'Chop off her head', and they chop it off. 'Ring up fair Rosamun'. Fair Rosamun answers the bell. Next morning 'Chop off her head'. He made every one of them tell him a tale every night; and he kept that up till he had hogged a thousand one tabs that way, and then he put them all in a book, and called it Domesday Book—which was a good name and stated the case. You don't know kings, Jim, but I know them; and this old rip of ourn is one of tile cleanest Ive struck in history. Well, Henry he takes a notion he wants to get up some trouble with the country. How does he go at it—give notice?—give the country a show? No. All of a sudden he heaves all the tea in the Boston Harbor overboard, and dares them to come on. That was his style—he never give anybody a chance. He had suspicions of his father, the Duke of Wellington. Well, what did he do?—ask him to show up? No—downed him in a butt of mamsey, like a cat.... (pp. 140-41)

Huck gave free rein to his knowledge of history of English Royal heritage and the war of Independence in America, a sharp contrast in style and attitude. He is correct, but in detail the whole anachronistic messing-up ludicrous. The essence of his analysis is "kings is kings, and you got to make allowances. Take them all around, they're a mighty ornery lot. It's the way they're raised" (*ibid.*). Jim's innocuous remark an intellectual judgement he did not know: 'But dis one do smell so like de nation, Huck'. If a king is like that (he means this king a fraud) the nation must be no less a bother. The American Constitution has no place of a king. They adopt Uncle Sam tradition, not figure head but a responsible family-guide. Huck describes his style and integrity of leadership. Democracy is not an irresponsible bandwagon.

These two frauds are rootless, no love-link, no social cement to attach them, outside an organized society, a statutory polity. Twain has introduced them to fill the fund of fun, their misadventure as a foil to Huck's adventure. At the next station the grossness of their fraud so shocked him that he swore: "Well, if ever I struck anything like it, I'm a nigger. It was enough to make a body ashamed of the human race" (p. 148).

Their fraudulently earned wealth made them afford to spend on good costumes, the king was dressed like a young gentleman, becoming a pious profession like a preacher, but shockingly exposed his abject meanness completely indifferent to others' discomfort and even disgust. The king took Huck to a considerable distance Huck alone to pilot the boat, telling him both could enjoy a journey on a steam boat. Huck saw it was a lie. He was hunting for a possible swindle, he immediately got 'an innocent-looking young country jake' with his heavy baggage, swabbing on a log, for a journey to Orleans. He volunteered to take the man in their boat and asked Huck to help him lift the load on to the boat. King got the story of one Peter Wilkis', tanner, by profession, like a prowling beast always on the scent of his prey. The stranger only said whether he was 'Mr Wilk's, a trail enough for him as for a trained hound. He shrewdly pumped out of the person details of wealthy Peter's death that day, his two brothers in England never visited him in America, they informed to pay a visit for a last get-together, before his death, his other brother with him in America already dead, his wife too, leaving three daughters, etcetera.

King took the clue, Peter's two unvisiting brothers, Harvey and William, in England, one a non-conformist preacher in Sheffield and the other deaf and dumb; and fixed the plan to impersonate and immediately sent Huck back to row down to take the duke and king's carpet bags. King and duke's last and most infamous misadventure, most scandalously exposed, Duke and king landed with Huck to reach the Wilkis, impersonated as Harvey, William and their page. From the landing station they began their mourning drama, weeping, sobbing, sympathic villagers all carrying their luggage, lending their bodily support to the collapsing bodies of the supposed brothers at their loss, a long journey across the Atlantic, expected meeting alive frustrated by the rude blow of destiny, villagers all sharing their sentiments, reception mournfully solemn. Huck alone to enjoy the creeping clandestine plan of another big fraud.

[7]

Huck's role in this fraud-plan is more intimate, and more fraudulently honest than anywhere else. What he could not in Grangerford family he does here; Sophia's single-line scrap of paper he could not read well and could not preempt a tragic elopement and consequent bloodshed. Here is a different kind of deception, a fraud he could read well and foil the fraud and save the family from a heavy loss. He defrauded the fraud. As narrator Huck here could use his close involved observation more thoroughly than elsewhere in the story. In the mourning family among the neighbours king in his lamenting address explored all the details of Peter's position, his concern in life, liabilities, and good relationship with important people, all by name; the girls and the assembled crowd were so much convinced that they were carried to conviction, and felt relieved, the girls most. He said clearly his brother Peter wrote to him all these. Now Huck's comment: "but that was a lie, he got every blessed one of them out of that young flat-head that canoed up to the steam boat" (p. 151).

The daughters of the deceased brother so believed them that the eldest handed the king, taken to be their uncle, a letter he left behind. The letter is virtually the will, the distribution of property and wealth, 'three thousand dollars in gold to Harvey and William', 'six thousand cash hid down cellar'. King read out loud to his audience, shedding tears over it. They played the three daughters and neighbours fools. The intimations, particularly of the place where money in cash lay, flamed their greed, and made them that very night—the night before the funeral—fix how to get it and befool them, apparently with dignity and usual show of honesty. They took Huck with them (otherwise as a narrator he cannot convince his audience), of course allowed no share. They took the cash in gold, counted, with a candle in hand Huck the only witness. The count revealed four hundred and fifteen dollars short, duke made it up from his own pocket, really to testify their reliability, to further harm to them they planned. It was pat to their purpose. King made a public demonstration of their selflessness, in presence of simple-minded neighbours he laid the six thousand on a table, counted and offered to part with their share, the money should be the unlucky orphans' alone.

A very ebullient public exposure, appreciation in the midst of attendant exhortation by the king, his enthusiasm duly distorting King's English, a Sheffield-preacher though, inviting everyone to the 'funeral orgies' (duke corrected him passing a slip 'funeral obsequies, you old fool' (p. 153). In his added enthusiasm made it more awkward explaining the appropriateness of the word 'Orgies' instead of the word obsequies' authoritatively claiming out of currency in England. Now among the audience the doctor took serious exception to his hollow show of a learned Englishman: "Keep your hands off of me!" says the doctor, "you talk like an Englishman—don't you? It's the worse imitation I ever heard. You Peter Wilkis brother. You're a fraud, that's what you are!" (p. 154). Other people tried to restrain the doctor, they were convinced he was Harvey, the girls too, but it wasn't any use, he stormed right along, and said any man that pretended to be an Englishman and couldn't imitate the lingo no better than what he did, was a fraud and a liar. The poor girls were hanging to the king and crying; and all of a sudden the doctor ups and turns on them. He says:

> I was your father's friend, and I'm your friend; and I warn you as a friend, and an honest one, that wants to protect you and keep you out of harm and trouble, to turn your backs on that scoundrel, and have nothing to do with him, the ignorant tramp, with his idiotic Greek and Hebrew as he calls it. He is the thinnest kind of an impostor—has come here with an empty names and facts which he has picked up somewheres, and you take them for proofs, and are helped to fool yourselves by these foolish friends here, who ought to know better.... (*ibid.*)

The doctor ripped through the impostors' trap, but the common villagers and the girls like them, simple honest but fools, did not heed the warning. They form duly a section of contemporary society, simple at heart, easy to embrace any one who may come to be intimate and friend. The doctor detected the fraud mainly by his awkward English which no Englishman, particularly a preacher, could claim 'obsequies' now obsolete and can replace it by 'orgies'! If he had consciously chosen the term, orgies instead of obsequies, as he claims in his free style of false pretension to his knowledge of Greek and Hebrew etymology, he exposed himself more to the learned doctor.

Mary Jane an honest fool to rely such a man and submit, "Take this six thousand dollars, and invest it for me and my sisters any way you want to, and don't give us no receipt for it" (pp. 154-55). Only the youngest Joanna seems a little clever. She had her supper in the kitchen with Huck, while her elders at the guest table. Out of curiosity she was talking about England, wanting to know how different their life was. Huck knew nothing, hopelessly less than what those frauds knew. Her first enquiry was quite intelligent, 'Did you ever see the King?' Mark Twain's fun is a sort of Bacon's wit, tricks to make good the deficiency of knowledge, here extended to its extreme, as almost everywhere; at a different level these frauds make free use of their ready wit. Huck plays a parallel role only innocently meaning no harm. Every time he is caught on the wrong foot Huck squirms into shape. He said, 'he goes to our Church', 'regular'. When she questioned, King lived in London, how he could, meaning if he at all did, Huck invented 'when he visited Sheffield'.

The whole series is fun indeed, but not ended in fun. The young lady rightly commented, even after he agreed to confirm all true by touching the sacred book he took for a dictionary: "Well, then, I'll believe some of it; but I hope to gracious if I'll believe the rest" (p. 159). Both of the same age, their lies and detection cannot be a serious offence, quarrel too, if any, is nothing but childish game; but the issue led to a serious breach of hospitality Question, the two senior sisters took it up like that and taught the younger so and corrected her by ruling her to beg forgiveness, which at once deepened into further seriousness: Huck's essential goodness, so long latent under frivolous lies, awakened. At once the decision:

> I said to myself this another one that I'm letting him rob her of her money. When she got through, they all jest laid theirselves out to make me feel at home and know I was amongst friends. I felt so sorry and low down and mean, that I says to myself, my mind's made up; I'll hive that money for them or bust. (p. 160)

Mark Twain paints an American scene so nobly endowed with human values and trust in human goodness, which these blackguards exploit even in their bereavement! They more terrible than blood-sucking bugs. They are professional cheat and Huck's adventure his conceit, a part of the shared national character, out of this character a nation is born. Huck's determination henceforth is to save the family, to keep them free from harm. His mind is now busy fixing how to cheat the characters. He would act the benevolent thief, theave on their theft. Duke and king debating between them the whole night, details not needed here, Huck bugging around to know where they decide to keep the loot.

We need not get into details, Huck managed everything without anybody's knowledge, stole the bag of six thousand dollars from under the feather-bed where king kept it and in the darkness of the night when the watchers gone lodged the bag secure on the corpse's stomach in the coffin, lid set again as it was. Day broke, undertaker began his work, Parson Reverend Hobson came, the scene altogether changed.

[8]

Huck's mission still remained a dubious success. He was fussing about with one thought in his mind, always watching whether king or anybody else traced the treasure to its hiding place. The day passed off through funeral rites, Huck watched carefully whether the undertaker probed into the coffin before sealing it, he did not; yet doubt haunted him if anybody, or king himself, 'hogged' it before the coffin was laid into the grave sealed. He kept watching, particularly king.

Next day the girls got the first shock, king began to sell out their niggers, the wife and children, each taken to different destinations, their family torn apart, a human cruelty that hurt the girls: "The girls said they hadn't ever dreamed of seeing the family separated or sold away from town" (p. 166). The king is the greater scoundrel of the two: 'the duke was powerful uneasy', neighbours too. The next day the auction day. But something dreadful already—the discovery of the plunder somehow plundered by some other, who, a puzzle! King detected it was, instantly he and duke came to Huck's 'Cubby' if it was by him, of courses sounded him shrewdly, if he was in his room, Huck had no lack of presence of mind, he could easily sell lies for truth, told them he found the niggers going up that way, the duke took the cue and accused: "It does beat all, how neat the niggers played their hands. They let on to be sorry they was going out of the region and I believed they was sorry" (p. 167). The sale of the niggers made the duke 'raspy', his series of banter readily his expostulation.

Huck reveals his true identity as a man, not as an adventurer—if adventure that is also his identity, his humanity —an exceptional character, a superior version of a bloodless Robin Hood. Those who want to assess and account for America as a nation at the peak of power, would find the qualities, not in one character entire, but diversified into so many here, their combined push behind led them to this prospect. Not because they are Christians but because the qualities of their characters could consolidate under an urge of a united nation. If for any reason the character-consolidation disintegrate that would be the beginning of a downward trend.

Huck's humanity as well as his inventive resources for human good is more clearly revealed when among the Wilks-daughters, a witness to the two frauds' impersonation-tricks, and inhumanity of their cupidity which could shame even Jonson's *Volpone*. They always selected soft target, gullible though honest; neighbours too are equally unenvious, honest, hospitable, cooperative but unintriguingly fallible. Such a community requires to be guided, and protected from cheats and frauds, and there are among them an enlightened section like Dr Robinson. This is the shape of early British settlement in America. A well-intigrated society with a selected heroic segment, people like Sherburn and Col. Grangerford to protect and lead, and adventurer like Huck, a modern Robin Hood to foil the frauds' swindling attempt from outside.

Huck stole the stolen treasure for those innocent orphans, and played an intriguing role to protect them, who were befooled by king and duke to such an extent that all the three sisters, younger two most, began dreaming of their original home England, for them Alice's wonderland! The eldest of them was partly disillusioned: She said the beautiful trip to England was most about spoiled for her; she didn't know how she was ever going to be happy there, knowing the mother and the children warn't ever going to see each other no more—and then busted out bitterer than ever, and flung up her hands, and says: "Oh dear, dear, to think they ain't ever going to see each other any more!" (p. 169).

This girl, aged only nineteen, seems not formally educated, had in her blood this sort of untaught humanity which these frauds altogether lacked and cold bloodedly fixed to deprive them of their honest share of wealth and tempted to take them home to England. The situation thus created made Huck feel absolutely uneasy, his humanity forbade him to remain an idle spectator. He chalked out a plan of rescue. Had there been no self-accepted obligation to a runaway negro he could boldly expose these frauds instantly, but he could not for Jim. He privately told Jane everything, but asked only not to disclose it immediately to anyone, not even to her sisters, he asked her to leave home immediately before they woke up, and stay away for sometime. He would fix everything here. Fixing is not easy, Mary Jane's sisters, particularly the hare-lip younger, are so taken-in for a journey to England that they began to ask desperate questions why Jane was out at this crucial moment! Huck continued to invent lies and finally persuaded them to believe and say to their Uncle Harvey—Jane was out to other villages to inform them of the auction sell of property in the evening.

Mark Twain's fun and firm formation of serious execution are coeval, inseparable. Huck's trying to convince the younger sisters with all his untenable lies is urgent, and to that extent serious, but the girls' finding it all follies, mainly misinformation, and contrary to their set purpose—a happy journey to their dreamland—I wish I could afford a long quote instead of a snatch here and there: "Shucks, and stay fooling around here when we could all be having good times in England whilst we was waiting to find out whether Mary Jane's got it or not? Why, you talk like a muggings" (p. 175).

These girls could definitely unsettle Huck's plan to save them, Huck had a difficult time, they won't allow any delay, England a great temptation, it brooks no delay. After so much bungling, this way or that, they agreed to tell their Uncle Harvey what Mary Jane asked them: "Tell them to give Uncle Harvey and William my love and a kiss, and say I've run over the river to see Mr—Mr—what is the name of that rich family your uncle Peter used to think so much of?—I mean the one that—" (pp. 175-76). The name and story Hucks instant invention, they helped him with the name.

Mary Jane out, really Huck sent her out of home, his plan in her absence what, we need not strain our brain, but definitely his honest love for the young lady, more than for the Grangerford girl, awakened his basic honesty to a well-planned execution which he lamented he could avail himself of in the Grangerford host family. He could get into more familiar an intimacy with the girls in this house, situation allowed it, their naked honesty erected no artificial barrier. He disclosed everything he knew, and everything did without their knowledge and gave Mary Jane a piece of paper with his written information where she could find their stolen treasure, only warning she must not disclose it to anybody, not even to her sisters, before the plan was fully executed.

Mark Twain is not a writer to wait for Huck's plan to be fully executed, Peter Wilks had written to his brothers in England, those two Sheffield brothers on their way to America, due any moment to land, and did land, baggage mistakenly sent to another village, a little up the river, a too mazy river course for any first-coming Englishman, Harvey's brother had in the meantime had his hand broken, just the one he could write with all Harvey's letters, eventually Harvey's own handwriting illegible to strangers. Now a little before fraud Harvey's auction-sale of Peter's property the British pair of brothers arrived to initiate another set of proceedings to the utter confusion of the whole village, including the elite section, lawyer Levi Bell and early-doubting Dr Robinson. A funny scene. Fun for all, young and old, one 'a big rough husky that came along and listened to all the old gentleman said, and was listening to the king now' cross-examined the king:

> 'Say, looky here; if you are Harvey Wilks, when'd you come to this town?'
>
> 'The day before the funeral, friend,' says the king.
>
> 'But what time o'day?'
>
> 'In the evening—bout an hour er two before sundown.'
>
> 'How'd you come?'
>
> 'I come down on the Susan Powell, from Cincinnati.'

'Well, then, how'd you come to be up at the Pint in the mornin'—in a canoe?'

'I warn't up at the Pint in the morning'.

'It's a lie.' (p. 178)

The stranger authincaped his account, he lived up there, and saw his landing from a Canoe 'along with Tim Collins and a boy', Tim Collins must have been the stranger whom they took upon their Canoe. Dr Robinson, and Huck in his own unknowing way, detected this new Harvey speaking British English and pronouncing it in the right kind of British accent the king was nowhere near it—The doctor already detected king by his distorted King's English, so a piece of humour, he asked Huck, 'Are you English too?'

The genuine Harvey-William Wilks wisely decided to put up at a hotel, the scene shifted there, the doubtful Harvey-William pair and along with their boy (Huck) was bundled up there for further verification. Now it is the turn of the lawyer Levi who had in his possession British Harvey's letters, the new claimant Harvey's signature did not tally with the letter's signature and contents, all those only copies of his originals which only his brother could read and write in his neat hand now dysfunctional. This led to a tattoo-test on the corpse, another adventure, all the way a crowd-pulling medley in the early hours of the night. All trotted to the grave-site, with spades and shovels, some whooping and howling, one sent for a lanter from a nearby house. The work done in no time, coffin unscrewed, and the bag of money found.

The double pair of Wilks-brother and Huck imprisoned for trial in a sort of People's Court, Huck tight-gripped by a stout sturdy fellow, but the lost treasure found gave a new flurry of curiosity where it was, all butted, nudged, jammed, shoved ahead, to have a sight of. The man who held him forgot his hold, let him loose, Huck gave them the easy slip in the dark. Twain outbid Huck's plan, what still remained was Mary Jane's sign of the light. He hurried off into the road, flash of lightning served better, storm and accompanied drizzle helped him no less, he could rip easy through straight without hiding into side alleys. He saw a candle burning on the window of Mary Jane's room. A sign that she had returned home.

[9]

Huck is back to his riverine adventure, the Mississippi is adventure itself like the Congo in Africa, the Amazon in South America, only Mississippi in Mark Twain's time assumed a different kind of puzzling character with a growing civilization of transplanted enterprising European settlement almost everywhere, varied in kind and quality, absorbing the negro population in their workforce, to a better economic stability, if conflict initially with the natives, that too getting gradually narrowed down to growing accommodating amity. Huck, back on the river, trying to get rid of a company so inhuman by nature he knew, sailed without them, but like an evil spirit they got them on the open river, they too like Huck slipped away in the melee and took any riverside Canoe they found and rowed beyond their reach, baggage left behind.

King at once took his boy, Huck, for a betrayer; he left them stranded among enemies, Huck pleaded his own fear to be caught again, Jim his extra dread, and he did not know, that they too got free! Duke saved him, starting his own charge against him, the king was an old fool, an ostrich in human form trying to gobble all, more than he could gulp down, now he raised the moot point who hid the money in the coffin, he must have planned to deprive him of his share, king accused him of this trick to deprive him; the heated exchange made them fight, Duke flew at him, his hands at his throat, he would not let go until he said he did! He was anxious to make up the deficit, a big amount from his pocket, now he was without a cent, a poor beggar! the quarrel may have continued long if they did not relieve themselves by a share of the same bottle, Duke first then king. It was also a relief for Huck and Jim. They were snoring in the wigwam side by side.

Two-three days they flowed down the river, no stop yet anywhere, then they thought they should try some village or town, pocket empty, beyond the trouble zone already they thought. The only art they knew was fraud, everything else only trick, nothing seriously, acquired—fortune-felling, mesmerizing, mountebanking, play-acting and all that! This time they fixed a village named Pikesville, the king first went ashore and told duke and Huck to stay behind, himself scouting there to see if they had 'any wind of the Royal Nonesuch'. Word left if by noon he did not return they should also join him there. Huck fixed this time he would give them 'a cold shake and clear out and leave them behind'. He did of course, but this time without Jim.

What happened to Jim is a piece of king's betrayal of trust, that is perhaps the reason why duke 'fretted' and fidgeted about, and was uneasy with everybody in king's absence. The king was found in the back room of a doggery tight among "a lot of loafers bully-ragging him for sport" (p. 190). Duke kept abusing him, and he cursing, Huck slipped away and reached the Canoe to find no trace of Jim, no response to his repeated call from anywhere! He turned around to ask people if they had seen a nigger, he saw a boy, he told him, some elderly stranger had got a runaway nigger and sold him to Silas Phelps, told also where the village was and how far.

Loss of Jim was for him a great shock that more than anything else in the story awakened him to a sense of sin and Providential dispensation, his two moral obligations: to Jim and to Miss Weston, one in conflict with the other. There is, therefore, a third line of action, no less moral. He thought first to write to Tom Sawyer, then direct to Miss Weston where Jim was, then thought how that benevolent widow would take it, he must be marked as a black sheep, an ungrateful scoundrel to at least help her negro to runaway. She was never unkind to him, gave him shelter when he had none, the whole town would take him for a common blackguard, hated:

> And at last, when it hit me all of a sudden that here was the plain hand of Providence slapping me in the face and letting me know my wickedness was being watched all the time from up there in heaven, while I was stealing a poor old woman's nigger that hadn't ever done me no harm, and now showing me there's One that's always on the look out and ain't agoing to allow no such miserable doings go only just so far and no further, I most dropped in my tracks I was so scared.... (p. 192)

Self pity, self-repentance shook his whole frame, he wanted to be a sin-washed good boy. His essential Christianity made him feel miserable! But there was this simple-hearted negro, now his protégé, he his only support, once his support withdrawn all his misery would be his sin, damnable sin, all his adventurous doings so long would be all to a miserable massacre! Horrible to think of! A living vision: Jim all the time with him, before him,—ready to embrace, "I see him before me, all the time, in the day, and in the night-time, some times moon light, sometimes stoms, and we floating along, talking, and singing, and laughing...I come back out of the fog; and when I come to him again in the swamp, up there where the feud was; and such-like times; and would always call me honey..." (p. 193).

He could also remember Mary Jane who cried for the nigger family king sold away, father in one remote town, mother another, child still another, whole family dispersed across far distance so that husband, wife, children could never meet; and could never reconcile to such an act as to part with a nigger who sought his freedom to bargain for wife and children's freedom! His final decision was if it was sin he would be ready to sin it out, even to hell!

He is for the Phelps, Jim is there; his canoe and raft to be kept secure somewhere, only his baggage-pack with him somewhere to be hidden; to get back again everything, the location to be closely fixed, so out to examine the lay out of the land. While a little ahead of a sign written Phelph's Sawmill Huck saw the Duke, before he could slip away he called him. His accusing story all, how they were left stranded the day before, no canoe, no raft, no trace of the boy (meaning Huck). Huck excused himself narrating his own story, some true, some made up. Jim missing true, his worries too, everything else made up. Duke told him how the king sold Jim for forty dollars, but lost every cent immediately to those bullyragging louts in the doggery, he too now with not a cent in his pocket. He asked Huck to give him ten cent—he earned he said. But warned him and Jim, and fixed him telling him half truth: "I'll tell you something. We got to be here days. If you'll promise you won't blow, and wan't let the nigger blow, I'll tell you where to find him" (p. 195).

The duke only said 'Phelp', then bit the word in the middle, then gave some other name and told him he lived forty miles back, misdirected Huck knew. He pretended he would immediately start. They would be these three days for the show Royal Nonesuch: Now Huck is free. Phelps's house reached and was received as their expected Tom, so Huck had no other way but to act the role of Tom Sawyer, his friend stylish adventurer Tom. The reception story highly dramatic, first canine reception, as many as fifteen dogs made a circle around him, Huck formed their hub, any moment could be torn to pieces, only not savage as Heathcliff's pets in Emily Bronte's *Wuthering Heights*; a nigger woman saved him timely restraining them, half the number then returned instantly, returned spanieling. Huck is now Tom. Mark Twain takes his opportunity to depict another tier of settled British migrants, a different position, different nature, a sharp contrast to Grangerford—Shepherdson type, even to

Sherburn colour. A little homely, unheroically polite, sweet and sober. A preacher—farmer, a tolerant-true gentleman type.

In such a man's house Huck entered a stranger, dogs' terrible reception ended, instantly started human reception, Huck had no time to say anything, the mistress of the house took possession of him, foredoomed his introduction: 'It's you, at last!—ain't it?' She grabbed him and hugged tight...then tears came into her eyes and ran down over, and kept saying: "You don't look as much like your mother as I reckoned you would, but law sakes, I don't care for that, I'm so glad to see you! Dear, dear, it does seem like I could eat you up! Children, it's your cousin Tom!—tell him howdy" (p. 198).

Huck's strategy, changed, now he is Tom, Jim imprisoned in that house! Tom expected any moment, he heard a steam boat 'coughing' up and thought he might be on it, so any way he must intercept him. So he wished them to allow him to go to take the baggage home (his baggage), and somehow persuaded, the gentleman not to accompany him. He met Tom on the way and told everything, he at once willingly took the charge of the situation. Tom managed in his own style of adventure; the whole story reveals how these people are tolerant, hospitable, forgiving and know only simple honesty. Just like the Wilks and their neighbours. These people are easy prey to people like Duke and King. Tom immediately after Huck had reached home with Tom's baggage appeared as a stranger misled, Sally his aunt would not allow a stranger to leave their door without breakfast, Tom obliged, but when he kissed her she fired up, a stranger's kiss out of common etiquette. These people pious and conservative, purity of character their standard of values. Even people like Huck, in spite of his adventurous mode of life, inherited it.

[10]

Now Tom and Huck together plan how Jim could be rescued. Before they could fix it they would have a clear idea of the settlement and escape-route in the house itself, they escaped out of their bedroom window to mix with the crowd going to the show that night duke and king were to put up. Huck saw the two frauds tarred and feathered and carried in a procession, in a pitiable plight. The whole adventure-story holds up how life in the Mississippi area was a long-extended adventure, the migrants of Europe had to be adventurous, but definitely the characters in the story, save only a limited few like the fake duke and king, demonstrate inherited as well acquired traits consolidated to lay the foundation of a civilization and a nation that America is now, if for any reason these values etiolate a declining trend will set in.

Tom and Huck—adventure pattern is a woof of free use of falsehood with a shuttle cock of wit well-designed and woven well, definitely fun but never a fraud, and surely not within the sin-area, rather a contribution to life as an adventure itself. Tom and Huck together working out the plan to rescue Jim, this togetherness was another problem, rescue delayed, planning consumed much deliberations, Tom guided by eminent authorities, Huck unlearned had no authorities known to him but himself. Tom's knowledge of authorities, partly affected, for Huck all Greek, yet he acknowledged his erudition and style. Tom made the rescue-operation of a simple negro a studied demonstration of his method. Mark Twain makes this studied thoroughness another piece of fun, like Lilliputian accuracy, Tom's adventure his art, Lilliput's mathematics; Huck's only passion to do good, even to barter away lies for good, even mischief for welfare, to steal a soul languishing for love (his wife and children).

Tom's style is always to make adventure amusing, as any real art is, and a well-studied process. So he involved in Jim's rescue operation the whole nigger-block and whole Kennel Company, no less than eleven sturdy hounds and terriers, and then the witch world of the niggers' usual phantoms of fear. Everything allowed to play roles yet the rescue-affair a close secret. Jim rotting long in his distressing suspense, no hurry for that, Mark Twain's usual adventure humour. The whole house mesmeric for Tom's planning, something lost, some had unexpected appearance, not wanted, aunt accusing uncle, uncle aunt, they were at their wit's end. Jim had to wait! Tom would have Jim go through all the eminent rescue-operation-details recorded in leading Adventure stories, the fun is he yet insists an ignorant runaway nigger must not be denied State Prisoner status for form's sake: "Jim's got to do his inscription and coat of arms. They all do" (p. 232). The prison here is a simple hut and no glamour of a State Prison.

Mark Twain allows Tom long to unload the stock of his knowledge of prisoners and their rescue-schedule, ironically the present prisoner, a negro, would have nothing of it, unsuitable for him, rather a bother! Thus book-learning and life are different, difference is due to the fact that life lives in its own way, not by book-learning, and book-learning is not in the book but derived from life so lived, life in a broader sense the whole Existence. Huck has no education, he is guided by life's realities, and has no fantasy of giving an artificial shape to life on a model found in books. Tom is amateurish, Huck is original, inventive, more suitable for success in realistic life. Only when Mr Phelps wrote to Orleans plantations to collect their runaway negro Tom turned realistically wise to plan Jim's rescue, wrote an anonymous letter for Mr Phelps's niggers' knowledge immediately, and ultimately to Mr Phelps's too, as one of the well-meaning cut-throats who had planned to steal the runaway nigger, time and plan disclosed, and as a penitent accomplice offered to help by a sound-signal indicating the time of their operation. This is the first concrete step to rescue Jim without further delay.

Tom and Huck fixed the plan of disguise, Jim already taught how to play his part and how they would, Tom would be in Aunt Sally's stolen apron, Huck to slide down the cellar, with the stolen food already stuffed in, where, a fun; in the early darkness of the night Tom and Huck traced the canoe and raft to their exact place and got assured they were where they had been left secure and now in the dead of night they were out of the house to give the signal 'ba' like a sheep. Huck was caught when he marched down with foodstuff hidden under his hat, butter-hunk and bread! Aunt Sally up with a candle! Huck had no option but to oblige Aunt Sally, be seated where she asked him to. Butter melted down his cheek, that saved him, she was melting too like butter. People who collected outside with guns, all uninvited, to help their neighbour out of the declared assault at that night, rushed inside to help the lady, someone took the hat off and off the stocked bread rolled down. Huck was saved the embarrassment: Brain fever, "Oh, what a turn you did give me! and how glad and grateful I am it ain't no worse; for luck's against us, and it never rains but it pours, and when I see that truck I thought we'd lost you, for I knowed by the colour and all, it was just like your brains would be if—Dear, dear whyd'nt tell me that was what you'd been down there for, I wouldn't a cared. Now cler out to bed, and don't lemma see no more of you till morning!" (p. 245).

Aunt Sally missed everything, Huck's plan and all, only out of her simple heart poured love and affection for the child and made a myth of her own. Is she a fool? No. She is a character always carried by her own unreserved kindness that easily blurs her own loss and harm and sees only the other side, its afflictions and predicaments all true and compared to it her own harm, loss—all insignificant. A character that won the heart of an apparently ill-principled child too.

Tom is a steady adventurer, intellectual, less emotional than rational, Huck quite appreciative. Jim for him a subject of pure emotion, for Tom an intellectual reorientation. These three characters together, of two different colour-divides, but united on a basic human plane in spite of varied others differences, Mr Silas Phelps another forbearing accommodative kind, honest well-principled, yet soft at heart, unhurting. A venture is a charming façade which engrossed a section of Twain-scholars who preferred the title Raftmen's Passage. But Mark Twain's interest seems further deep inside, the River itself a mute expectator of a transplanted population and a gradual change in the topography and demography of the whole valley, the change itself not a windfall, not by the Divine assurance to the Believers, but by the resurgence of indomitable energy; every section of this population contributed to this campaign of undeclared crusade, finally unitedly, a spirit that Rabindranath hailed in an Indian community, the English rendering of the original verse: 'On the five courses of the

River, as if in the twinkling of an eye, the Shiks rose up with braided hair on their head, inspired by the gospel of the Guru'.

The innumerable courses of the Mississippi threw a challenge to these people, and they took it up like a crusader, with a Crusader's character, a Chivalric faith. And they won; a vast number of lakes, signs of extra-terrestrial calamity in the long past waited for them to explore, like another Prince of Hell to build a Pandemonium, unlike Rabindranath's Raja in *Red Oleander*, difference with Indians obvious. Rabindranath fell upon his faith, his king was converted to this faith, the king abandoned exploration and surrendered to love, a sort of spiritual love. Satan did not do it, he knew hell was not a comfortable place, his fall from the glamour of heaven never extinguished his essential virility, he would rather explore and exploit the hidden treasure of hell and build a new capital, and reign there supreme. An English poet Shelley for this reason perhaps considered Satan as the best character in the entire epic.

Rabindranath translates modern Indian trend when he says 'creative output thousand offspring of idleness', if he means 'leisure', no substantial difference. Western world, America most, discards idleness altogether, even no spiritual dependence to shirk exigencies of the material world. So a thorough religious minded Milton could allow glamour to a character like Satan. Mark Twain creates two Satans without glamour, those fake duke and fake King who deserved no fall from heaven, they never were angels, mere frauds they fell into the hands of men, adventure-loving and active. Huck and Tom mainly Huck, without any education and formal religion devoutly to follow, religious no less actively. They rescue a negro, though later he was again captured as a runaway nigger and brought to his owner Mr Phelps. Mark Twain could end the story with Jim successfully rescued by Tom and Huck, but he did not, did not because it would have been a cowardly betrayal of trust, a serious breach of morals, particularly on the part of Huck. That fraud king could do it, he had done it everywhere, most blatantly the Wilkses.

Tom's bullet injury only literary a feat to avoid it, the doctor attending him honestly accompanied the wagon in which Tom was brought home on a mattress and returned the nigger to the owner, and nobly certified Jim's fidelity to Tom, and recommended fair and kindly treatment to him. Tom Huck and Jim together represent a new generation of unity among colour divides, and Tom-Huck separately further developed white generosity towards the black, a new phase of development towards a well-organized nation, which yet the old generation could hardly appreciate, Aunt Polly, for example, wondered aloud: "I couldn't ever understand, before, until that minute and that talk, how he could help a body set a nigger free, with his bringing up" (p. 260). Even Huck doubted with that professed kind of up-bringing Tom could help him free Jim out of slavery!

Aunt Polly made a journey of eleven hundred miles down the river prompted by a confusing letter from her sister that Sid was with them along with Tom though Sid was at home. Aunt Polly's sudden appearance on the scene made Tom—then recovering from injury—disclose his fake identity and Huck his. Aunt Sally got her brain messed-up, in all those days things happened so forbiddingly dreadful that never before she thought the place so unsafe to live. Tom owned up in a detailed narrative how he got his share 'I got my share' (p. 258) and declared 'Jim was a free man', 'we done it all by ourselves'. Aunt Sally, now relieved, reproved:

> Well, I never heard the likes of it in all my born days! So it was you, you little rapscallions, that's been making all this trouble, and turned everybody's with clean inside out and scared us all almost to death. I've as good a notion as ever I had in my life, to take it out o' you this very minute.... (*ibid.*)

He is already Aunt Sally's proverbial Old Harry. She only wished no more meddling with the runaway nigger. Tom, still not fully cured, sat upright authoritatively to say: 'They hain't no right to shut him up! Shove!—and don't you lose a minute. Turn him loose! he ain't no slave; he's free as any cretur that walks the earth!'

'What does the child mean?'

> 'I mean every word I say, Aunt Sally, and if somebody don't go, I'll go. I've knowed him all his life, and so has Tom, there. Old Miss Watson died two months ago, and she ashamed she ever was going to sell him down the river, and said so....' (pp. 258-59)

[11]

The end of Huck's adventure, Huck's narrative, Mark Twain the spinner sends a message of United America with a lot of States of regional peculiaries, and a population of different colours and customs, flexibility allowed, yet under one overall central control. It is a big adventure story, adventure all out, every man adventurous in their own roles, a section essentially chivalrous, crusader in their faith in chivalry, all in general engaged in a war against every kind of opposition to a fresh establishment, uprooted people to strike root there, to make it their own land, the river theirs, woods, where needed, cleared for farm land. Finally everyone for everyone, a discipline thus of an integrated community life emerged, their faith duly nursed, at home women too kept up their integrity of simple honesty, initially though they made the natives their slaves, they duly accommodated them as their hands, gradually absorbed in an extended establishment, granting essential freedom for humanity's sake, as Miss Watson did to Jim, and amongst the young generation people like Tom and Huck to help it a step further to progress.

Tom and Huck got Jim immediately free, and the Aunt's whole family rejoiced over it when they learnt "how good he helped the doctor nurse Tom, they made a heap of fuss over him, and fixed him up prime, and give him all he wanted to eat, and a good time, and nothing to do" (p. 261).

All the families of the riverside towns where Huck had been are different kind and qualities, though of the same migrant class, of the same faith more or less, are people of principle, hospitable, accommodative, even for a stranger, most a farmer class Phelps family; not to speak of the people of St Pitersburg who adopted two orphans as their own and tried to raise them as civilized members of the society. Even Aunt Sally, a mother of children, felt like adopting Huck who along with Tom subjected them to their adventure mischief quite long. This adventure revealed what kind of people they were, also revealed how the people around made their trouble their own and all unitedly fought it, no one asked them, they came, for they must, to standby, and share it with them. Everyone came with guns, risked their life. The family's good-natured dealings deserved it and they too deserved their kindly dealings.

Their woman folk flocked around Aunt Sally, apparently gossipy, but their shared worries not the less pronounced. Aunt Sally got assured she was not alone an isolated victim. This assurance lightened her sense of unprotected helplessness. Their men-folk already took up the charge of the safety of the house. Her preacher husband could enrich her sermon as he never did before. Their faith in God's mundane Mercy well within their power of appreciation. The whole life is His programmed protection! What Huck said to conclude his narrative is the author's own reading only transferred to his narrator: "and so there ain't nothing more to write about, and I am rotten glad of it, because if I'd a knowed what a trouble it was to make a book I wouldn't a tackled it and ain't agoing to no more. But I reckon I got to light out for the Territory ahead of the rest...."

The last sentence in the quote represents Huck as an adventurer, and his author as a visionary who must have seen the future waiting, a land new-won, made their own, its awaited prosperity; his characters in this adventure story assuring him to realize the dream of that Territory, the target fixed, for which no waiting for comfort of an adopted orphan, no hanging around for ease, once orphan, denied shelter, no need for another's benevolence, let one stand on own feet. War after war, inside and outside, for a consolidated unity amongst race divides, colour divides, an adventure all the way. A Nation thus at the centre of the authors dream! Attainment not then, but awaited, adventure the price!

6

The Story of 'Beloved'

[1]

Mark Twain's Negro is rather a favoured friend, friend of white men though a slave, two adventurous white boys' completely; in *The Adventures of Huckleberry Finn*, Jim features as a runaway nigger for fear of his suspected sale to an unknown master, a sort of Pre-Christian problem of a Thegn's fear of the loss of a Master's protection. Protection, love and respect, whatever due to a noble servant, then lay in the service of a powerful wealthy chieftain, a warrior or authority. In post-Independent America Jim's position a modern version of the risk and relief of that primitive stage. Additionally a colour-distinction comes to intrigue the relationship, which was gradually loosening its tight twist, a stage of such an easing process is presented in Mark Twain's story. A young generation like Tom and Huck its sponsor. Just beside such a story Toni Morrison's *Beloved* appears entirely a Negro-story, their misery with a snatched bit of happiness now and then, a soft contact with nature, then scarcely noticed efflorescence, as well as human tenderness of touch, however secret, however deeply thawing, the rock-rude load of sorrows in their slave life.

The story is better centrally set with a woman than a man, 'Beloved' a woman better than a man, the author too better a lady than a male counterpart. Sweet Home a sort of Wuthering Heights, hundred years later, its modern version, its American Counterpart, there Catharine here Sethe with a different kind of crime, more bloody than a psychological fixation, left the

House, now 124 haunted, crime-reproval of a sort. Emily Bionte's more complex an obsession, Toni Morrison's love retrieved in 'Beloved'.

The Story begins with where it will end, Naipaul's method in *A House of Mr Biswas*, with some individualistic variations. Here the year is 1873, in the background 1861-65 Civil war, the action in the story consolidates in the aftermath. The eleven-State Confederate fought against the Northern State Combine on the issue of Slave-Law liberalization claim. Negroes are free in Northern State Ohio since it was declared State. Sethe's family fled Kentucky to Chinchinati across the Ohio river, their 'run' is a tragedy, 124 is 'Sweet Home' soured in a prolonged painful miscarriage of every sort. The story starts with:

> For years each put up with the spite in his own way, but by 1873 Sethe and her daughter were its only victims.

Paul D came to meet Sethe at the fag end of the story to see, no Beloved, none other but Denver and her mother, Denver the only child who did not desert her mother, mother too changed, not at all effusive to Paul D as she was in the opening chapter of the story to the utter disappointment of the only child then with her. Paul D's visit too long after eighteen years of separation from their Kentucky days of Sweet Home recapitulated—they five boys and Sethe then a thirteen year old only girl among them brought home to attend widowed Mrs Garner then ailing, and a thorough change in the farm discipline with the new dispenser Mr Garner's brother-in-law, a school teacher! Sweet Home getting soured under the new master's unkindly rigidity, which, of course, could not suppress altogether the boys' (all in early twenties) romantic flutter with one blooming beauty among them fleeting fairy-like beyond reach all the time!

Paul D's appearance in the first chapter is a throw-back recollection, so is everything else of the Kentucky Sweet Home days, Sethe the central figure, Paul D the link, with his eighteen years of varied experiences in other fields outside Sweet Home, to connect it. Here is only one in this chapter how eighteen years after Paul D met Sethe, not in Kentucky Sweet Home, but in Chincinnati Blue stone Road sweet home with a number 124, to live several days in that haunted house dreaded by everyone, in close intimacy with Sethe, in the repulsive presence of Denver, then ten years old, Baby Suggs dead when Denver only a two-year old baby, Halle Sethe's husband untraced, fate unknown, two children Howard and Bugler left home when one thirteen another twelve, baby daughter throat-cut dead, house haunted! Throat-cutting mother's throat-cut baby now 'Beloved', though it hardly could prevent its turning her nemesis!

Paul D's this visit is not the last visit, of course the first after they all ran away from Kentucky, so after eighteen years of her run Paul D's visit gave her occasion to narrate the run-story, obviously in 1855 and Denver's birth on the way during the cross-over. Now in this sweet home they are 'twosome', Paul D is for Sethe the only memory of their earlier life of six negroes, she the only female, in the Sweet Home establishment, he her husband's friend; Paul D too, in spite of enormous changes in life and circumstances, cherished the same unfulfilled desire for their only girl finally appropriated by one amongst them. Sethe to could not but melt down to accommodate with some apparent decency and demure, which made Denver a little reserve, and a little unhappy and restive, if not it turned to open hostility immediately.

[2]

A curious device adopted by the author: the story unfolded itself through ragged memory of the mind, Sethe's presently in and through her closest possible intimacy with Paul D, the surviving Sweet Home man, now her guest. Baby Suggs's life, her eight children by six unknown fathers; her last son Halle, Sethe's husband "she was able to keep the longest. Twenty years. A lifetime. Given to her, no doubt, to make up for hearing that her two girls, neither of whom had their adult teeth, were sold and gone, and she had not been able to wave goodbye. To make for complying with a straw boss for four months in exchange for keeping her third child, a boy, with her—only to have him traded for lumber in the spring of the next year and to find herself pregnant by the man who promised not to and did" (p. 28).

Sethe considered herself lucky "Sethe had the luck of six whole years of marriage to that 'somebody' son who had fathered every one of her children" (*ibid.*). It was being recounted when she and Paul D played their erotic game, "She started to turn over on her stomach and changed her mind. She did not want to call Paul D's attention back to her, so she settled for crossing her ankles" (*ibid.*). Paul D too having the twenty-five years past revived, Sixo's meeting with 'Thirty-Mile Woman', "his two thirty-four miles round trips' and 'three months' total time his cost. Sethe's changed posture dulled his 'appetite', only 'felt obliged to try again'. Present and past meet. Sixo's whole story and Paul D's 'yearning for Sethe' along with all the rest of the boys' twenty-five years before ruminated, yet presently 'his foolishness made him smile and think fondly of himself as he turned over on his side, facing her. Sethe's eyes were closed, her hair a mess" (p. 30). Then a close review of their present position, a long-awaited realization or a near-flop! Both tried in their own manner. It is very difficult to isolate Author's own overview from, theirs.

More so when Paul D and Sethe in bed ruminate, almost at the instant, the same thing in the past, Sethe's coming together with Halle in the cornfield: "they coupled...the first two having been in the tiny cornfield.... Both Halle and Sethe were under the impression they were hidden. Scrunched down among the stalks they couldn't see anything, including the corn tops waving over their heads and visible to everyone else" (pp. 31-32).

On page 28 she 'crossed her ankles', now on page 32 remembering the scene "Sethe smiled at her and Halle's stupidity. Even the crows knew and came to look. Uncrossing her ankles, she managed not to laugh aloud". Paul D recollected likewise early days and took his turn with uncrossed-ankles Sethe late:

> Paul D sighed and turned over. Sethe took the opportunity afforded by the movement to shift as well. Looking at Paul D's back, she remembered that

> some of the corn stalks broke, folded down over Halle's back, and among the things her fingers clutched were husk and corn silk hair. (p. 32)

Very difficult to identify the narrator, Author or Sethe? Better leave the attempt. For Paul D it s rightly Sweet Home, Sethe's too in a way, flocked memories of sweet days alive, in her ostracized life, Paul D's society, more intimately than a daughter's can be, they can share their sweet past together, their minds tuned together, experiences in and out in the past swelled up on the surface, a togetherness even physically effected, in a ghost-house though! Denver singled out apart in that house with her lonely reserve to nurse, mother snatched away by the man to himself.

[3]

A time shift, Denver in Paul D-entry—before period, among other children of her mother and the old Grannie Baby Suggs, growing not happy for that unless in her boxwood bower, presently recipient of the woeful story of her birth. This time Denver's flash-back story she its narrator, how her mother with all her children bundled-up in a wagon sent ahead of her, herself alone trudging up and ahead heavy in her stomach, she said, with 'an antelope' horning inside, feet and belly swollen, as if to burst; how she met a white girl mistaken for a boy, who 'straddled her' in the canoe crossing the Ohio river. Denver, while returning from her private asylum, a green bower, to their home, ruminating, saw her mother on her knees praying clasped around the waist by two white sleeves, a vision of the girl's clasp at the time of her birth: "It looked just like you. Kneeling next to you while you were praying. Had its arms around your waist" (p. 43).

Denver got the story from her mother. Presently she is the narrator, Amy's story in relation to her mother's meeting and what she got from her, she on her way to Boston, hundred or so miles away, for an item of velvet nowhere to be found but Boston, then a piece of her story: "My mama worked for these here people to pay for her passage. But then she had me and since she died right after, well, they said I had to work for'em to pay it off. I did, but now I want me some velvet" (p. 40). On land Sethe crawling to a lean-to, "just a crawling graveyard for a six-month baby's last hours" (p. 42). Sethe could not communicate all to Denver, something she withheld, so Denver had to surmise and make her reconstruction. Sethe only came up to Schoolteacher's appearance on the scene, Mr Garner's sister's husband; why she would not go beyond is a question Denver did not find immediately the answer to, had to wait until Paul D arrived. His arrival exorcised the Home finally of the ghost's visit. Why? Is it related to the answer Denver sought?

One is to wait for the answer. Paul D complicates mother-daughter relationship, this relationship requires author's interference, narrative then authorial, just a sort of impartial mediation. Denver's reading of mother's silence over something to be linked to the white shadow kneeling beside her kneeling mother taking her waist in a close clasp. Denver received Paul D well initially as Mother's Kentucky friend, her father's friend, but three days later her reading changed, he came not for a visit to the house, in Paul D's own language addressed to Sethe, "It's not the house. And it's you!" (p. 17). Denver "flat out asked Paul D how long he was going to hang around" (p. 52). Paul D took serious exception, "Hang around?"

Paul D-Sethe relationship within three days roused a sort of whimper in Denver's mind, Paul D explained it to Sethe in a way that hurt Sethe's motherly feelings: "I can't hear a word against her" (p. 54). An accommodation problem arose: Sethe and Paul D, none of them quick and clear at heart, I however much they might say, one 'I quit' and the other 'I can't hear a word against her'. Perfunctory adjustment was a 'carnival in town', Paul D proposed for all the three at his cost, they agreed to avail themselves of. The strained relationship could have still continued with a temporary elasticity because of carnival conviviality, if some other more absorbing thing immediately did not face up. It was 'Beloved' they met on their way back home, a strange young lady suddenly came up, as if a Nymph from the river flowing by, crossed their way then seated upon a stump, apparently dead-tired, speechless. They three circled her, to help her if she needed! They helped her to their house within hailing distance. She could not tell them who she was and where from, except for her name 'Beloved'. Significantly this supplies the title of the novel.

Beloved—a riddle. Is she Sethe's daughter come? Is she a spirit embodied? A fraud or real? Coleridge's Geraldine? At night lovingly dear to Christabel, in the morning an object of jealousy; her father's fond care for her, royally escorted to her father's castle under order—all these not taken in as chivalric courtesy! Yet the story of the night does not match well with the story of the day! Coleridge an acknowledged poet of the supernatural, so no one questioned it. Morrison evades it realistically in the story. One is to remember Sethe's conscience-prick made the dead child Beloved, a life-long oppressed memory, a constant ghost haunting her mind, distressed her soul, a Biblical massacre of Innocent with her own hand! The murder a victory over her enemy whom she could not fight to protect it, her due right; she must not allow her enemy to win if she can, but the murder is the murder of the Beloved!

In one sense it is a Negro-book entire, a negro woman its centre, other stories conglomerate around her, Beloved a victim, victim of love turned extreme cruelty, like Othello who killed love, without love he could not kill, loved and killed, no tragedy can be more tragic! Sethe is not heroic like Othello, neither has she any Iago to riddle her into a confused jealousy though she is confused and jealous too, she killed like Othello her love, killed and loved, her confusion is extreme, a kind just this: "As a small girl, she was unimpressed. As grown up woman Sethe she was angry, but not certain at what" (p. 74). Sethe's position is a pitiable generic Negro woman's position of her time. Denver tells Beloved what Sethe could not tell her, the story of her mother, she was her child whom her mother spared as did Sethe Denver, but could not Beloved, she killed her own child as her mother did hers. Nan a Negro woman was with her mother, Sethe told once what she told her: "She told Sethe that her mother and Nan were together from the sea. Both were taken up many times by the crew". "She threw them all but you. One from the crew she threw away on the island. The others from more whites she also threw away. Without names, she threw them. You she gave the name of the black man. She put her arms around him. The others she did not put her arms around. Never. Never" (*ibid.*).

Sethe's mother did not find time enough to face a repeat of 'Beloved'—problem in her life, her stage of Negro-history was over, Sethe's a trail of post-Civil War stage; what Sethe's mother did was a protest in the form of hate, hate for the unloved white father of her children; Sethe's was a variation of a sort, that is why she is uncertain of her anger, at what? She killed love, Sethe's mother did not feel so. Moreover before she could feel so her life was cut short, she was 'hung' (p. 73). Love and sex are different, though love may include sex, sex may not include love, often does not, when does not, it breeds hate. This happened to Sethe's mother. Sethe's difference is a part of the change in history, though not a thorough change of human behaviour. American nationhood remained fissured at bottom by an ethnic coloured-conflict, initially by a combined overpopulated advanced race from abroad since the Renaissance in a spirit of conquest, developed thereby a social and cultural conflict. It was first a conflict which took time to change into co-operation between the colour—divides, the civilized and the savage; the story depicts one phase mainly and sad history, with a still unsteady flicker of a democratic prospect of nationhood. Sethe is the latest victim.

[4]

Her Beloved whom she buried and raised a crude memorial curved an epitaph 'Beloved', her love memorialised though killed by her own angry hand, if she were to be enslaved and embraced the fate her mother, latest she herself, had to go through, better she died by her mother's hand! What her child escaped she could not, only hope Denver was helped to be born by a white woman, herself too was not spared the ignominy of an uncertain paternal parenthood and rude whip-hand, she pitied her lot and suggested the born child named after her own Amy Denver! Denver had reason to tell this story of her life to 'Beloved', now Sethe's self-pitying exculpating pleading to Beloved—a measure Sethe does not owe to Denver, but definitely to Beloved when she had come from the 'other side of life' come to her mother to identify her by the sign on her back, a chokeberry tree, cruelly carved! Sethe's own mother gave her sign to see below her breast but she was not allowed to see the mark on her dead body! Nan took her away.

Beloved essentially differs from Christabel's Geraldine, she is not a spirit of the dead night, but a re-born real entity with continued memory of the earlier birth though with some mist to befog the chain here and there, which Paul D had no patience, nor the head either, to understand! Denver is not Christabel who never took Geraldine for a sister Beloved, never questioned who she was except for once; but Denver questioned everything, some very significant, and the answers too equally revealing:

"Why you call yourself?"

"In the dark my name is Beloved"

"What's it like over there, where you were before? Can you tell me?"

"Dark...small in that place. I'm like this here." (p. 88)

Revived memory in the next birth is like torn fleeting fragments, in them only something can be fixed, Beloved is mostly unsure, fixed only on one sure object, unbeclouded: "What did you come back for?" Her answer clear: "To see her face." "Ma'am's? Sethe?" "Yes, Sethe" (*ibid.*).

Denver and Sethe believed, they have reason; Paul D could not believe, his experience of women all his life taught him they had only sex, and sought only men for it; even presently he could win Sethe on his side only for that, he forgot women are mothers too. Sethe is a mother, Denver knew what she had done for her birth and staked her own life and comfort after birth; Beloved's return whichever way possible, appeared to them a fulfilment, a mistake mended, even a divine trick played well! Paul D and Beloved fought a silent, momently open, battle over Sethe, one for sex, another for love. Five boys' romantic obscurantism got Sethe at the centre, only one could marry, Paul D only survived all the rest to seek her for sex, if possible to fix on her.

All memories of the past crowded in Sethe's mind with Paul D's entry into her skeleton family, Paul D himself is her past as Sethe is to him, early romance and loss, everything; now their present sweet and sour at the same time. But Denver and Beloved do not belong to this loss and romance. They have duly constructed their confidence exclusively between themselves, theirs only the present, Sethe their moorings but appropriated by Paul D, envy brewing, an air of hushed, and sometimes open, hostility prevailed. 124 their present abode itself a history with Baby Suggs, a sort of holy, with her past slave life, then freed to Chincinnati, Sethe's entry with her baby tugged to her breast, all a private history. Baby Suggs an 'unchurched preacher' to the blacks who came to hear her. Now all changed.

Baby Suggs is no more, but her preaching pattern could be memorialized. Sethe accompanied by two daughters, Denver and Beloved, reached Baby Suggs' preaching platform, if any voice could help her out of the present ordeal. There she felt Suggs's spirit clasping her throat tight as if to choke her breath leaving finger-print thereon. Both Denver and Beloved rubbed their hands to undo the marks left there. What she learnt from this unlucky incident appeared to her an immediate suggestion to solve her problem with Paul D in their midst.

Baby Suggs's hostility seemed strange to Sethe: she nursed her like Amy Denver, that white girl, when she came to 124 with her one-day baby tied to her chest; but Baby Suggs queried her about her ear-ring: "Going-away present?" She answered, "Wedding present." Baby Suggs insisted, "Be nice if, there was a groom to go with it" (p. 111). She could not say clearly where Halle her husband was. Now in Chincinnati she had already twenty-eight days of 'unslaved life'. Only Paul D could tell her where he last saw Halle butter-smeared face, further information he either suppressed or could not keep track of. After eighteen years of Sweet Home acquaintance when Paul D came to meet Sethe, their romantic indulgence of their mind for the only girl moving around unavailing then, now seeking fulfilment, though so late, he must have taken advantage of Halle's long absence, yet untraced existence, if existence at all.

Sethe did not repulse, then encouraged, Sweet Home memories and her starved womanhood and a little of Paul D's inviting gesture opened a new chapter in her life. But a smooth passage was not her destiny, Denver earlier, now Beloved along with her claimed her unshared love:

> She could bear the hours—nine or ten of them each day but one—when Sethe was gone. Bear even the nights when she was close but out of sight, behind walls and doors lying next to him. But now—even the daylight time that Beloved had counted on, divided by Sethe's willingness to pay attention to other things. Him mostly. Him who said something to her that made her run out into the woods and talk to herself on a rock. Him who kept her hidden at night behind doors. And him who had hold of her now whispering behind the stairs after Beloved had rescued her neck and was ready now to put her hand in that woman's own. (pp. 118-19)

In Sethe's home a ghost is exorcised by a male's arrival who can meet Sethe's womanly need, but another ghost is duly invited to invade it, the ghost of jealousy! Beloved bitterly takes exception to Paul D's encroachment upon her claim of a different kind of love, different from his male love for a woman! It has been taking too serious a turn! "Sethe has now to decide whom to oblige!" "Sethe and Denver tried to call up and reason with the baby ghost, but got nowhere. It took a man Paul D, to shout it off, beat it off", but curiously, "to take its place for himself" (p. 123). Another ghost! Denver's reaction to this replaced ghost: "Carnival or no carnival, Denver preferred the venturous baby to him any day. During the first days after Paul D moved in, Denver stayed in emerald closet as long as she could, lonely as a mountain and almost as big, thinking everybody had somebody but her; thinking even a ghost company was denied her." She decided "whatever her power and however she used it, Beloved was hers" (p. 123).

She began thereafter to read Sethe in a new light. Denver recalled what Nelson Lord, her acquaintance during Lady Jones school days told her, "Didn't your mother get looked away for murder? Wasn't you in there with her?" (*ibid.*). Denver would not ask her, but she saw clear turtle-mating where Beloved landed in the water of the river, she must have intuited Paul D-Sethe mystery in the house. Sethe too decided: "It only a tiny disturbance anyway—not strong enough to divert her from the ambition welling in her now: She wanted Paul D. No matter what he told and knew, she wanted him in her life. More than commemorating Halle, that is what she had come to the clearing to figure out, and now it was figured. Trust and memory, yes, the way she believed it could be when he cradled her before the cooking stove. The weight and angle of him; the true-to-life beard hair on him; arched back, educated hands. His waiting eyes and awful human power. The mind of him that knew her own. Her story was bearable because it was his as well—to tell, to refine and tell again. The things neither knew about the other—the things neither had word-shapes for—well, it would come in time; where they led him off to sucking iron; the perfect death of her crawling-already? Baby" (p. 116).

Morrison with calm restraint and evocative decency makes out a woman's personal distress and starved urge, rare in modern writer, even in modern Indian writers wanting. Sethe's hard-won freedom wasted, her decision an untimely assertion, envied eyes and unshared affection, call it love, affirmed. Paul D too came to 124 to pick up the thread of Sweet Home memory, the only surviving male member, to another surviving only female amongst them, and of course to renew the romance effectively, after long years of tortured slave life and several months of fiendish trudge to the North.

[5]

Paul D in 124 is getting more and more complex as he gets three women now, young and aged complex, his relationship with Sethe immediately, first appeared as easy as a plane, but slowly, unexpectedly, imperceptibly for himself, was turning serious in the first undetected prying eyes of two young women, Sethe's daughters one at home already, another got any way (Beloved), in the house; then affectively arrogant, their secret relationship got assertive, then submissively repulsive. As usual Morrison gives everything an evocative sober touch—Sethe—Paul D exchanges:

> "I thought you went out somewhere," she said.
>
> Paul D moaned, surprised to find himself exactly where he was the last time he looked.
>
> "Don't tell me I slept in this chair the whole night."
>
> Sethe laughed. "Me? I won't say a word to you."
>
> "Why didn't you rouse me?"
>
> "I did, called you two or three times. I gave it up around midnight and then I thought you went out somewhere." (p. 134)

Two starved souls in the same house together, satiety or sense, or both in interaction, or anything else intervening, they parted ways, direction changed, decisive or not. The present position is Paul D is out, but close beside in a separate shed which made Beloved's sudden visit to him possible. The visit is meaningful, not apparently what one may mean, at least not the whole. She offered herself to Paul D: "You have to touch me on the inside part. And you have to call me my name" (p. 137).

Paul D's position is better in Author's language: "If he trembled like Lot's wife and felt some womanish need to see the nature of the sin behind him; feel a sympathy, perhaps, for the cursing cursed, or want to hold it, or want to hold it in his arms out of respect for the connection between them, he too would be lost" (*ibid.*). Total confusion, even stupefaction! He inert, she insistent! Finally he had to obey, but horror broke loose: "Red heart. Red heart. Red heart" (p. 138).

Sethe and Denver could not decode the riddle of Beloved, neither could they her outrageous approach to Paul D. Denver was sure she was "the white dress that had knelt with her mother in the keeping room" (p. 140), her mother questioned her and got only scraps "she remembered a woman who was hers, and she remembered being snatched away from her", "she one white man". She concluded she must have been "locked up by some whiteman for his own purposes". She concluded so, supported by Ela's similar account and explained "Beloved's behaviour around Paul D, whom she hated" (*ibid.*).

Paul D's reading is still more confusive, his own confusion the final source of confusiveness. He wanted to tell Sethe 'about his last three weeks' experiences. He recalled school teacher in Sweet Home how he described himself: a veiled reference to Sethe's relation, in his self-brooding: "If schoolteacher was right it explained how he had come to be a rag doll—picked up and put back down anywhere any time by a girl young enough to be his daughter". Sethe only is not so young, neither is he ill-matched, but turned to be a rag doll all the same. "Fucking her when he was convinced he did not want to" (p. 148). He came to meet Sethe to tell her inconveniences mainly, no fixed place for him, now out, all contact barred, his problem with Beloved was of a different nature, he wanted to be fixed with Sethe. He sounded Sethe, "I want you pregnant, Sethe. Would you do that for me?" (p. 151).

Three weeks stranded from Sethe's close association, now a schedule like this would fix him, otherwise "you make me feel like a girl, coming by to pick me up after work. Nobody ever did that before" (p. 150). Whatever he may have had in mind to tell Sethe, if at all, about Beloved Paul D had forgotten under Sethe's gestured softness and spell; but now for an extra appeal he had to mention Beloved as a part of his plea: "the words flock in his head like kids before lining up to follow the leader":

> Well, ah, this is not the, a man can't, see, but aw listen here, it ain't that, it really ain't, Ole Garner, what I mean is, it ain't a weakness, the kind of weakness I can fight 'cause' cause something is happing to me, that girl is doing it, I know you think I never liked her nohow, but she is doing it to me. Fixing me. She's fixed me and I can't break it. (p. 149)

A sort of self-pitying monologue follows for Paul D though in Author's language:

> What? A grown man fixed by a girl? But what if the girl was not a girl, but something in disguise? A lowdown something that looked like a sweet young

> girl and fucking her or not was not the point, it was not being able to stay or go where he wished in 124, and the danger was in losing Sethe because he was not man enough to breakout, so he needed her, Sethe, to help him, to know about it, and it shamed him to have to ask the woman he wanted to protect to help him do it, God damn it to hell. (*ibid.*).

Paul D was restored to his coveted sanctuary, Sethe too nods "You come upstairs. Where you belong...and stay there" (p. 154). But that cannot solve the problem at home, her personal need-based liking not isolated from the situation, immediately two daughters, they are more closely together, though Beloved yet a mystery! Denver needs Beloved more than she does her, mystery or no mystery. She points to a slit of a sun-lit crack where, she says, her face. Denver sees nothing (p. 146) Sethe with Paul D in her room, in close embrace too, broke into a sort of monologue: (in Author's word)

> ... She thought quickly of how good the sex would be if that is what he wanted, but mostly she was frightened by the thought of having a baby once more. Needing to be good enough, alert enough, strong enough, that caring-again. Having to stay alive just that much longer, O Lord, she thought, deliver me. Unless carefree, mother love was a killer. (p. 155)

The other side of the situation:

> What did he want her pregnant for? To hold on to her? Have a sign that he passed this way? He probably had children everywhere anyway. Eighteen years of roaming, he would have to have dropped a few. No. He resented the children she had, that's what. Child, she corrected herself. Child plus Beloved whom she thought of as her own, and that is what he resented. Sharing her with the girls.... (*ibid.*)

She cannot be decisive, neither way! This is her position, this is human weakness! Unless situation compels, decision is difficult. Yet something made her act: "Right after she saw the shadows holding hands at the side of the road hadn't the picture altered? And the minute she saw the dress and shoes sitting in the front yard, she broke water. Didn't even have to see the face burning in the sunlight. She had been dreaming it for year" (p. 156). The daughters are isolated from mother. Paul D and Sethe left together, left them to talk between themselves, Denver said, "She likes him here". Beloved retorted, "Make him go away." Denver, "She might be mad at you if he leaves" (p. 157), Sethe and Baby Suggs had their past in Sweet Home, under an easy white master before Schoolteacher replaced him, Schoolteacher's arrival changed the scene and prompted them to runaway. Mr Garner, Sweet Home master, gave Baby Suggs freedom, helped her in Cincinnati to secure a job and a convenient home; but Sethe could not be trouble free though comfortably sheltered in Baby Suggs's home, Schoolteacher pursued her with his nephew, a slave-catcher and a Sheriff.

[6]

Sethe-Paul D relationship had already turned to an intricate enigma, more to Sethe who now drifted back to the memory of Sweet Home under Schoolteacher, and a part of it, to take up to face Paul D direct. The story of Schoolteacher's invading army of four white men on horse back within a month of her free life in Boston Road house. Freedom gave her natural power to love, Paul D too acceded: "He knew exactly what she meant: to get to a place where you could love anything you chose—not to need permission for desire—well now, that was freedom" (p. 191).

For 'freedom', then for 'safety', then for 'love' she did the self-pitying horrible deed—with her own hand, with a hand-saw. Cut her own children, one a daughter dead, another not a month old thrown to the wall planks and missed, second attempt averted by Stamp Paid's timely intervention! She had no remorse! She explained further to Paul D: "They ain't at Sweet Home, Schoolteacher ain't got them" "to keep them away from what I know is terrible. I did that" (p. 194).

Sethe turns more brooding in her mind, tracing back to the Sweet Home, all souring, Schoolteacher's entry changed all, in a gentleman's disguise a tyrant, she mother of three children one coming, never in Garnet's time they thought of running away, never felt like slave. Paul D a friend of that time, now he is going, two daughters, Denver and Beloved make her present position with Sweet Home-sweetness in the easy flush of her womanhood revived in Paul's presence, as far as a slave girl's married life can. In a sort of monologue Sethe explains to herself as well to her daughter-pair, their response not needed.

Stamp Paid's life another skeleton in the cupboard, he "misnamed himself and there was another debt he owed. Born Joshua, he renamed himself when he handed over his wife to his master's son. Handed her over in the sense that he did not kill anybody. Thereby himself, because his wife demanded he stay alive. Otherwise, she reasoned, where, and to whom could she return when the boy coming through? With that gift, he decided that he didn't owe anybody anything" (p. 218). This turned him a runaway-rescuer, "he ferried them and rendered them paid for, gave them their own bill of sale, so to speak. 'You paid it; now life owes'" (*ibid.*).

Paul D and Stamp Paid both in their different ways showed their interest in Sethe, Paul more actively with partial success, Stamp with no success, Paul now out, stranded, Stamp Paid tried as usual to offer a stranded coloured shelter, Ella not so willing, took exception to Sethe's old story, a killer mother, and showed due reservation for Stamp's frequent visits to Sethe's family. Sethe narrated old Sweet Home story, partly in a monologue form, to justify her extremely tragic act, one piece here: Sethe and Halle her husband talking between them in their bed, Sethe recounted, the white people's apparent softness was not soft, only not open brutality, but shocking all the same, Schoolteacher proposed a suggestive deal, not open, Halle too presented it to Sethe suggestively Stamp's shocking submission to his master's son's offer repeat, a life-long tragedy could have been, but evaded by an uncertain risk on the other side of the river Ohio:

"He could of said no. He didn't tell you no"

> "No, he didn't tell me no. She (Halle's mother) worked here for ten years. If she worked another ten you think she would've made it out? I pay him for her last years and in return he got you, me and three

> more coming up. I got one more year of debt work; one more. Schoolteacher in there told me to quit it. Said the reason for doing it don't hold. I should do the extra but here at Sweet Home"

"Is he going to pay you for the extra?"

"Nope"

'Then how going to pay it off? How much is it?"

"$123.70"

"Don't"

"He want something."

"What?"

"I don't know. Something. But he don't me off Sweet Home no more. Say it don't pay to have my labor somewhere else while the boys is small."

"What about the money you owe?"

"He must have another way of getting it."

"What way?"

"I don't know; Sethe." (p. 231)

'I don't know' repeatedly to his young wife is a bitterly felt whimper adequate to no less a language, no less a communication of heart in revolt than language can, when body cannot, voice cannot work! Such is the misery man in bondage shared by a particular coloured community. Sethe tries to convince her daughters, particularly Beloved. Her cruelty is a rage against an extremely distressed slave life she would prefer her children's death to life, if not in any other way, by her own hand, to avoid. Her own life and her husband's mercilessly agonized inability to protect her from abominable shame are presented in expiation. Her womanhood starved, an outrage upon natural human need, they are of age to understand she expected, Paul D out ghosts reappear. In a sort of monologue then Sethe convinced herself killing spared her intolerable death in tortured subjection, usual destiny of a slave: "Why I did it. How if I hadn't killed her she would have died and that is something I could not bear to happen to her" (p. 236).

[7]

In the successive two short chapters Sethe and Denver are given to monologuing, intense in tone as monologues need be. Both explain to themselves their apparent sins and their deplorable compulsions: Sethe's intense love for her children sought them spared a slave life, more tragic than death itself, every moment death-like torment helplessly unbearable borne, sooner inviting soul's release from body; Denver's anti-mother impulse is fear of Sethe's 'die-witch' immediacy any moment to kill. She too found reason why Sethe's such an unmotherly cruelty: "but maybe there is something else terrible enough to make her do it again. I need to know what that thing might be, but I don't want to" (p. 244). She does not want to know, yet she feels the need to know, is a pathetic something, more terrible, better not known: Sethe would have had reason enough to feel that at Denver's age when she had no death in life bit by bit, moment by moment, lifelong death a white woman's slave, who gave her a beady ear ring at her wedding, a slave girl's wedding who is denied love for children, pleasure in husband's company, if any attempt to assert by the slightest disobedience, like Sethe's, the ring-giver white woman's fury Denver better not want to know: in Sethe's language: "Can't wait. I tried to make her. She said. Can't do it. Come on. Hoo! Not a man around. Boys scared. You sleep on my (you meaning Beloved) back. Denver sleep in my stomach. Felt like I was split in two. I told her to take you all; I had to go back. In case. She just looked at me. Said, woman? Bit a piece off my tongue when they opened my back. It was hanging by a shred. I did not mean to. Clamped down on it, it come right off. I thought, Good God, I'm going, to eat myself up. They dug a hole for my stomach so as not to hurt the baby" (pp. 238-39).

Sethe identifies the reason for Denver why she 'didn't want to know': "Denver don't like for me to talk about it. She hates anything about Sweet Home except about how she was born" (p. 239). Denver harks back to Baby Suggs's experiences as a woman slave, her womanhood sold out to different masters of her body: "Slaves not supposed to have pleasurable feelings on their own; their bodies not supposed to be like that, but they have to have as many children as they can to please whoever owned them. Still, they were not supposed to have pleasure deep down" (p. 247).

Beloved's really a soliloquy verging on Colerigian supernatural type, her face inheriting Sethe's, his teeth more charming; her unusual death by mother's hand a deep agony out of no less deep a love from the core of her heart, won Beloved's love, a really loving mother killing her own child to spare her brutal orgies of a slave's tortured life day in and day out, body molested, heart oppressed, as Sethe knew with her own life and seen own loving mother's distressed hanging at Beloved exact age of having been killed—an explosion of protest in this way, humanity's last instrument of protest in its utmost wretchedness when no other better alternative available! This when thus appreciated the mind is tossed into a semi-supernatural trim, she no longer could arrest herself from essentially being anything but unnaturally supernatural, her return too supernatural, not then Coleridgian kind finally!

Beloved's continued next chapter natural supernatural mixed, not really a soliloquy but monologue proper, involving two other characters one after another, Sethe mother and Denver sister, Denver and Sethe immediate realities, but Beloved is half-submerged in her mysterious account of the other side of living realities, sometime she blends in it Sethe, but leaves alone Denver, as if Beloved's killer mother joined her in that killing, her soul was transported with her soul only Sethe's ghost remained on earth among too many ghosts haunting around her soul-shrived body-cloak. Beloved describes her-thrice-lost, to her: "Three times I lost her; once with the flowers because of the noisy clouds of smoke: once when she went into the sea instead of smiling at me; once under the bridge when I went into join her and she came toward me but did not. She whispered to me, cheated, and swam away" (pp. 253-54).

Sethe and Beloved are in a bewildering maze in their love and cruelty struggle, the force behind is another loveless cruelty they mutually understand in their depth of feeling only cannot express in their clear language, a human trap, they cannot wriggle out of it, though their souls want, a crisis that makes both of them desperate to revolt, they have not Shelley's power of language, nor Byronic puissant potency, so they go weird, as if in a world of vision uncommon altogether: if reborn in that state vision likely to be dream disarrayed on the borderline of supernatural cruelly loving mother's face constantly appearing as though her own face, and behind it all figuring out 'men without skin', they "came and took us up into the sunlight with the dead and shoved them into the sea" (p. 254). Sunlight and the dead—a sharp contrast. Sethe close to it, yet not, is another contrast!

[8]

Paul D distressed in dry-goods church for his shelter out of Sethe's household where he was roosting lately, alone seated on the porch, recalling the past, their Sweet Home days, their sweetness evaporated when Schoolteacher came, after Garner had died, to take care of the estate and the Sweet Home establishment. Paul D, youngest of Paul brothers, is absorbed in memories of sweetness in Garner's time soured in Schoolteacher's taking over. The whole lot of Negro slaves in Sweet Home secretly planned their escape shortly after Sethe was subjected to an extreme form of cruelty, behind filed, stomach holed, for a simple disobedience to stay too long to attend sick Mrs Garner when her nine-month old child languishing for mother's help and husband's earlier tenderness shown to her was not anything but formal; Mrs Garner's true colour exposed. Paul D and his three half-brothers born of the same mother but by different fathers were "sold out to Garner and kept there, forbidden to leave the farm, for twenty years" (p. 258). In Author's language Paul D—remiscences are presented, not virtually different from Paul's own ruminations, his past along with the escapade-plan and sad bloody miscarriage, which decided Sethe's fate on the other side of the river.

Sweet Home chapter closed, 124-chapter opened, Paul D now neither there nor here; in Sweet Home they were a sort of family together, now family broke into bits, he envied and still does, "the families of slaves who had all been together for a hundred years: great-grands, grands, mothers, fathers, aunts, uncles, cousins, children. Half white, part white, all black, mixed with Indian" (*ibid.*). Curious he made them identify over and over, in Maryland, who belonged to who. Mark Twain's later picture in sharp contrast with the 1861-65 story, his Jim had a family Miss Weston never thought it to disturb, neither was the fake uncle's sale of Miss Mary's Negroes tolerated, their families disintegrated.

Another fellow sufferer Stamp Paid, his assumed name, originally Jasua, his wife his master's son appropriated, a sad thing in his life, a thousand such things happened in the coloured class, undislodged as heavy a stone upon his soul, he could not carry any longer; Paul D and Stamp now sail in the same boat, unfixed, stranded, male life, nowhere life take a feather in the air, Sethe in her female life, they in their wasted manhood! Is it that God decreed! Their Bible re-written for them, they could say! They are neither 'fruitful' nor could 'multiply'. They are slaving their manhood and womanhood, as well as their body. Paul D and Stamp Paid had their confidential exchanges, now back to Beloved mystery. Stamp told Paul: "You don't say? Hup. Was a girl locked up in the house with a whiteman over the Dear Creek. Found him dead last summer and the girl gone. Maybe that's her. Folks say he had her there, since she was pup" (p. 277). Thus far conjecture could go!

Beloved Morrison's creation, supernatural as much as an unloved hated daughter turned humanly supernatural to the extent of a flaming dragon in Rushdie's *Shame*, here only instead of unloved 'dearly Beloved' daughter—Sethe could not add 'Dearly' to her epitaph for want of means—an utmost loving mother's kill, the extremest possible challenge to the Sweet Home turned too bitter to her humanity, her liberty as a woman who would not allow her children to be anybody's property, her body anybody's unloved ownership, her challenge to any such mischief, if not by other means, frustrating such an attempt, then even by killing them whom Schoolteacher or anybody may have had the power to trap in her enslaved wretchedness, more shameless than Shelleyan in *Masque of Anarchy*!

Beloved her love-kill, if returned, is due to be ghostly in presence, her love too cannot but be all too concentrated, claiming in a measure on the verge of an extreme form of selfishness, even cruelty; how this extends to what effect the Part III of the novel clearly reveals. Seethe readily responds at the cost of her personal comforts, then gradually at the same rate of transaction demanded love exclusive! Sethe provided everything she wanted, everything even she did not want, but she lost her job for frequent delay, for late attendance, Beloved demanded her exclusive attention and constant active intensity of love, which Sethe willingly provided in a sense of atonement, a sort of Raicharan's love for Khokababu (baby), he thought returned after death for his neglect, his master's son born as his own, in a poor family, yet he tended him as he should have been nursed in opulence, he without means, spent his all to expiate his sin. Rabindranath's Raicharan's a sin of omission, Sethe's a sin of commission, Raicharan withheld due care as a servant, constant attendant, Sethe a mother—killer of her own baby! Her conscience more excruciating than Raicharan's, though the end-result the same. The baby lost, now her own, more when returned grown up, and she continued to give signs of her earlier memories when memories not normally expected so accurately developed, so something supernatural, which Raicharan's boy was not, Sethe has further reason to be confirmed and further prone to be inhumanly exploited, one here which made Denver take side with mercilessly exploited Sethe. "She sat in the chair licking her lips like a chastised child while Beloved ate up her life, took it, swelled up with it, grew taller on it, And the older woman yielded it up without a murmur" (p. 295).

Denver reacted, 'seeing her mother diminished shamed and infuriated her'. The most terrible reprisal of unretaliated wrong in human history is a self-killing sort of love-kill: "That before she could make her understand what it—what it took to drag the teeth of that saw under the little chin; to feel the baby blood pump like oil in her hands; to hold her face so her head would stay on; to squeeze her so she could absorb, still, the death spasms that shop through that adored body, plump and sweet with life—Beloved might leave. Leave before Sethe could make her realize that worse than that—far worse—was what Baby Suggs died of, what Ella knew, what Stamp saw and what made Paul D tremble. That anybody white could take your whole self for anything that came to mind. Not just work, kill, or maim you, but dirty you. Dirty you so bad you couldn't like yourself any more" (*ibid.*). Sethe had better spare Beloved that self-hatred finally.

Denver begged for mother, then stopped and looked for work, Nelson Lord her school friend warned her when casually met in his grandmother's house "Take care of yourself, Denver" (p. 297). She understood late, moved outside home looking for work, meeting Janey at Mr Bodwin's house. Janey perhaps provided her a job, a night attendance, but a hush in the manner of the service, Janey cannot be open, so shrugging she simply said, "Don't ask me what white folks need at night" (p. 300). Denver's coming out of home was in fact wide circulation of the Beloved episode at home and her equal amount of experience of the outside world, Ella's experience for example: "Cogitation, as she called it, clouded things and prevented action. Nobody loved her and she wouldn't have liked if they had, for she considered love a serious disability. Her puberty was spent in a house where she was shared by father and son, whom she called 'the lowest yet'. It was 'the lowest yet' who gave her a disgust for sex and against whom she measured all atrocities" (p. 301).

Sex never a pleasure in such an enforced possession of the body, rather enslaved agony, unwilling wildness, more cruel love-killing than Sethe's, born beastly more than beast's is. Sethe wanted to keep her love-born children free from such a brutal ownership. Denver saw poverty brought her close to it, now Denver to pick a job at their former benefactor, the owner of 124, Mr Bodwin's house, her mother would resist Denver from slavery joining Bodwin's house, the extreme measure of resistance armed with ice pick to hit Bodwin, Ella saved further harm "Before Denver and them grabbed her and Ella put her fist in her jaw" (p. 312). Ella "was a practical woman" (p. 301), "Sethe's crime was staggering and her pride outstripped even that" (p. 302); yet she could indulge Beloved to an extreme no return possible from, Ella made a practical assessment, Sethe to be rescued. But rescue a practical process, Beloved out, Denver in Sethe's love, when Paul D makes the reverse journey, Stamp Paid following halfway.

On the day of Bodwin's visit to his old house 30 years later, left a young man, now an old man of seventy for the visit on purpose to take Denver to his house to provide a job there. Thirty black women gathered Ella among them, in the planned rescue of Sethe out of her self-made mess. They take Beloved at the root of her problem, her weak surrender to her bargain for love, love at the cost of her life which is cruelty. Ella doubted she was Sethe's daughter come back, rather 'a pretend' she was (p. 305). At the same time Bodwin appeared, a confusion whether "a hill of black people falling" (p. 309), Sethe Beloved together, apart, alone. Bodwin with a whip in hand!

Around 1987 Morrison cannot but be a realist, she takes a turn, finally free from the supernatural unreality, to a realistic good sense. Sethe waked up to realities, everyone around did, Denver early from inside, Sethe's immediate protector, Ella from outside, Paul D interested for a different to reason, reason a silver link of love, Paul met first Denver, "he was on his way to work and she was leaving hers" (p. 313), then Sethe, in her absence Beloved gone. Paul had left behind memories of the Civil War (1861-65) serving on both sides, now a different memory, Sethe the centre. The visit is a fair rounding off of the story, a story of unfulfilment in Negro life, the story of freedom an agonized trial of the still continued slavery in every possible way, Ella-Stamp—Sethe memories of the past still haunt Denver, Sethe's revolt and her rescue-effort armed with an ice-pick in hand served no purpose, Denver had to take a job at Bodwin's house, job itself a white man's mercy to a Negro who needed it.

Sethe-Paul D meeting towards the end of her unfulfilled life of ineffectual rags against concealed tyranny, more than the open, declared kind, both sufferers, both eager to compensate mutually for what was not, both missed when time was, now time's up, chance missed, yet the picture of prospect vivid in the author's presentation is drawn to a close:

> Sethe closes her eyes and presses lips together, She is thinking: ... There's nothing to rub now and no reason to. Nothing left to bathe, assuming he even knows how. Will he do it in sections? ... She opens her eyes, knowing the danger of looking at him. She looks at him. The peach stone skin, the crease between his ready waiting eyes and sees it—thing in him, the blessedness, that has made him the kind of man who can walk in a house and make the women cry. Because with him, in his presence, they could. Cry and tell him things they only told each other: that time didn't stay put; that she called.... (p. 321)

Thus Sethe looked in and at Paul D and repented she had lost her black-beauty, "that Amy was scared to stay with her because her feet were ugly and her back looked so bad; that her ma'am had hurt her feelings..." (*ibid.*).

But Paul D sees the woman, beside him, Sethe is, "There are too many things to feel about this woman". He tries to describes in Sixo's langues 'what he felt about the thirty—Mile Woman "She is a friend of my mind. She gather me, man. The pieces I am, she gather them and give them back to me in all the right order. It's good, you know, when you got a woman who is a friend of your mind". Sethe was to Paul D. But now all lost, nothing stays put. Paul felt "only this woman Sethe could have left him his manhood like that. He wants to put his story next to hers."

"Sethe," he says, "me and you, we got more of Yesterday than anybody. We need some kind of tomorrow."

... "You your best thing, Sethe. You are". Sethe's reply short, cryptic: "Me? Me?" (p. 322).

The reply meaningful, only language cannot convey it. What follows is "a loneliness that can be rocked. Arms crossed, knees drawn up; holding, holding on, this motion, unlike a ship's, smooths and contains the rocker. It's an inside kind—wrapped tight like skin".

Thus the story ends. Sethe's story, Sethe 'Black is beauty'—type, her story, 'not a story to pass on', history—neglected desert-bloom, no oasis to nurse her, she is not Wordsworth's lonely Lucy 'a violet by a mossy stone, half-hidden from the eye', made eternal by a poet's love, Sethe has no such chance, Morrison laments. Sethe is not a soft soil violet, like Lucy, nature-nursed beauty. She could have been Pygmalion girl of Shaw's making under so suitable circumstances, but that was not her lot, her position is "Although she has claim, she is not claimed. In the place where long grass opens, the girl who waited to be loved and cry shame erupts into her separate parts, to make it easy for the chewing laughter to swallow her all away" (p. 323).

Sethe's and Paul D's beauty lent rapture to love when Halle's absence and untraced long existence, if existence at all, created a vacuum, something quite human and mundane reality. Morrison makes it a part of Negro-slavery's common tragedy, mostly yet undetected tragedy, if less discerningly observed. Everything yet in a continuum of change, the past yielding place to the present, the present to the future, one effacing the other. So in it Sethe's tragic history along with her existence at all passed beyond memory. An author who so frequently weaves the supernatural into the woof of her story cannot overstep hard realities of life, life has duly corrected its blunders so long done in the continuum process. A lesson remains within life itself, life teaches in time. America in Morrison's time is not the Civil War period America, far ahead of the blunders of the past, from Hawthorne's Mark Twain's time till today, Morrison's time included, a panoramic change, with a bundle of newer problems figuring out.

7

Walker's Color-Beyond Great Mystery

[1]

The Author's personal perception counts initially, but cannot end there, Eliot believed, it leads to history, his tradition, where he can blend into impersonal universality—everyone's embraced shared truth, where past is present, future too no longer seems future, rather assumed in the present itself. Creation thus an Eternal present, only colour change, only variation variegated. Morrison's Sethe and Walker Celie are not of the same kind of victims, the difference makes all the differences in their stories, Sethe's is a slave woman's fight to assert her innate womanhood, against white master's hegemony, Celie's a Black woman's more acute an inside story of ugliness, an outrage that can be addressed to 'Dear God' alone for amendment of this His Dear Creation, creation of His own image, the last day of His creation thereafter His Sabbath, and no creation.

Sylvia Plath's Daddy-hate confession, in her poetry clear at least, sets the revelatory pattern anyway in the elite level, in *The Color Purple* in the lower, an unspoken agony in the male-dominated society, more at the lower level, savage. In modern fiction sex is a major human truth, more acute in American perspective, but this acuteness better in relation to another universal truth, Love. Celie is caught in a savage mesh of sex, rescued by love into fluttered freedom. She has more reason than 18th century Pamela to address her agony to Dear God. The whole story is set in Richardson-style in letters addressed to God in utmost helplessness the only available Person who knows everyone's secrets and everyone's sorrows and sins and who is everyone's support when no one is available to stand by, we believe when no one is there so finally to believe, when all trust in mankind is reasonably lost; Pamela had her family to bear with her, Celie had none, her sister could a portion bear with her, but shame stands in the way, unless she encourages, she does, yet shame persists, Nettie encourages in words replete with utmost sympathy feelingly articulated:

> I remember one time you said your life made you feel so ashamed you couldn't talk about it to God, you had to write it, bad as you thought your writing was. Well, now I know what you meant. And whether God will read letters or no I know you will go on writing them. (p. 117)

Yes, she does, because she cannot help it, one cannot. Nettie too cannot. Celie's initiative 'is guidance enough for me', she acknowledges, 'when I don't write to you I feel as bad when I don't pray, locked up in myself and choking on my own heart. I am so lonely, Celie'. Her reason not like Celie's enforced sin made to commit; but imposed sin uncommitted. Corrine, wife of Samuel, suspected their adopted children were Nettie's and Samuel their father.

The extra burden of sin, circumstances imposed on a sacred soul, that turned to the Ultimate Source of solace to its smarting wound, thoroughly justifies, the Author's claim and Celie's addressing her burden of sin, though misconceived, to the Unreached Invisible:

> '...a rebirth into strong feeling of Oneness I realized I had experienced and taken for granted as a child; a chance for me as well the main character, Celie, to encounter That Which Is Beyond Understanding But Not Beyond Loving', in that state of submission alone possible to 'say: I see and hear you clearly, Great Mystery, now that I expect to see and hear you everywhere I am, which is the right place'.

Yes, the right place to see and feel the Invisible visible. The only way to invoke in your presence His presence by your inmost love, you can talk too and He hears. Celie adopted this sure method, and it did not fail her. Her uncommitted burden of sin, was unloaded sooner by human medium, that is also His Mercy, she should have felt. Walker's story is built up around sin a story of purest blessedness, thus the tricks well played. Morrison's story of the coloured people in the transitional period of the Civil War (1861-65)—a tragedy; but Walker's is not a tragedy, the line of approach seems reaching back to a secret corner of the coloured home. The historical perspective is Post Civil War America, Celie's family re-union on the day of the celebration of 'independence from England July 4th' (p. 261), a national holiday Nettie back home from Africa with her husband and Celie's children. Racial and colour-ill feeling still persists, inside the colour rot not aplenty, woman in particular the suffering lot, sometimes most wretchedly, at its extreme stage even Sethe-like revolt not possible. In such an extreme stage woman has only God to unburden her unshared load, man though can escape such a situation far more easily.

God-seeking in this story is an important major issue which leads to where and how to seek Him, or at all to be sought or not; the story does neither represent God-free modern extremism, nor God-myth cultism altogether, but just a middle path of rationalized faith, faith in available everything, leaving anything unavailable, unapproachable, intangible—so love inside one's own being for everything around, extended to even what is apparently unlovely, so Celie now tolerate Mr—and Albert too can see something loving in Celie, in all Shug and Sofia, Adam in Tashi a scarified Olinka African, everyone every tree, every green field, colour purple.

[2]

Black is beauty, Richardson's Pamela could not go so far, she had no scope for so complex a modern world training; her experience was too limited. At Pamela's age Celie lost family's protection entire, father lynched off, mother crazy, her second husband passed for father, father's property now his, home under his rule. Pamela was a maid in an 18th century English home, Celie a daughter of a coloured American home in the post-Civil War period. Alphosno her mother's husband describes clearly the kind of coloured freedom:

> Your daddy didn't know how to get along, he say. White folks lynch him. Too sad a story to tell pitiful little growing girls, he say. Any man would have done what I done.
>
> Take me, he say, I know how they is. The key to all of 'em is money. The trouble with our people is as soon as they got of slavery they didn't want to give the white man nothing else. But the fact is, you got to give 'em something. Either your money, your land, your woman or your ass. So what I did was just right off offer to give 'em money. Before I planted a seed, I made sure this one and that one knowed one seed out of three was planted for him.... And when I opened up your daddy's old store in town I bought me one white boy to run it. And what make it so good, he say, I bought him with white folks' money. (Celie's *Letter*, 164)

Old habits die hard! The salve-owning white, could not still completely cleanse them of the long-standing habits of exploitation and inhuman cruelty, which one section among them thought seriously to amend. American Civilization thus slowly emerged. Walker too did not take an exclusively angular view, her story does not escape rottenness inside the coloured community, in America as well as their original home, and as well their native simplicity which is evident in some of the characters, in some as a subdued flicker amidst their accumulated junk-heap. The story is finally a message of hope, humanity always is.

Celie's real father was lynched, mother too a demented woman, her second husband a wretched lusty young man appropriated their parental property quite easily, Nettie her younger sister quite a Black beauty, these two sisters lost their father, how, they did not know, a coloured fell victim to white rage in the transional unsteady stage of slave freedom, they knew their mother's second husband for their own, but his dealings with them seemed repulsively low, mother died early, left them easily victims to this stepfather's lust and his second wife's neglect, Celie practically the family cook and second wife's children's maid when their mother was 'kilt' by her earlier lover. A position for Celie and sister, immediately for Celie, an outrage upon their original pious sense of humanity. Her extra responsibility again to protect Nettie from his raging lewdness. She kept her with books, her crazy mother died seeing her 'big' suspecting some outside promiscuity.

Celie most sufferer, excruciating for secretive imposition, her one baby already 'kilt' in the bush, stolen away while she was asleep. The next baby a boy she thought must have been "sold to a man and his wife over Monticello" (p. 5). Celie's all three babies, one killed, the other two sold out early, definitely to keep the passage clear for another lady, immediately 'a girl from round Gray' (p. 6), 'She be my age but they married'. The situation in his house was an air of mistrust. In Celie's letter: "He be on her all the time. She walk round like she don't know what hit her. I think she thought she love him. But he got so many of us" (*ibid.*). He tried Nettie behind Celie's back, in the Church, where Mr—too haunted regularly to try, Nettie for safety perhaps picked a boyfriend. Nettie Celie both withdrawn from school, both Celie and Nettie now unwanted liability, Celie graceless, Nettie yet not, when Mr—came with a proposal for Nettie he told Mr—clearly all the scandals of his family and why Celie would better suit, then in the course of negotiation both the families were exposed however caution may have been taken on this side.

Their Pa told "Mr—got too many children already. Plus what about the scandal his wife cause when somebody kill her? And what about all this stuff he hear about Shug Avery? What about that?" (p. 8). To convince Mr—that instead of Nettie Celie would suit him better Pa told him pretending his disgust with Celie: She spoiled. Twice. But you don't need a fresh woman no how. I got "a fresh one in there myself and she sick all the time" (p. 9). This Pa always kept a straight façade, he withheld Celie from school when she first 'got big', he told Celie, 'you too dumb to keep going to school' (p. 11). He is a confirmed pretender, when their teacher Miss Beasley visited his house to "say long as she been a teacher she never know nobody want to learn bad as Nettie and me" (p. 12). She could not read Pa's tricks when he called her to appear before pleading Miss Beasley, who saw big and without saying anything instantly withdrew.

Mr—knew from his own experiences what could happen to Celie in her Pa's custody, so he wanted to see Celie bodily once more, Mr—is not Miss Beasley, he flatly told him what she looked like: 'That cow still coming', Pa 'He say, Her cow' (p. 13), no bar to how he pleased to explain to himself, no shame.

Walker does not see any White role-play in a coloured community, lately out of slavery, amongst themselves they are not less tyrannous. Celie and Nettie fell victims to two male coloured blackguards' insatiabfe sex-orgies, to save Nettie Celie offered herself, yet that won't do, she was already unattractive, Nettie fresh, charming. Pa planned anyway to discard Celie, her marriage to Mr—(Albert real name) the ready way. Both around Nettie, Pa would appropriate Nettie, his wife often sick, Nettie fresh, youngish, their shared attempt failed, Nettie vomiting on the porch, Pa's wife weeping—ugliest possible scene in a coloured's home! No Lawrentian 'Eros the Sacred Mystery', a savage scene. Celie has none to tell her story but her God, whoever wherever He may be! Celie is a black victim of her own society! God alone her support, no question of His existence or not, she has nothing or none else to seek:

In this story God is an important issue, as in India Rabindranath's almost every play his concealed subject, yet everything weaves around it, Rabindranath cannot locate where, but sure there is, hence his is only a flight after a search, eager and urged not to remain idle and unstirring, Walker's only a support-seeking of the supportless helpless. These two sisters are of this class, victim to no white master, but a class of masters from amongst the earlier slave class. Oppressors and tyrants are of no class-definition but by itself. This way Walker's is a tilt towards humanity and humanity's last resort Divine Dispenser.

[3]

Wife's position in a coloured home is a foregone conclusion—an oppressed slave class, life and body at the master class their husbands' mercy, Nettie's African experience of Olinka community confirmed it, women, as a class, field slaves of their owner husband's lands, in, addition their children's mothers, ownership always husband's, children and mothers his. Celie's marriage to Mr—hardly changed her subjugated exploited position, children of the previous wife a wild lot, son eldest twelve, on the first day threw stone and hit her head bleeding, this was her reception. All the four children like wild cats in her keeping one kind of torture, husband another, a body-beating beauty, his beauty itself a ready lure for women, one already declared Shug Avery, no secret. Then another discovery lately, Celie found her baby girl, taken away when two months only, 'now about six' in another woman's possession, chance-met at her visit to town. Six year old child's mother Celie when recalled how mercilessly baby taken away from her milking breast, only she knew what the memory was like! Was it less cruel than a white master's selling his slave's children to another white master?

Celie escaped one tyrant's possession of her body and mind into another tyrant's possession, only her soul remained alive to submit to whom she believed to be God, the Final Dispenser. All her letters addressed to God are submission, Nettie lacked that power, she left home behind, fled to her sister's home, earlier she was under sister's protection, without protection she was unable to protect herself, neither could so entirely submit to God all the perpetrated outrages upon her, like Celie. Celie's husband tried Nettie every way he could, before Celie's marriage one way, now at home another way, when he failed he disapproved Nettie's stay there. Nettie's meeting Reverend Mr (Samuel) at his house for the lady whom Celie met at the store with her lost baby a turning point in the story.

The visit of Albert's two sisters to his home another turning point in the story, these two sisters appreciated the value of neglected and tortured Celie amidst the wild brood of

Albert's children and her husband's scattering wild oats outside, one Shug Avery a scandalous woman known to all, they warned Celie, advised her to assert herself, and packed off immediately; his earlier wife Agnes Julia suffered a lot, herself too not a clean woman, not a home-keeping type, they warned Celie, and left. One sister clearly told her "you got to fight, Celie. I can't do it for you. You got to fight for yourself" (p. 22). But she is not a fighting sort. Harpo the eldest son, seventeen, a brute, father's own piece of a block, picks up a 15 year old girl, he is not sure, that she loves him, yet he would have her! Harpo is a piece of his father's block, Nettie rightly presumed he would one day kill his father. Alphosno and Albert are a representation of a class from amongst the coloured no less than the white class of tyrannous masters. They are slave-owners of their own, both of the same block. It is no matter of colour or racial specification, it is humanity run rot. Walker's finger seems to point to that basic truth.

Harpo, though of father's copy, does not rely on father's wisdom, he confides to Celie, quite natural. He knows he father, unsteady, unreliable, unsympathetic tyrant. Celie's softness, tenderness must have had an unsuspicious natural appeal even to her open enemies. He told her everything about his love and her determination to have her. From the very beginning Celie stands out an exceptional coloured outstandingly uncoloured by a rotten community of the coloured. Her faith in God kept her alive, her sinless mute protest against sin causing silently a change in the order finally in her favour.

Harpo an overdeveloped young man, a lover, asking father unpleasant questions, relationship getting strained quick. His father left Harpo and Celie to do the field work, Celie chopping and Harpo ploughing, "Harpo complain bout all the plowing he have to do" (p. 28), asked his father, "why you don't work no more?" The girl's daddy rejected him, he was not good enough, so he asked his father why he was not; his father told him, 'your mammy', 'what wrong with my mammy?' His father answered, 'Somebody kill her' (p. 29). Harpo's marriage after the birth of his child, a trick he played with the girl. His father too was befooled, he rejected Sofia on the plea she was already big, even when she clearly told him, the father of the baby was Harpo. Both his son and himself are being paid in their own coin, Sofia a fighting woman since her childhood, her father of the same colour and conduct, a tyrant, her mother oppressed like Celie, he had 12 children all doubted but that by her mother. Sofia came aggressively to accuse Celie that she asked Harpo to beat her, but was readily corrected by her plain confession, to her guilt-conscience. She pitied her sufferings like her unfighting mother's. They six sisters fought together all the male members of the family, and formed an idea: "A girl child ain't safe in a family of men" (p. 39).

The two women are of the same colour, but their difference is very sharp: 'Well, sometime Mr—get on me pretty hard. I have to talk to Old Maker. But he my husband. I shrug my shoulders. This life soon be over, I say. Heaven last all ways. "You ought to bash Mr—head open, she say. Think bout heaven later" (p. 40).

Celie cannot be taught, Nettie could be, but not she, an exceptional character, far ahead of Pamela, Clarissa, here Lovelace too many, here Shug Avery round the corner everywhere, out of slavery, now they are slave-owners in every home, secret and open, Avery their 'Honeybee' Queen Honeybee, Albert drone. Avery now in their town, a show to be held, drone Albert dressing up, which set could suit him, failed repeatedly to decide, Celie to help, then Queen Honeybee fell ill, none to take home, which disease not known, all afraid, may be ugly female disease. Albert ordered Harpo to fix up wagon, he did with a sly look and subdued simper, father brought her home five days later, under a makeshift canopy, she alighted supported by one side son other side father, Celie was ordered to fix up the spare room for her, she did, now Queen home for two months, her three children a subject of gossip, she a free woman, they are under her mother's care, she carefree, worried Albert nestled in one corner, care-worn, of the Queen's room.

Two visits one after another, Albert's old father, and Tobias his brother, came, the old man to warn, his home his land, his garden, all his, here a scandous woman, with filthy disease, her children no one knows whose, where none knows; brother Tobias came with a packet of choicest chocolate for offer, the angry father's quite opposite gesture, a farcical response too, Shug sagging into a butter lump, diseased lady waddled to ease! Fun. Mr—son and his old daddy in debate over Shug: "Old Mr—clear his throat. Well, this my house. This my land. Your boy Harpo in one of my houses, on my land. Weeds come up on my land, I chop 'em up. Trash blow over it I burn it'. He told his son: "Her mammy take in white people dirty clothes to this day. Plus all her children got different daddys". Son says "I vouch for that. All Shug Avery children got the same daddy" (p. 53). He had reason to so strongly vouch.

Tobias a different scene, Avery at her ease with him, Celie too enjoys the fun. They quilt-sewing Celie, Albert her husband, engaged for Avery's comfort, Tobias and Avery witnessing them to do it eagerly, a lighter moment for all. The old father out in a huff. Celie in a lighter mood exceptionally, "I see myself sitting there quilting tween Shug Avery and Mr—. Us three set together against Tobias and his fly, speck box of chocolate. For the first time in my life, I feel just right" (p. 55).

[4]

Walker is very rarely in a lighter tone in this story of entire Nigroid mismanagement in their own house, hardly any white interference in their own home except from outside incursion into their own territory for modern industrialization, in their usual commercial expansionist zeal as in a Renascence spirit adventure, America itself their New England. Walker writes here Celie's story, a homey coloured girl, tragedy in her early blooming life home-miscarriage without any white interference, as not in the Sethe-Shug family of the Black. Their humanity stunted spoiled altogether by white adventurism. Celie a victim of her own people, Albert Alphosno Shug Avery her own people, they are not slaves, if not of their own degraded propensities. They are themselves to blame. They are slaves to themselves, let them wage war against it, in Islam Jihad is exactly that, Rasul preached Arabian nomads this

Jihad, they only misexplained it to themselves. Bal a poet of Rasul's time excelled in satire, which infuriated Rasul, why could he not sing in praise of Al Lat Allah? So, Rasul called poets liars, poets like Bal.

Walker's coloured community slaves to their own bestialities, their males make women their slaves, like they themselves are slaves to their loveless brutal body-possession, body-ownership, Celie told Sofia's husband, not merely for projected peace and harmony: "Mr—marry me to take care of his children, I marry him cause my daddy made me. I don't love Mr—and he don't love me" (p. 61). A woman like Shug cannot be made to 'mind', Celie told Harpo, Sofia cannot be, if you try she would 'beat' you back, and make you her slave, Mr—Shug's slave. A new chapter of slavery in their life, no role of the white people here though! A new slave-circle is created from amongst themselves, sometimes women to men, again on occasion men to women, as for example men like Albert and brother Tobias to Shug Avery, Albert with confidence certified to his old father all Shug-babies had but a single father, even Celie too did not fail to 'feel just right' (p. 55).

In Albert's own home Harpo failed to assert her authority over his wife Sofia, an amazon type like all her sisters, he tried like his father, trickily gained possession of the girl's body, married her when a baby was born, just father's liaison-episode with Shug only marriage missed, babies born of unsure obscure parentage. A community of so reckless use of freedom seems to have gained the way of slavery of their own creation, an unintegrated unloved unrelated co-existence unnatural, discordant, struggle for existence bound to assume an air of war, no one secure; Celie alone in the whole story forms the basic stay, herself for all, for her, if no one, at least her unknown unknowable God, support-seeking, if not by anything, her unfailing love, her greatest surest possession! Love withholds no confidence, so hers are all love-letters to Him.

This tangible offer makes the intangible invisible real to her, lends her a force to which even Shug's coquetry surrenders. Her coquetry conquered every male heart, Celie's husband most, but conquered by Celie's love.

Shug's superior Indian version is Rushdie's Vina Apsara, her song and charm not of Apsara grade as Vina's was, obviously less glamourous. She gave Juke-joint show at Harpo's porch—not rock and roll—which suit her taste and nature. She is Celie's best friend, yet could seek her permission to sleep with her husband though she declared openly to his face, "Good thing I ain't your damn wife" (p. 69). Her husband, Celie says, "love looking at Shug. I love looking at Shug. But Shug don't love looking at but one of us. Him" (p. 70).

Shug's love for Celie not for look, but her response to Celie's love. Her husband could not love her then because she was not a beauty and not able to love her love and care for him and lost her love by his unloved outrage upon her as on other women where he could. Only he could not venture upon Shug, as his son Harpo could not upon Sofia. Harpo was his father's son, Sofia left him with her children, returned with her lover and one child extra and openly declared: "I got six children now, Miss Celie", she "tossed her head, look over at Harpo. Life don't stop just cause you leave home, Miss Celie. You know that" (p. 77). Harpo too in Sofia's absence picked up a girl friend whom he called Squeak, Sofia accompanited by a 'Prizefighter' friend came, who to possess Harpo-house, the immediate result of a fight, Squeak bruised, two teeth lost, upon the floor bleeding, Harpo helpless, fondling Squeak, Sofia and Buster friend left easy, as if nothing happened, Albert reported "Both the girls bigged and gone. Bub in and out of jail. If his granddaddy, wasn't the coloured uncle of the sheriff who look just like Bub, Bub be lynch by now" (pp. 76-77).

Albert has not yet learnt the lesson, he is yet at ease with Shug, Celie at home patient witness to Shug. Albert hugs, a freedom they take under Celie's uncomplaining untwisted nose and unblinking eyes, yet with an unease inexplicable in her forsaken bed! Did they care? This is the kind of freedom from slavery! Shug among them Queen Honeybee, if she cares for anybody, it is only Celie, she sings Celie-song, Albert beats Celie, because she is not Shug, fool he is, Shug would not leave until he no longer ventures to beat her: "I won't leave, she say, until I know Albert won't even think about beating you" (p. 72). This is love's silent conquest, Albert her conquered guy, but she is Celie's conquered girl, a different charm, different from that which enthralled Shug and Albert each to each.

Celie finally wins in the story by a kind of 'God Si Love', Love your God, when God you don't know where, so God, if Love, the only available substitute. Everything else in the story fails, God does not know colour, love too doesn't. Sofia in prison, her fighting spirit fails, fighting Mayor's wife and Sheriff brought her to prison in broken body and crushed spirit, from five to eight a laundry woman in the prison, most obedient to order. God manifests Himself as Love, the whole Creation is He for your love. Sofia's imprisonment changed her a bit, her fury learnt to adjust though not for love directly, but guided by self-love, avoiding self-destruction. She saw her husband, husband's father, her rival woman Mary Agnes, Celie, Shug all came to try how to early take her out of prison. Mary Agnes (Squeak) acts a major part in this rescue drama, to the extent of her scandalous obscure birth brought to light.

The divulgement drama is as intriguing as her played part. They are at the prison-gate wanting the warden's 'black kinsfolk', their eachone's supplementary information taken together located one Henry Hodges, his brother Jimmy Hodges. Celie's husband meaningfully asks Squeak 'you know them?' She knows, first says 'cousin', then 'Daddy' when Mr—asks further whether Jimmy knew it, she says "one time he live with Mr Jimmy, he give us all quarters say we sure look like Hodges." "He got three children by my mama. Two younger than me" (p. 86). They sent her to the warden. How she succeeded a scandalous story, the warden recognized her when she referred to "you come by the house with my mama friend, Mr Jimmy", then finally more than recognition, the cost of the success:

> He took my hat off.... Told me to undo my dress. She drop her head, put her face in her hands.
>
> He say if he was my uncle he wouldn't do it to me. That be a sin. But this just little fornication. Everybody guilty of that. (p. 90)
>
> Six months after Mary Agnes went to get Sofia out of prison. (p. 91)

Unattached women and children a vast lot thus created, moral support of a healthy society, purity of human birth thus lost, marriage can never remain a sacred bond, all finer qualities of human life, like love, respect, wisdom, compassion, all get stunted; out of slavery they remain long—if not ever—no better than slaves. In sharp contrast Celie is a sacred light, her existence in such an unholy, depraved society, is a constant torment, her sole support is God whose existence she feels in love, the only tangible expression that she does is Purple shrubbery, green foliage, graceful human body, all God's expression she loves, even ugliness by contrast His love, loving this love living Celie has no lack of God's love, her love too a living response. Thus she can live even in so depraved a community, earlier slaves got free only to indulge their slavish sanction to the full.

[5]

Sofia took a haughty stand she could not serve as a white woman's maid, perhaps thought, once out of slavery no longer a slave; right determination possible only by a determined principle of improvement. But these slaves adopted a hate-haughty stance and made use of freedom for unchecked indulgence of base propensities so long held in check before white masters' insolent eyes. They rather degraded themselves, and became more worthless to be even servant or slave. Sofia came back to become maid to the Mayor's wife, Shug a woman, in spite of her worth, knew nothing of love or moral discipline, if she did not find Celie to love, she must have ended loveless, in body-recreation, call it pleasure. Shug confessed everything to Celie. She repented she hurt Celie's feelings seeking her permission to sleep with Albert, she did not repent so when she appropriated Albert from Annie Julia, Annie too slept with another man who finally killed her. Shug had three children by Albert, the third one caused a stir at home, she had to leave and had to stay up with her wild aunt in Memphis, she made her confidence to Celie, now she sleeps with Celie, her present lover Grady and Albert over drunk, boozy in another room, she told everything to Celie, this aunt "She just like me, Mama say. She drink, she fight, she love mens to death. She work in a road house Cook. Feed fifty men, screw fifty five" (p. 111).

Shug clears everything she did, she harmed Julia "She was pretty, Black as anything, and skin just smooth. Big black eyes look like moons". She harmed Celie "I treated you so mean. Like you a servant. And all because Albert married you. I did not even want him for a husband, she say. I never really wanted Albert for a husband. But just to choose me, you know, cause nature had already done it.... But what was good between us must have been nothing but bodies, she say" (p. 112). Shug is Vina Apsara's early Black junior version, her conquest at a less glamourous lower lever. Less captivating than Rushdie's, but more single mindedly effective towards a pious humanity, conversion easy and straight, Celie-central. Not Rushdie's rock and roll, but juke-joint. No Vina glamour but Celie-sober! Celie's silent sobriety wins all sub-human inhuman outrages to a genuine human evolution clamping down Black-White barrier, among themselves the coloured quiddities, to calm. The shift is physically Shug now from Albert's bed to Celie bed, a submissive mother to her.

Shug is now on Celie's side, Celie's confidante like Celie hers. Celie could recover Nettie's long held-up letters in his possession and the contents, including all his mischiefs with Nettie in the past. Nettie's letters to Celie serve a different purpose in the story, their unknown part of their life brought to knowledge for the audience, and for themselves too, a fuller view of life in evolution. Celie knew where her children were and how, and how luckily Nettie too was with them their aunt without their knowledge. In addition a close view of African Black inside from the coast and the recent days missionary efforts to civilize them, and Europe-American response to them from the slavery stage to their freedom, limited to Nettie's experience and information. Two sisters' accounts, one side the coloured community, the other outside amongst the missionaries in England—America and Africa, taken together edit a picture with a close bearing upon white and colour relationship, better decided by human values, which is finally the trend of the story. Celie a coloured character with firm faith in God, her faith is made easy and translated into a working order by love, which alone can reach wherever He is, otherwise unreachable, everything God's Creation, everyone His, this very attitude makes her disclose everything to God, even things which she cannot disclose to anyone else on earth, a little to Shug because of her love for her and vice versa.

Another male character from the coloured group, Samuel, only human standard of judgement makes him stand out prominent amongst his fellow coloured, even beside all those white in America and England, even his fellow white missionaries there and in Africa, projected European civilizer Kurtz, for example in the Congo (Conrad's Heart of Darkness). Celie is a character anywhere a leading light. Nettie, next to her, another glowing coloured character in the story, late slavery-free unsteady period's free-coloured community's victims they are. Their response different, difference qualitative and in degrees only.

[6]

All Nettie's letters deeply informative, and of a nature that it unweaves the tangle towards a happy resolution on the one hand and on the other weaves a fresh knot very difficult to undo unless true sense of humanity dawns on the growing civilization in the West and anywhere else, no question of coloured or uncoloured. Colour and quality can be varied, even as varied as there are individuals, but basic humanity is almost the same.

Nettie's voyage to Africa opens the window to another part of the Dark continent not covered by Conrad and Naipaul, not the riverine region, but the inside dry Western region away from the coast, a little nearer our time, slavery-free America's contact with the original slave-source, people who did not have personal knowledge of slave life. If it is still darkness it is by their adaptation to dark environment, but a light-bringer, if any like fire-bringer Prometheus, must be a true friend, not enemy. Nettie's description of a British Rubber-factory magnate is an enemy's invasion, a total unsettlement of the basic support of their life. The American missionaries in the Olinka area led by a well-wishing coloured a sharp contrast, they are their friends, they too could finally realize they were. They came neither like the British conquerors nor got converted like Kurtz, they shared their discomfort of darkness and gave light, without being converted they could convince them of the benefit of light, Tashi's father died unconvinced, but her mother and many like her were convinced of their good will.

Local healers with their limited knowledge of herbal medicinal properties and witchcraft could not cure Tashi's father's simple malarial fever, he died; all his wives unprotected, only Tashi's mother with her five male children for protection could decide not to marry again. Women are in their society field workers, their husband a sort of drone, only breeder, wives are amongst themselves in the field at their ease, free to talk in the midst of their work and their children with them under direct care and attendance, if any ill-feeling that too reasonably there at play without husband's knowledge, everyone afraid of being identified as having witchy ill-feeling towards another's children, husband their sole authority to decide what punishment of such a crime should be meted out for which offence, even to the extent of death. Women are virtually a slave class in their male-dominated society. Tashi's one aunt revolted and she was sold out to slave traders. Women safe in their community from dishonour and adventurism by others, but slaves to their husbands. Daughters are protected from adolescent male allure by scarification of faces and female circumcision. The missionaries could not protect Tashi from this unnatural debeautification.

In America the whole of the coloured history is quite different, in one word from slavery to freedom, tortured life in slavery turned them slowly on the path of revolution against their white masters, revolting spirit urged them to be equipped, the dispossessed to be in a position of possession, they could not remain stagnant as in their undisturbed home land. In their homogeneous society women remained under male rule, only a little better than slaves, their males were not slaves, females were their own slaves without their own freedom of choice, even within home, love affection within limited range, almost of a uniform pattern, conjugal relationship not a shared partnership of confidence and love. They are guided by an unwritten uniform code. The whole society is guided by an unwritted accepted code. Exceptional human attributes are acknowledged in their Chief. They felt no use of female education, rather considered it as a breach of rule.

Nettie's letters to Celie convey this idea, Samuel a coloured missionary from America felt estranged by the difference: "the women share a husband but the husband does not share their friendship, it makes Samuel uneasy. It is confusing, I suppose. And it is Samuel's duty as a Christian minister to preach the Bible's directive of one husband and one wife" (p. 150). Freed American Negroes by competitive race are modern and hardly make any difference from earlier slave owner white Americans. Harlem in New York is all coloured-dominated, they may be diasporic, may feel nostalgic for their original home, but they would never go back to darkness from light. This is civilization, Celie, Nettie, Samuel would not go, though they may feel kinship for them, for their self-forged shackles, weakening themselves to be conquered too easily. The whole American coloured community learnt from their own experiences since their days of slavery how to improve their position, definitely not remaining steeped in their age-old incompetent obscurity, Samuel-Corrine-Nettie and the children with them learnt how to assert themselves. This is struggle for existence. They saw still in spite of freedom they had to travel in a separate ill-provided Rail compartment exclusively for them. They are taught by their straggling experiences, which the Olinka community had no occasion to learn till the oppressive British industrialists invaded their lands and destroyed their leaf-roof plants they knew for their God providing them shelter so long.

Walker narrates this sad and sweet story of evolution of the coloured. A step ahead of Morrison's story of another earlier period of transition. Walker's is more of an inside story of the coloured. Sethe and Celie are victims of two different kinds of tragedies, Sethe could not survive, but Celie could for a different quality of character, more ideal than emotional, more unraging, more patient and persistent, more inside the coloured community, her parents a step closer to Sethe's tragic trappings. Christianity weaned them away from roof-leaf God or death deciding Kanaima, Celie, and finally Shug, made proper use of faith, on a line that links one to another for undisturbed peace, by love. Thus you know or not you can love God. Though Nettie belongs to a missionary group abroad Celie was taught more by life to seek support of faith, that was the reason that she could stay alive.

Celie's letters to God are confessional, but letters to Nettie are personal informal, and everything in relation to Shug a woman-to-woman sharing support only not through letters, as between Clarissa Harlowe and Miss Howe. Apparently Shug and Celie are quite different in their style of life, yet somewhere there is a secret link for their mutual closeness and appreciation, difference without hostility may be one reason, enforced by mutual need—though of two different kinds—might have been steadied into love. Finally they detected a deep spiritual basis of their unity of mind, which seems to be Walker's focus of centripetal diversions. A point to take up later.

[7]

Nettie's letters carried to Celie relieving information, two at a time, how? the design of the story makes it a life-like natural development: Celie's meeting with Corrine in a town store, a baby girl with her, the child awakened curiosity. Nettie's job-seeking brought her to this lady, Celie suggested her, when she was out of her husband's favour, to visit this lady who may require her service; more importantly Nettie's fondness for the children and children's for her awakened jealousy in Corrine. Later developments are the natural continuation of this related series of events.

Corrine fell ill, Nettie had extra duty now, to nurse her; while Nettie "was changing her as she lay in bed, she gave me a long, mean, but somehow pitiful look. Why do my children look like you? she asked". She would not hear any reasonable explanation. She accused, "you could have spit them out". And went so far in jealousy that she asked, "when did you meet my husband first?" (p. 155). Mistrust began growing in her, not the less in her husband. She harassed Nettie every possible way, got her to swear by the Bible, even Samuel too, and he got out of the sick room, she made her show her under belly. Even after she asked her not to use her wearings and meet Samuel alone and let the children call her mama Nettie. Samuel apologized to Nettie for all that crazy things.

Samuel thought Olivia and Adam were Nettie's children, that is why he took Nettie when that woman who was to go to take care of the children was married and her husband would not go with her nor would allow her to go alone. Now the position is, Samuel had to explain to Nettie how he got the children from a man and the story he narrated at the time of parting with them; and Nettie to tell him what she knew. These two stories together enlightened both of them and Walker's readers too what the real position was and how face saving tricks the person played. The story he narrated to Samuel was from Nettie's letter:

> Once upon a time, there was a well-to-do farmer who owned his property near town. Our town, Celie. And as he did so well farming and everything he turned his hand to prospered, he decided to open a store, and try his luck selling dry goods as well. Well, his store did so well that he talked two of his brothers into helping him run it, and, as the months went by, they were doing better and better. Then the white merchants began to get together and complain that this store was taking all the black business away from them, and the man's blacksmith shop that he set up behind the store, was taking some of the white. This would not do. (p. 157)

Morrison took up one transitional period of Civil War, Walker another transitional slavery-abolished period when White masters could not fully reconcile to the changed order. They envied Black-prosperity, and did what they were used to do in the slavery period, destroyed the store and smithy and hanged the three brothers in the night. This coloured farmer storekeeper Celie's father left then mother horror-shocked demented, one daughter born another coming, the whole property passed into this stranger's possession, and the family itself through mother's marriage.

This stranger was known to Samuel in the course of his preaching contact, he told Samuel a false story:

> The man had a wife whom he adored, and they had a little girl, barely two years old. She was also pregnant with another child. When the neighbours brought her husband's body home, it had been mutilated and burnt. The sight of it nearly killed her, and her second baby, also a girl, was born at this time. (pp. 157-58)

This part of the story is true; then the rest truth and falsehood mixed. These two girl children were Celie and Nettie. Their mother was also 'a good looking woman', 'while the second child was still a baby, a stranger appeared in the community' also true. They married too. But this stranger purposely misinformed Samuel about this lady living long enough to have given birth to two babies a girl and a boy, before she had died, nor 'were they named Olivia an Adam' (p. 158). Olivia and Adam were Celie's children, Celie thought born incestuous. The riddle of these lost children is unriddled in Nettie's letter:

The stranger who married the widow was someone Samuel had run with long before he found Christ. When the man showed up at Samuel's house with first Olivia and then Adam, Samuel felt not only unable to refuse the children, but as if God had answered his and Corrine's prayer (*ibid.*). Celie relieved, no sin of incest at least. Shug offered to take her immediately to Memphis. And she too decided to pay a visit to Pa and her parent's grave, Shug to accompany her. The visit only revealed, he was steeped in sinful gain satisfied, his earlier wife left him with her children, a new one, a young wife, almost a girl, over indulgent, over satisfied apparently. No sin-sense, no repentance, no usual formality, rather behaviour of a confirmed, cunning, criminal winning assured security, satisfied.

[8]

Nettie-Celie correspondences reveal a change in Celie's quality of faith in God, human support from Shug and sister must have caused this change, her softness too no longer remained so soft, behaviour even turned a little aggressive, women of the story all took side against male obstreperous oppressive oddities. She is found assertive. She declares to her husband, she is leaving, Shug too not so soft to Albert. All the women at Odessa's table made fun of men in their helplessness against their combined force—perhaps a possible modern reprisal trend in male dominated womanhood so long.

Celie stopped writing to God, she had a human confidante to write to and get response, which one cannot expect from God unless self-contrived; Nettie seemed to her a better substitute. That was foolish to think God's substitute, Celie could have thought it God's gift, free offer for her relief; she thought quite otherwise: "what God do for me?" A challenge to which Snug replied: "He gave you life, good health, and a good woman that love you to death". Celie accusing "he give me a lynched daddy, a crazy mama, a low down dog of a step pa and a sister I probably won't ever see again. Anyhow, I say, the God I been praying and writing to is a man. And act just like all other mens I know..." (p. 173).

Whatever Shug might say she would not be convinced unless she saw reasons. This really happens: "But it ain't easy, trying to do without God. Even if you know he ain't there, trying to do without him is a strain" (p. 174).

Shug took the cue, she said, "I is a sinner. Cause I was born. I don't deny it. But once you find out what's out there waiting for us, what else can you be?" (*ibid.*).

The debate over God continues. To sum it up: everyone makes God in his own image, so white people's God is white, they go to the Church to share a white God, "and all the coloured folks doing is gitting cursed?" (p. 175). Whatever different in the Bible they don't care. Biblical Ethiopia is Africa, and 'Jessus' hair like lamb's wool', but they take it to be like white man's finally the faith and vision are coloured by one's preoccupation. Shug is Walker's representation here, realistic: "Aain't no way to read the bible not think God white, she say. Then she sigh. When I found out I thought God was white, and a man, I lost interest. You mad cause he don't seem to listen to your prayers. Humph! Do the mayor listen to anything colored say? Ask Sofia she say" (*ibid.*).

Shug is man with human limitations. Her reading realistically human reading, Author's approach too realistic, finally true. God has no colour, Indian age-old concept 'Niranjan Purus'—colourless, yet every colour, white as well as every other colour. When Purus indifferent no colour, when in everyone individually He is every colour, every form. Shug presents it for the Author and for all:

> Here's the thing, say Shug. The thing I believe, God is inside you and inside everybody else. You come into the world with God. But only them that search for it inside find it. And sometimes it just manifest itself even if you not looking, or don't know what you looking for. Trouble do it for most folks, I think. (p. 176)

She affirms 'yeah, It. God ain't a he or a she, but a It'. She further extends It to Love—God Si Love: "My first step from the old white man was trees. Then air. Then birds. Then other people. But one day when I was sitting quiet and feeling like a motherless child, which I was, it come to me; that feeling of being part of everything, not separate at all. I knew that if I cut a tree, my arm would bleed. And I laughed and I cried and I run all round the house. I knew just what it was. In fact, when it happen, you can't miss it.... You praise God by liking what you like" (*ibid.*).

Celie is reconverted: "Now that my eyes opening I feels like a fool. Next to any little scrub of a bush in my yard, Mr—'s evil sort of shrink. But not altogether. Still, it is like Shug say, you have to git man off your eyeball, before you can see anything a tall" (p. 177).

In Shug's home Celie and Squeak, all women together, Grady to manage outside work. Women together, apparently their closeness without any man to interfere with male authority, no husband, no lover, an exclusive women-world. Only Shug sometime out of home for outside programmes private or public; Celie engaged in her pant-making for a living her indepence thus contemplated. After all her bitter experiences with man an exclusive female world of intimacy made possible, Shug too enjoys a change, in her arid life of adventure, a freedom of a kind for women as women. Celie's letters to Nettie depict one kind in America, Nettie's to Celie another kind in Africa, Walker a woman, a different kind of British Jane Austen in New England, coloured too.

Celie got remaining lot of Nettie's letters held up by Celie's husband, under Harpo's advice. Sofia's mother died, her funeral was attended by Celie and Shug, Shug did not come to see Albert, but Celie came and on that visit she learnt from Sofia what happened to Albert in her absence, he was then a solitary forsaken man, worried, house haunted at night, Harpo to attend and even to sleep with him, his house to clean. He advised him to send Nettie's letters. After that no ghost visit! Celie should have known God, though invisible unknown, can make Him visible and known in many varied ways through His creation, all that happens in her favour are God's response, His sanction.

[9]

Nettie's longest letter to Celie contains vital personal intimations as well as blunderous Euro-American deal with African black and the African's sneering attitude to the Euro-American coloured whom originally they sold out to them for slaves and caused much gruesome tortures silently to bear long enough before they gathered courage to revolt. This section of European American coloured are virtually double victims of mistrust of their own people in the homeland and the white in hostland, and even more wretched are those who are harmed, tortured, and cunningly exploited by their own people in the host countries. Walker takes the entire complex issue in this story.

Nettie met Doris Baines on the ship back to England from the Olinka community of Africa, hated, or at least, mistrusted them coloured from America, mainly because they were out of the homeland and stuffed with a borrowed culture or custom; in one word they were different, Tashi's father directly accused. Doris told them, they too saw, how the natives of Olinka were mercilessly ousted from their homes, their lands, with guns and in an invasion style, and they submitted helplessly with a concealed grudge in them ever nursed secretly for the opportunity to retaliate in the same measure of merciless cruelty. Doris foretold: "But big war is coming. Bigger than the one they were starting when I left. It'll go hard on England, but I expect we'll survive. I missed the other war, she said. I mean to be present for this one."

Why this coming war? She accounts for: "Why, she said, the signs are all over Africa. India too, I expect. First there's a road built where you keep your goods. Then your trees are hauled off to make ships and captain's furniture. Then your land is planted with something you can't eat. Then you're forced to work it. That's happening all over Africa, she said. Burma too, I expect" (p. 206).

Doris-reading is right, Nettie's eye-witness account of forcible occupation by a British industrialist of Olinka, their submission under the threat of guns, their fury left fuming, waiting for the time of explode. Doris showed the method how to civilize the savage, if civilize they should. Doris an upper class white lady, spent her whole life in Africa, knowing the details of the Black life, and formed her own idea of civilizing the savage, the method implemented duly by a love conquest, she sent two women to England, got them back duly educated to serve their people, she remained there their children's grannie, Harry now with her on her way back home. She sensed the European conquest policy a mistake, the ultimate fall-out a bigger war that she had known. Doris learnt their language, studied their life and culture and wrote books on them. She won their trust and brought about changes. No European or American did it. The white people on the Olinka sea-coast were adventurers, Kurtz's generation, either traders or conquerors, women their bait, Tashi's father told Samuel and Nettie.

Doris fooled the Missionary, she did her own work, she became a reputed writer, made money, the Africans were so pleased with her that one of them made her a present of 'a couple of wives' whom she educated in England and "gave them away in marriage to two young chaps who were always about the place" (p. 208). She was the grannie of their children. Tashi and her mother could finally appreciate after

Tashi's father's death that women too required some freedom, some choice of their own, but their society would not still allow them to assert. Olivia and Adam, Samuel's adopted children, originally Celie's, offered Tashi adolescent company. She, and eventually her mother, would not have known anything better than their own stifled subjection; outside contact was needed, even uninviting aggression with a trail of shocking cruelties eye-opening to them, as an enforced lesson, that they cannot remain static in their self-cherished solidarity. The weak always encourage the mighty to conquer and exploit and oppress. The sold slaves in America and other parts of the world are now in a far better position, Harlem Club in New York is a glowing example. Situation did not allow them to remain self satisfied, and indifferent to the outside world.

Walker warns women in the coloured community, and all in the home land, that they can no longer afford to remain as they were, completely isolated from the outside light, locked in their self-contrived darkness. God created all everything, but left the best use of His creation to anyone; awareness, ability and use only own responsibility, creation is God's performance, colour is God-given, Saxon Cedric's plea to Prior Aymer and Bois de Guilbert 'If God can endure him we can,' Let him be what he is, he would not harm you, you need not interfere in his being so. A simple truth.

Any variation is a piece of beauty, let us love it as His Creation. Walker makes this plea of love 'Black is beauty' as much as white is. What's the harm to accept this truth, this acceptance is love, God is Love, His presence is Love, otherwise no lively presence humanly possible to find. True Christianity Christ preached. Adam from America, Tashi from Africa, an Olinka, one loves another, her beauty her own identity as much as Nettie's to Samuel, Love for beauty, one need not spoil beauty, it is God's gift, if love is lost, what remains for mankind to enjoy? Walker appears to make this plea. Doris wins Africans, a bloodless invasion, Harry is with her, munching a piece of biscuit to testify this visible truth. The British Bishop took it otherwise. He misread: "Instead of even mentioning the Olinka the Bishop wanted to know how long it had been since Corrine's death, and why, as soon as she died, I had not returned to America" (p. 209). Thus Nettie reported to Celie her sister. She wrote to her sister in America what Doris Bainees did: "she cultivated a pious interest in heathens. Fooled her parents. Fooled the Missionary Society, who were so taken with her quick command of languages they sent her to Africa (worst luck!) where she began writing novels about everything under the sun" (p. 207).

Nettie's letter elaborates further what this woman told her: ...Anyway "when I get to England I'll put a stop to their bloody encroachments, I'll tell them what to do with their bloody road and their bloody rubber plantations and their bloody sunburned but still bloody boring English planters and engineers. I am a very wealthy woman, and I own the village of Akwee" (p. 208). Hers a love-conquest.

What the learned Bishop missed Celie's children mended. Nettie told Olivia and Adam the story of their mother, and they eagerly waited for their aunt's marriage to their foster-father. They eagerly attended the simple ceremony at a church in London. Women are always a tormented lot among the coloured, whether free from slavery or not, even in their own home not the least a slave, a slave to the male community at home and outside. In Morrison's *The Bluest Eye* to the father, in Walker's story Celie to her stepfather, she knew long to be her father. In the slavery stage they all slaves to a white master, in their African homes they slaves to their savage customs, in the O.T. stage circumcision was a male baptism with a different meaning, but in African custom it was a protection against male adventurism, that at the cost of natural female beauty and womanhood.

Tashi could have been a rebel, but she had before her the sad story of her aunt, she was sold to traders. Adam from America in love with Tashi, her beauty and natural wisdom made her a real Black Beauty. Adam from a dear-earned freedom world—Naipauls Free State—reasonably felt she should also be free from their savage customs, like debeautification of maidenhood and enjoined 'promised marriage'. During their absence from Olinka she was perhaps persuaded to undergo the ceremony of scarification and circumcision. So Adam and Olivia found no trace of Tashi for two days, and when she appeared Adam was in a rage, her beauty wilfully abused and bloom arrested. It is not the kind of puberty-worship in Rushdie's Grimus, it is a physical cruelty, Axona Amerindians in a ceremony of joyous recognition, but this is an outrage upon nature. Tashi too felt ashamed. Olivia saved the situation, she embraced Tashi more closely when her brother turned around. In spite of the community's total ban of female education Tashi's contact with Olivia opened a secret lane for her education, she is intelligent enough to absorb imparted knowledge easily. Doris successfully experimented. British planters' attack upon their preserves created a stir in their static society. This time journey to America is not to be a slave, but a loving partner of life.

[10]

The British planters had already unsettled the whole Olinka community, though America and Olinka had formed a silent love-link, their two coloured sects. Tashi and Tashi's mother Catharine fled their already razed homes for the far-away 'mbeles' (dense bush area). Their curative crop Yam variety, resistant to malaria and chronic blood disease, all lost. They were helpless, they knew no other remedies, death-toll alarming. They left, and Adam pursued them, he was missing, Samuel Nettie and Olivia worried where he was. Nettie's letter to Celie extremely distressing. Two sisters far apart 'Nearly thirty years have passed without a word between us' (p. 232) Nettie wrote. Letters written, but held up by Celie's husband. The only communication immediately passed on to Celie by her husband was a telegramme by American War office, the ship that Samuel Nettie and children took for their journey home was destroyed by the Germans and they were drowned. The report fortunately proved wrong.

All these letters, save only the telegram, are old and not instant information, so all that Celie wrote to Nettie remained one-sidedly informative and too few in number, only answer to earlier few letters stealthily readout with Shug's help and restored to Mr—'s personal box. Information limited to changes on her side in the family and her new found friend Shug's movements, one lately her staying away with a nineteen year old boy lover, one-third her age, one Germaine, Walker does not propose to make Celie a Saint or Convent Nun, but only a patient human being, under extreme duress befriending God and relyind on His support when support was not there, and only shows the way how this trust could be realistically love, love for the unavailing unapproachable God through love for available ever present created things as His visible manifestation. She wanted immediate benefit, at least benefit, if not immediate. Shug is a character Walker created to teach her further realistically that she could not do otherwise, Celie wrote to Nettie how ungodly Alphosno died and ill-gotten property ultimately passed out of his grip to Celie and Nettie, even the house he rebuilt more fashionable, as their parents' legal heir. He died too unpredictably early and supposedly an unnatural death. For all these gains God's personal appearance is not needed, definitely it is God's duly acknowledged return of her love, only Celie did not know that it was.

God has no colour, again He created every colour and was in every colour, this is the mystery of His creation, Walker seems to drive at that basic unity for all mankind, no scope for hatred there remains. Be in peace and have the due return of peace. Celie writes the longest letter to Nettie her sister, though the Telegram carried the message of their death. She now got the encouraging feeling: "Mr—seem to be the only one understand my feeling. I know you hate me for keeping you from Nettie, he say. And now she dead. But I don't hate him, Nettie. I don't believe you dead. How can you be dead if I still feel you? Maybe, like God, you changed into something different that I'll have to speak to in a different way, but you not dead to me Nettie" (p. 235).

This quality of peace lovingly nursed in her makes everyone peaceful to her, everything, including her hateful husband. She writes now to Nettie in the same manner she did to God. Goodness has no colour, a property anyone can own, anyone can claim God as much for him as any other. A white lady, Celie narrates to Nettie, claimed it for a child. A debate over this issue between a white lady Eleanor Jane and Sofia their coloured maid. Miss Eleanor Jane is raised by Sofia, but she "herself that baby she went and had. Every time Sofia turned round Miss Eleanor Jane was shoving Raynolds Stanley Earl in her face. He a little fat white something without much hair, look like he headed for the Navy" (p. 238).

Miss Jane's claim 'Ain't little Reynolds sweet?' Sofia keeps silence, 'stand there ironing some Susie Q and Henrietta's clothes', Repeatedly urged to call baby Reynolds 'sweet' and 'smart', though she does not think so, Sofia had to say "no ma'am, say Sofia. I don't love Reynolds Stanley Earl. Now. That's what you been trying to find out ever since he was born. And now know" (p. 239). Disagreement! Debate, heated. Sofia clearly tells the truth, clean truth—"I love, children, say Sofia. But all the coloured women that say they love yours is lying. They don't love Reynolds Stanley any more than I do. But if you so badly raised as to ast 'em, what you expect them to say? Some coloured people so scared of white folks they claim to love the cotton gin" (p. 240).

Very common two women speaking, the debate not quarrel, but free-feeling subdued, one-sided assertion-imbalance, exposed, assertion-attempt or wished-for sanction no-good, unless willingly approved. Approbation cannot be a claimed approval, if not unclaimed acknowledgement, Eleanor Jane claimed it, Sofia rejected because she would not conceal, other coloured maids only concealed, disapproved, but flatteringly offered open approval, a sort of purchased commodity. So Jane could claim: "All the colored women I know love children. The way you feel is something unnatural" (p. 240). She should have known love is natural, one cannot claim it. Slavery is a purchased service, praise too a purchased merchandise. Love, if you call it natural, is salvation. Though apparently Celie's longest letter gossipy, it conceals yet some important issues to take care of, one Sofia-Jane exchanges, the other Celie's informed knowledge of original Black community.

Sofia clearly told Eleanor Jane they should not expect, as before, the coloured people would consider them all whites excellent because of their whiteness of the body, they must individually by their qualities to deserve love specially and respect. Jane is not immediately convinced, she wanted whatever her qualities, body represents a kind which claims respect, even love. Shug's three children, two already ashamed to recognize their mother, her character a vital question for them, they are not ready to acknowledge publicly her as their mama; only one child decided "he want to see his mama no matter what" (p. 242), but 'He a schoolteacher work on the Indian reservation. They call him the black white man...they so far gone nothing strangers say mean nothing" (p. 243). 'Everybody not a Indian they got no use for'. Shug 'hate to see his feelings hurt, but that's life' (*ibid.*). Lack of 'understanding' still persists between different communities in mixed American population, not only between coloured and white, but even between different grades in the coloured communities. Shug's a different experience, different from Sofia's. Walker tries to strike up a note of basic unity among all varieties of human beings, perhaps as humans. Politically America adopted Democratic system for a solution, but at the more basic human level some layer of unity is yet to be cemented, Walker must have thought.

Celie now finds Mr—quite 'understanding' her position, Shug was his 'well-beloved' all along, she too no longer a steady support, that phase of his life a closed chapter, she is now with her child Germaine in tow, stable in her free-spirit way, Celie now remains only one to disclose his burdened soul. They together talk about the original history of Biblical Eden, the Negros' own version of Black and white, whites are naked, Black a colour interpreted as wearing, colour covered their nakedness, two species, clothed in colour, and naked white. Black species claim they were original, white naked savage. Thus a conflict arose. "In fact, they gon kill off so much of the earth and the colored that every body hate them just like they hate us today. Then they will become the new serpent". Olinka community makes a history of their own.

Celie seems to represent Walker's voice. Colour-conflict must find some solution, some meeting platform. Celie suggests: some kind of Black-bigotry. They think the first Man was Omatangu meaning un-naked. Their meaning is colour-clothed. A white man's Adam is white, Christ too white, though Ethiopians (Africans called then Ethiopia). Bigotry on either side is wrong, God created all, let them all be as they were created, only take them for varieties of God's creation, and be at peace, if you can't love, don't hate, Sofia could not love Jane's baby but wants herself free from harm. Politically democracy assures it. Now is needed a Divine Democracy, God has created Celie and Shug, Mr—and Alphosno, so does Sofia and Eleanor Jane and her baby, let them be as they are, if the baby 'sweet' her mother would be happy, if not she is to suffer, Sofia cannot resist it, no interference needed, ill-will or otherwise. Jane would raise it as she has made it!

Celie now finds Mr—reasonable, open to her, she cannot expect, nor can Mr—that Shug would be always hers or his; she has her own ways and stake in life, choice her own. God leaves everyone to act his or her role and reap harvest as they have sown. Celie has retrieved her due—house and property. Mr—has to detect his mistake: "Took me long enough to notice you such good company, he say. And he laugh". Celie too realizes: "He ain't Shug, but he begin to be somebody I can talk to" (p. 250).

God cannot appear in person, He leaves His whole Creation in its proper order, including all our fellowmen, to—act freely in harmony or not with the order, what is thus done we must take proportionately our deserved share, God is not expected to play a partisan part, which may cause a disturbance in His created order. Order is ordered to maintain it. To accept this truth is submission, God expects it from everyone in His Creation. Celie's world is now in her favour, Shug rather out of sorts, her boy, third of her age, she says 'like a son. Maybe a grandson' (p. 258) went to his college, she back home, perhaps nothing more to do. Nettie coming, her children and along with them Tashi, a happy addition. Love is a universal knitting thread, Tashi responded to Adam's love; Adam was two months and a half untraced, long remained a cause of worry to his friends in shattered Olinka, he came back with Tashi.

Adam-Tashi love story is very simple and open, Tashi was afraid she might not be accepted, and she might fail to accommodate to an entirely different culture and community, far away from her mother and people, even Adam could finally dislike her; she would then be an unloved miserable misfit. Such was Adam's love that he voluntarily scarred his face as she did hers and assured her that whatever would be her life he would always remain a willing sharer.

Walker marks out the kind of conclusion to her story significantly with a reunion of the long-parted near and dear ones, and not at a moment in the continued long period of sufferings, but at the end of that period, to strike up a positive note in life after a stormy darkness of the night a calm sunrise at day-break in the clear sky. Celie too felt like young herself and all around her, though old.

Both Morrison and Walker initially take the coloured issue, but then diverge, Sethe an earlier stage, slaves not free yet; involvement direct in the transitional stage, bitterly oppressive to a woman's basic freedom of choice out and inside home; Celie's situation is against her inside the fresh liberated coloured community, her individual choice as a woman still not ensured under male domination, a sort of inside-community slavery, as Olinka women in their community in their homeland are, Tashi is now liberated by Adam's offer of sincere love, a step ahead and encouraging: "Everybody make a lot of migration over Tashi. People look at her and Adam's scars like that's they business. Say they never suspect African ladies look so good. They make a fine couple" (p. 261).

Celie's final letter's address-pattern too symbolic attitudinal change of direction "Dear God. Dear stars, dear trees, dear sky, dear peoples. Dear everything. Dear God". She begins and ends with 'Dear God'. She felt one support for her constant and unfailing, first and last, everything else are gifts of the Final Dispenser to her, as to all mankind, to stand by, only invisible Dispenser in visible ministrations in varied forms.

8

Faulkner's 'Bear' and Hemingway's 'Well-lighted Place'

[1]

Both 20th century contemporaries, major American novelists, Nobel-winners too. Short stories their relaxation area, as for other major writers of fiction of all ages. I select here one from each for a close look into the secret of their style of presentation and their line of approach to anything beyond style. Writing is out of a subjective reaction duly objectified for all to share with the writer, the writer's expectation of sharing with them cannot be exhaustively fulfilled because of his audience's subjectivity yet intact, it is difficult to 'make them see', if not in their own eyes as it appears. Still no harm from the writer's side to play the tricks in his command. Not like Conrad, who claimed to have made his audience see, Faulkner and Hemingway do in their respective ways. One common factor in their efforts is luxuriant details. Faulkner is one degree above Hemingway, due to his closest approximation to the European drill in Stream of Consciousness, less catchy for an eye to miss; Hemingway reduce himself by a sparing dive into mind's abstraction and less frequent shift in time and space as in *The Old Man and the Sea*.

Faulkner's 'The Bear' could have been another *Animal Farm*, only a bear-led hounds and horses instead of a pig-led animal-revolt of a Farm. But Faulkner did not want it to be an allegory, his truth does not need any allegorical cover, truth is better open, if imperceptible, the duty of the author is to make it perceptible. The subject is serious enough for concealment, even if by an amusing allegory superimposed. Frequent time-shift cannot here obscure the development of the subject undertaken. Man and his pet appear on the scene from the beginning: the hunting party and their hounds and bear a big lot in a November forest. Two beasts and two men presented at the opening, Boon Hogganbeck had a plebeian strain in his blood, "only Sam and Old Ben and the mongrel Lion were taintless and incorruptible".

The boy who comes next in the story, presented 'sixteen' then, already 'a man's hunter' 'for six years now'—time shift set in, he began at ten and under Sam Fathers' training. The wood itself a controversial possession, who was the original possessor very difficult to detect. That was the primary stage of original European settlement in America, for them exactly the New World. In Hawthorne's *Scarlet Letter* we saw only some Indian Sagamores present in the crowd to settle ransom over Chillingworth's release from captivity in the forest their own territory. Faulkner reaches back to that stage: 'It was the wilderness, the big woods, bigger and older than any recorded document—time and space—jugglery is not only possible but also should be the accompanying divisive train. Unknown uncertainly can be suggested but cannot be presented in certainty. The woods Major de Spain's possession now, but whose it was then unreclaimed, Ikkemotubbe the Chickasaw chief's or whose, no one can tell, the woods were older than him.

Faulkner does not mean going back to the palaeolithic age, but definitely from a pre-settlement drawing down to the settlement stage of America, from a man and beast together in a contest of survival in the forest, equally shared, to a life only a step ahead, ownership demarcated, still hunters, forest-lovers, gamesters, Major de Spain owns hundred square miles forest, every year in November encamped too hunting with friends and staff and pet animals—that developed stage: Not he the boy more remarkable a heritage of the unrecorded bygone age than a beast, the Bear, that gives the title of the story. He is an anachronism as Faulkner describes: "the old bear, solitary, indomitable, and alone; widowed childless and absolved of mortality—old Priam left of his old wife and outlives all his sons".

Faulkner here refers to *Iliad's* story, Trojan progenitor, sometimes Old Testament times, Abraham and Isaac. Is it only part of his metaphor? He is exceptionally metaphoric in his style no doubt but has not blurred his basic stand, rather helped it stand out: a stage of American growing civilization at its earliest evolutionary process, Eden—Abraham stage its right metaphor, a mythical stage of man and beast close neighbourliness in constant cooperation and conflict, yet in a state of uncertain possession. India too long long ages evolved out of that stage, only difference is it gave the land a rich literature and culture. Indian civilization evolved out of the forest, from a foresty seclusion, their Eden for closeness to God. America created a culture by a progress in evolution away from the forest, forest left behind as a trophy. Major de Spain, Walker Ewell, General Compson, of this stage of colonial culture, frequently visit this their early won trophy every year regularly, the boy narrator among them takes a critical interest, early alive to their interest as in his own, then disinterestedly critical.

Man and animal creature-qualities equally shared join the march, breed-difference blurred in adventure, killer and the killed. The Bear (Ben) and Lion (Mongrel) in the forest forget their lesson they learnt, the Old Ben missing, Sam said: "He do it every year. Once Ash and Boom say comes up here to run the other little bears away. Tell them to get to hell out of here and stay out until the hunters are gone. Maybe. The boy in the forest the first time, still not in forest lore taught well, his novitiate under Sam Fathers intensified his urge and forest did not seem to him as alien territory, pet or not forest animals did not stir dread in him, rather Ben and Lion's loss, particularly Ben's left him on a trail of eager search. Faulkner very often does not leave alone his narrator, he intervenes too often with substantial help in competent language to express his responses. He does it more with the boy than anybody else in the story.

For the boy it is a belated Eden scene, only God and Peace lost, man and beast together in the forest, in a hard competition for survival, man in addition for conquest, cooperation when sought from whichever corner, the conquered cooperation. The boy is asked to learn and be trained in that lore, within three years (now thirteen) he has learnt his own lesson. Time-shift frequent, past-present-future sequence shuffled and swapped too easily. The boy an interested observer and actor too among the aged, hunters all, the woods meant for that. Pets and games hardly to be distinguished. The Bear once their pet, now game, Lion once a game, found in the forest, trickily trapped, now pet set on the betraying bear. Human roles diverse in nature likewise, sudden shift, even in apposition.

[2]

Big Ben the bear disobeyed, even betrayed his master's trust, destroyed his property, a colt was his feed, pack of hounds reduced in number. Lion is Sam Father's pick, wild domesticated, now Boon's pet, from others dogs separate, feeding also Boon's fond care, keeps watch beside him at night, shares even a portion of his pillow, fierce, uncontrolled by anybody else, even Sam now alien. Everything different from the canine family. Major de Spain to order Lion now to trace the mischievous Bear, the boy worried, Sam knew something more than anybody else. Lion on the scent, ran Ben ten miles down the stream, bayed, yet failed to jump him. The animal world in conflict, Lion after the Bear, a dog-bear fight expected. A different issue from Orwell's Animal World.

The bear is an unluky pet 'wifeless, childless, himself his own ungendered progenitor'. Faulkner seems to pity him, now a disgraced deserter, himself his own protector; his master vindictive, sends a dog to bay for his blood, not Orwell's Farmer Jones. The hunting party all up against him, the boy and Sam mum, the camp got two hounds killed, they were sure it was Ben, the mare foaled and the colt missing, the mare mother restive and wild; Faulkner's in a very complex relationship, between man and animal, and between different species of animal, love and hate lacing them up in contradictory responses and reactions, none there to over rule and accommodate. The end-result decided by their complex part-play. Under the same master, in the same fold or forest, they are let loose to act or react, to obey or disobey, thus they decide their destiny. This is Darwin's Natural selection, finally evolution. There are things man and animal to share, in spite of wide difference in kind and character.

Only Sam remained unadulterated original Chickasaw, Boon a plebeian, grandfather original, his mother's side 'half-white', 'six-foot four inches', ruddy, not red, more akin to the woods and animal world, Lion his pet, almost his constant company carries his order, a blue dog strong and irresistible, almost an over-match to Ben the pet bear, now a betrayer, Lion on its trail. Major de Spain got it from General Compson years ago, but he broke the law. Spain offended. The aborigines who met them in their camp easily got free hand to run and shoot if they find him. It was Ben's disowned insecurity: Boon sent to the city to collect provision for four days' overstay; but Boon in the city turned a little boozy, Ike the boy with him the witness, now on their way back. The human world back to the woods, retraced to their early stage of evolution, now a game, a reminder. Ike the boy an actor as well as observer, fit to be the narrator, but blurred in the quick shift readily adopted by the author.

Major de Spain's party ready, Ash to help ride, hounds to follow. General Compson wished him among them though recommended Ike the boy in his stead, but Mecaslin pleaded 'Ike's got the rest of his life to hunt bears in' (p. 86). The Majors party reminded him of 'the last darkening days of '64 and '65', the days of Civil War, General Compson pleaded his 'old age', preferred to man the 'stand'. A war in the woods, not a bear-baiting game. A game for man who has already left the woods behind to build a new civilization, built on wounded nature and offended fellow-men-and-animals, yet there is a secret love-link unsevered. Animal world too responds, nature does if man can feel.

The animal instinct teaches them who are their natural enemies, they react for self-security, either to avoid confrontation or to fight for a victory or to secure their territory safe from the intruder. Lion and Ben, a dog and a bear, both pet, but natural enemies, other dogs in the pet-pack kept safe distance from the bear, but Lion would not permit him to encroach upon his privileged position. A fight royal between dog-Lion and Ben-bear, the fight ordered by their master, now their instinctive enmity could work free. Now in Faulkner's word:

> This time the bear didn't strike him down. I caught the dog in both arms, almost lover like, and they both went down. He (Boon) is off the mule now. He drew back both hammers of the gun but he could see nothing but moiling spotted hound bodies until the bear urged up again. Boon was yelling something, he could not tell what, he could see Lion still clinging to the bear's throat and he saw the bear, half erect, strike one of the hounds with one paw and hurl it five or six feet and then, rising and rising as though it would never stop, stand erect again and begin to rake at Lion's belly with its forepaws. Then Boon was running. The boy saw the gleam of the blade in his hand and watched him leap among the hounds, huddling them, kicking them aside as he ran, and fling himself astride the bear as he had hurled himself onto the mule, his legs locked around the bear's belly, his left arm under the bears throat where Lion clung, and the glint of the knife as it rose and fell. (p. 88)

A fight among beasts, man wanted it, wanted bear beaten and killed, he betrayed, left the flock, disobeyed, broke rule, man-made rule. The bear followed his own rule, his master would not like it, so he should be shot or somehow killed, he allowed the swamper aborigines to do, if they could. But Lion is Boon's pet, he cannot see Lion harmed by anybody, far less by the disgraced betrayer bear. So among the beastly fight he intervenes. The beast too had to protect itself, so enemy too, not only pet. A relationship too a natural law, Darwin's *Origin of Species* stands. The one-eyed mule, mare and horse are domesticated as well as other animals, even wild animals from the forest. They are protected from harms by their master, taken care of, for their service to human life. Mutual relationship outgrows transaction-relationship, obedience, love and affection develop. But it cannot absolutely neutralize their instinctive urge, their natural habits and behaviour. Man and animal equally share love of freedom, family affection, society, and self-preservation instinct.

The story opens significantly: "There was a man and a dog too this time. Two beasts, counting Old Ben, the bear, and two men, counting Boon Hoggerbeck", the other man is Sam Fathers, Boon's plebeian 'strain of blood shares that which runs in Sam. Sam, Old Ben and mongrel Lion are 'taintless'. The taintless blood originally belonged to the forest. Withdrawal from that original home led them into the mixed-breed area. This beginning is significant; it sets the tone of the story. America is now out of the woods, or better cleared the woods for human settlement and plantation cultivation and built up industrial complexes; a civilization seems to have emerged from Biblical Eden, built up out of Eden, in the Biblical trend breed got mixed up, Abraham's one wife Egyptian the other Israelite, incestuous inbreed too persisted for some time; in modern America Federal system of Democracy is a natural evolution.

The two characters initially, one mixed blood the other pure, from the coloured species came into the white dominated area, the two animals, originally of the woods, eventually fell into the domesticated civilized area to act their part. The story is a mute critique at bottom. The fight is done, man and animal, both sides wounded and dead, no truce conclusively. We have proceeded thus far.

[3]

They concluded bloody: "It fell all of a piece as a free fall, so that all three of them, man dog and bear, seemed to bounce once." The fall of the Old Ben, a bear, like Sam wifeless, childless kinless. So Sam's 'shocked' fall from the mule, the doctor diagnosed aright, was at the sight of the bear's fall, a sort of kinship he felt for him. Sam and bear seemed to be more to the boy than to anybody else. Boon's secret hostility to the bear was due to his love for lion deflected. The boy Ike's love for the Bear obvious, for Sam too clear, but to account for not so easy particularly when Faulkner's well-calculated use of suggestively expressive details, most of the mind curtained over for shifty clearance now and then. The boy did not want the old bear dead, nor did Sam; Sam wanted him free in the forest, forest his real home, Sam's too. In bed-ridden state he begged release from his master: "Let me out, master. Let me go home. Only this in his master's language, otherwise he talked here in the language of the old father".

The boy's love for the bear and Boon's love for Lion are love, but caused misery to both the sides, both the animals dead, McCaslin asked Boon repeatedly whether he killed the bear, the boy was the witness, Boon's sharp knife flashed when Lion and Ben fighting with other hounds whirling around yelling, a noisy wood-scene for hunters to enjoy. Now Boon denies, but the boy reacted without any word except finally:

> "Tell the truth" McCaslin said. "I would have done it if he had asked me to." Then the boy moved. He was between them, facing McCaslin; the water felt as if it had burst and sprung not from his eyes alone but from his whole face, like sweat.
>
> "Leave him alone!" he cried. "God dam it! Leave him alone!" (p. 93)

The boy prayed his uncle 'he to stay', they all to leave though. The boy had missed his lesson at school a whole week. McCaslin insisted he must not stay behind, General Compson mediated for the boy. General Compson read the boy's instinct aright, he had learnt already what they had not even in their old age, learnt lesson in the own line. Why should the boy stay behind in the forest alone may appear a riddle, to read it one must know how his kinship is made clear in the possession-transfer story of the forest Faulkner narrates immediately:

> ...the land which Carothers McCaslin his grandfather had bought with white man's money from the wild men whose grandfathers without guns hunted it and

> tamed and ordered or believed he had tamed and ordered it for the reason that the human beings he held in bondage and in his power of life and death had removed the forest from it and in their sweat scratched the surface of it to a depth of perhaps fourteen inches in order to grow something out of it which had not been there before and which could be translated back into the money he who believed he had bought it had to pay to get it and hold it and a reasonable profit too: and for which reason old Carothers McCaslin, knowing better, could raise his children, his descendants and heirs, to believe the land was his to hold and bequeath since the strong ruthless man has a cynical foreknowledge of his own vanity and pride and strength and a contempt for all his pet: just as, knowing better, Major de Spain and his fragment of the wilderness which was bigger and older than any recorded deed; just as knowing better, old Thomas Sutpen, from whom Major had had his fragment for money, just as Ikkemotubbe the Chickasaw chief, from whom Thomas Sutpen had had the fragment for money or rum or whatever it was, knew in his turn that not even a fragment of it had been his to relinquish or sell. (p. 93)

Just the post-primitive age transaction type, unrecorded transfer of ownership, Chickasaw Chief Ikkemotubbe the original owner, latest Carothers McCaslin owner, ownership though his money managed from a whiteman, land-yeild yet to be the money-lender's commodity against money. Ike, the boy, may claim ownership—as it could be at that old time of unrecorded deal—"He could say it, himself and his cousin juxtaposed not against the wilderness but against the tamed land which was to have been his heritage" his grandfather had bought....

Faulkner's stylistic vagueness is quite appropriate to convery the idea of an undeeded deal's vagueness of the time. 'During the two decades before the Civil War' his father Theophilus and his uncle Amodeus wrote 'on the yellowed pages' of the older ledgers 'clumsy and archaic in size' 'the manumission in title at least of Carothers McCaslin's slaves'. The American story of evolution in comparatively modern times, the Civil War marking behind, reminds Faulkner of Old Abraham's time, even before that the Eden Expulsion stage in God's Creation, a story sad and sweet mixed, evolution inevitable though! Carothers dropped out of count, only McCaslin remained, Ike's grandfather's line gone and snapped, McCaslin's fourth generation before woman's descendants retained the lineal streak. In God's world no bequeathing: "he created man to be His overseer on the earth and to hold suzerainty over the earth and the animals on it in His name, not to hold for himself and his descendants inviolable title for ever, generation after generation..." (p. 94).

Dispossessed of Eden man's sad story, Ike's is. How it happened Faulkner makes a new myth that explains a new world out of the old, or metaphorically out of an Egg (out of the Void)—a different story, different from the old. Post-expulsion story of the Bible, America a close parallel. Faulkner's few lines: "He saw the land already accursed even as Ikkemotubbe and Ikkemotubbe's father old Issetibbeha and Issetibbeha's fathers too held it, already tainted, already tainted even before any white man owned it by what Grandfather and his kind, his fathers, had brought into the new land which He had vouchsafed them out of pity and sufferance" (p. 95).

Out of the void, from Noah to Ham, a second generation with a new system, unrecorded possession annulled, 'So these men transcribed His Book for Him' but they 'were sometime liars', they had human limitations. Head worked. Lord wanted 'heart', because heart cannot miss. Truth must be told, and must continue from generation to generation, an unbroken chain. The narrator not the boy now who was only born late, did not know the transcription story: "the yellowed pages scrawled in fading ink by the hand first of his grandfather; then of his father and uncle, bachelors up to the past fifty, then sixty" (p. 96), "and continued to do it even after his twin married and the boy himself was born" (*ibid.*). Then it is their family Bible, the generation following being recorded, as in the Holy Book.

From Carothers to McCaslin the link severed, the boy alone the kink on the loop. His closeness to Sam is not an aberration, his love for the bear is not a bear-hug but Nimrodic reminiscence. General Compson early detected it and allowed him to stay in the woods, he did not require any school lesson. A natural Nimrod among them. He humoured the boy: come not Sunday but sun-day. Faulkner follows Genesis pattern in modern American evolution, Old Testament history is ultimately a civilization of Egypto-Israelite, even Philistino-Israelite, mixed blood.

[4]

America is going that way, first conflict then cooperation, finally consolidation their destiny, if no one God saw it and vouchsafed. The early recorded account is a concrete picture, only in Faulkner's usual artistic twist: the year 1880 or thereabout..."the slaves which Carothers McCaslin had inherited and purchased—Roscius and Phoebe and Thucydides and Eunice and their descendants, and Sam Fathers and his mother for both of whom he had swapped an underbred trotting gelding to old Ikkemotubbe, the Chickasaw chief from whom he had likewise bought the land, and Tennie Beauchary Champ whom the twin Amadeus had won from a neighbour in a poker game...Percival Brownlee which the twin Theophilus had purchased, neither he not his brother knew why apparently, from Bedford Forest while he was still only a slave-dealer and not yet a general..." (p. 97). The boy read the record in the book and knew it was his father's hand.

The record here has hardly any Biblical sacredness, it has no closeness to God, in their faith at least, it is out of primitive inability to protect them from natural inclemencies, and aggression from fellow human beings. Modern life, more in American history, cannot have an exact repeat, what it can, and America have, is a progression all through phases of inhumanities and ugliness to sobriety and sanity. The boy here with his white and coloured mixed blood scrutinized the record of late 19th century Civil War around American story, his birth itself a concrete evidence. God vouchsafed but never expected it all holy or all hell either, He saw Genesis and Exodus, and all other stages in progress. The hero is caught in one stage of evolution, a sad stage though. Negro slaves on a white man's plantation estate could shame the sins of Sodom Gomorrah of Abraham's time. The account in ledger book was very short, that too was as the white master pleased to spell and record, no one could challenge and none could know what he suppressed.

The whole slave-deal in the two brothers' ledger-account appeared to the sixteen year old boy murky, he assumed more than what he found recorded: "not alone of his own flesh and blood but of all his people, not only the whites but the black one too, who were as much a part of his ancestry as his white progenitors, and of the land which they had all held and used in common without regard to color or titular ownership..." (p. 99). The boy's urge to know further and confirm assumption remained unfulfilled, the "thousand-dollar legacy to the son of an unmarried slave-girl, to be paid only at he child's coming of age, bearing the consequence of the act of which there was still no definite incontrovertible proof..." (*ibid.*).

When record did not help, the boy could but no way resist the temptation to conjecture. Secretly at night in the McCaslin commissary he was turning the yellowed pages, his Biblical Genesis, not in its Biblical clarity, the boy at his responsible age saw something and surmised more, built up a picture Faulkner helps him to: "There was the old man, within five years of his life's end, long widower and, since his sons were not only bachelors but were approaching middle age, lonely in the house and doubtless even bored since his plantation was established now...there was the girl, husbandless and young, only twenty three when the child was born..." (p. 100). More secretive than Biblical, Faulkner's tricks for the boy's guess, so perhaps "he had sent for her at first out of loneliness, than out of necessecity", so 'summoned' her, 'bade her mother send her' regularly, mother 'acquiescing since that was probably understood', and already planned, because "the child of the couple who were not field hands and who held themselves something above the other slaves, not alone for that reason but because the husband and his father, and the white man himself, had traveled three hundred miles in...to Orleans...and bought the girl's mother as a wife for" (blank not filled up).

Faulkner's taste held him back from Biblical openness, in an age of achieved culture and civilization, yet truth to be told, so with an incomplete sentence of the preceding paragraph in the next paragraph begins in the middle of a sentence 'and that was all', Biblical directness once avoided artistic twist needed to speak the truth, Faulkner seems a master of such a device. The present reader of old ledgers got to brood over some blanks, "His own daughter His own daughter. No No Not even him back to that one", the mother, "not even a widower then", never stirred from home, did not need another slave yet "had gone all the way to the New Orleans and bought one."

One need not go further, still the boy goes, he was ten when Tomey's Terrel was still alive, "he knew from his own observation and memory that there had been some white in Tomey's Terrel's blood before his father gave him the test of it". The boy could presume "the fact of his own nativity" (p. 100). Thereafter entries in the ledger were his uncle's hand, his slave-dealer father was later about that time "a member of the Cavalry command". When the boy is fourteen year old orphan, under his uncle's care growing he needed no more geneological history. Plantation slave history, quite elaborate in Naipaul's *El Dorado*, reveals not only cruelties of every sort but also a diabolical shift from the Biblical openness of early inevitabilities to wilful sins and crimes in utmost secrecy, in American history otherwise a mixed generation growing towards true modern democracy. Black and white are not alone and apart clean, everyone, whatever his colour, is individual, rights apportioned to everyone, male and female, equally; and given to live and let live to build a nation, to protect it and contribute to its prosperity responsibly.

Still it is growing around 1886 to that grand goal, the nation to be. The boy found in the old ledger suspected in his father's further weakened hand written: Miss Sophonsiba birth 1869. In 1886 she was seventeen. McCaslin to receive a marriage offer for Fonsiba from a Negro stranger from Arkansas, he asserts his right as equal. The exchanges between them about 1886 record a considerable change, his mixed blood stature and appearance a change, as in their assertive expression in words and approach, a fragment here:

'To live in Arkansas I believe you said'

'Yes. I have property there. A farm.'

'Property? A farm? You own it?'

'Yes'.

'You don't say Sir, do you?'

'To my elders, yes'

'I see. You are from the North'.

'Yes. Since a child'.

'Then your father was a slave'.

'Yes. Once'.

'Then how do you own a farm in Arkansas?' (p. 102).

The dialogue above is a fragment of the Civil War residue. The farm is a State grant for service in the 'Yankee army'. A change in the Slave-master relationship. The stranger insist 'Call aunt Tennie', 'I don't ask your permission'. 'After all this is your house', then, assures 'Be easy. I'll be good to her'.

McCaslin felt a little unsettled—the relationship changed. The stranger speaking to him as an individual to another individual, nothing prevented him from doing so. He wondered: "Even their parents don't know until too late how seventeen-year-old girls ever met the men who many them too, if they are lucky" (*ibid.*). He wondered, but it could happen, Time cannot halt. Faulkner's 'boy' is an eye, he can see far, and his far-sight covers from Old Testament days down to theirs. He and the stranger lost to McCaslin next morning, and lost also Fonsiba. The boy only pursuing them with a money belt furnished, to meet them in their den eight days later on his journey, but the journey was made five months later. Time-sequence in Faulkner's treatment is tossed into a mesh, one requires unmeshing.

[5]

From Grandfather to the boy and McCaslin, the development a mixed family tree reconstructed by the boy's effort, better his curiosity, makes him the natural narrator of this story, which begins with a man in the woods, in his company a lot of animal pets, the Bear and the Lion among them, and then emerges from the forest into the open early civilization of man. In that Faulkner finds a close parallelism of the Biblical story of Abraham. The boy now a responsible member. Five months later he made this journey, with one third of the amount due to Fonsiba, the address now confusive, letter Post mark misleading, not the same address that the stranger left with Tennie, now in 1874 Father and Uncle dead. One thousand dollars in a money-belt for Fonsiba his kin, money her due. The journey took eight days, a journey from Jerusalem to Jericho type, quite tiring. He found them in their new Canaan, the assured land of freedom. He saw them in a single uninhabitable room, mouldering, icy fold, dark and a sort of kennel or hencoop, plantation unworked, no planning for an independent comfortable life, no earning of his own, depending on father's monthly pension banked by his creditor, yet he accused all their misery caused by white men:

> 'Don't you see?' he cried, 'Don't you see? This whole land, the whole south is cursed, all of us who derive from it, whom it ever suckled, white and black both, lie under the curse?' (p. 103)

True! But there is another truth. The visitor sees an ugly sort of New Canaan', not that Biblical Canaan:

> 'Freedom from what? From work? Canaan? ... damp, heatless Negro-stale, Negro-rank sorry room—the empty fields without plow or seed to work them, fenceless against the stock which did not exist within or without the walled stable which likewise was not there. What corner of Canaan is this?' (*ibid.*). Yet when asked: 'Fonsiba. Are you all right?' she answers 'I'm free'. (p. 104)

This is a scene, applies to India now! I am an Indian, our democracy on a wrong track. Our Jims depend on a white man, a full-scale well-meaning adventurer, Huck. Our Jims waiting for a Huck to win his freedom! No. It cannot be, unless Jims win it for themselves, they must know Huck did not depend upon Jim, his witchy wisdom; he worked his own freedom, and his too; his brain, inventiveness, untiring activities won it for him and for Jim too. Democracy gives freedom to workout everyone's destiny in his own way, freedom to that end, without any idle dependence. America is to that end a success story, India is yet to attain it.

Faulkner's story is more for Indian readership than for Americans, they have passed through the dark days, theirs rightly the New Canaan: "1874 the boy: 1888 the man, repudiated denied and free: 1895 and husband but no father, unwidowered but without a wife, and found long since that no man is free and probably could not bear it if he were;"... (*ibid.*).

Faulkner juggles here with his language pattern, twisted meaningfully, one knows: married then and living in Jefferson in the little new jerry built bungalow which his wife's father had given them: "and one morning Lucas [Lucas Quintus Carothers McCaslin Beauchamp Last surviving son of Tomey's Terrel and Tennie b. March 17, 1874] stood suddenly in the doorway of the room...He's twenty one today" (pp. 104-05). Claiming practically the other two shares of the money 'what's that rest of the money' (p. 105)—Carothers McCaslin money! The irony of Fonsiba's freedom euphoria! At his twenty-first year the boy reasonably explains: "More men than that one Buck and Buddy to fumble-heed that truth so mazed for them ..." Mazed mixed blood. "But not enough. Not enough of even Father and Uncle Buddy to fumble-heed in even three generations fathered by Grandfather not even if there had been nowhere beneath His sight any but Grandfather and so He would not even needed to elect and choose...."

Three generations mixed blood race. American socio-political system evolved a mechanism of adjustment. Almost the Old Testament problem in modern times. Abraham too married an Egyptian as also an Israelite, incestuous relationship and concubinage common. Then Faulkner's language tricks: one explains two—Americans and Abraham-Israelites:

"That having Himself created them He could have known no more of hope than He could have pride and grief but He didn't hope He just waited because He had made them: not just because He had set them alive and in motion but because He had already worried with them so long: because He had seen how in individual cases they were capable of anything any height or depth remembered in mazed incomprehension out of heaven where hell was created too so He must admit them or else admit His equal somewhere and so be no longer God and therefore must accept responsibility for what He himself had done in order to live with Himself in His lonely and paramount heaven.... He saw that they were all Grandfather all of them and that even from them the elected and chosen the best the very best He would expect...would be Bucks and Buddies..." Father and Uncle and they are.

The twenty-first year old claimed "If He could see Father and Uncle Buddy in Grandfather He must have seen me too—an Isaac into a later life than Abraham's and repudiating immolation: fatherless and therefore safe," none to offer him on the altar and no 'Hand to supply the kid' in his stead. Far ahead of Abraham's time though similarity was there. God too let them develop their civilization out of a savage dark stage. The entire South their Canaan, but they were to make it fruitful and themselves to multiply. Abraham's sheep to be herded, fertile land to be cultivated, savage to be civilized. It was in Civil War's time, Lincoln's leadership made a bold step, slaves granted freedom. McCaslin then sixteen, the boy inherited from them as their descendant, the change God wanted to see. Fonsiba's husband Lucus raised the point of an uneven War with the North, to which the present head of their family answered, theirs a close Biblical analogy, God-overseeing everything that happened:

> ... This was chronicled in a harsher book [he means family ledger] and McCaslin, fourteen and fifteen and sixteen, had seen it and the boy himself [the present, head of the family] had inherited it as Noah's grandchildren had inherited the Flood although they had not been there to see the deluge: that dark corrupt and bloody time while three separate peoples had tried to adjust not only to one another but to the new land which they had created and inherited too

> and must live in for the reason that those who had lost it were no less free to quit it than those who had gained it were.... (p. 107)

This is America's New Testament growing out of the Old. Christendom is American 'wisdom', 'suddenly freed but misused': "Apparently there is a wisdom beyond even that learned through suffering necessary for a man to distinguish between liberty and license" (*ibid.*). America is world's true Democracy now, but it passed through phases of wrong idea of freedom, from the O.T. State to the N.T. State, had to pass through "Promiscuity, Violence, Instability and lack of control. Inability to distinguish, between mine and thine". The Bible took two thousand years, and America only 'two hundred years' to learn "pity and tolerance and forbearance and fidelity and love of children" (p. 109).

White and Black only pigment of the body, servant and master their apparent relation, underneath they kept no distinction, propensity made them unite, secret, though suppressed, came open in their record book illegibly written, their descendants to read and understand, if not whole, at least in part, and claim share. They got it because colour distinction became obsolete, when blood mixed. Faulkner's brooding mazed style of discordant revelations tossed into a relevance, a family record corresponds to a nation's history, as does the Bible basically. The final linkage serves like Keats's 'Grecian Urn's images: man to man, one races to another: McCaslin, read aloud: "She cannot fade, though thou hast not thy bliss For ever wilt thou love and she be fair" (p. 110). While asking Sam Fathers why he could not shoot the Bear Ben, and while opening the rotten mouldy pages of the Ledger entries he read aloud the above stanza, his mind played him to do, the intruding truth, the inescapable bender of Sam's mind, as everyone else's, Love. Once they together lived in the same woods, hunted them in their haunts, all Nimrods, also loved them as their pets, now white men too do in their farm kennel dogs like Lion and fyce, Ben too. Their slaves sometime their love, the boy's father walked three hundred miles to buy

Eunice, paid a high price 650 dollars, no slave-like work their part, the boy's uncle saw sixteen years before his birth. (p. 98)

A trend like this has a deep secret, a truth like love claimed its high price, its sweetness and sin also its pay. Secret or open truth is truth, as Keats's Grecian Urn tells McCaslin. Though not Urn-image, Ledger-record is also a record, likewise a truth to tell, the way not wayward as it may appear. Hence the Book, O.T. or tattered Tomey-tale. 'Truth is one' which is the whole story of this Nation's building:

> ...the whole plantation in its mazed and intricate entirety—the land, the fields and what they represented in terms of cotton ginned and sold, the men and women whom they fed and clothed and even paid a little cash money at Christmas time in return for the labor which planted and raised and picked and ginned the cotton, the machinery and mules and gear with which they raised it and their cost and up-keep and replacement—that whole edifice intricate and complex and founded upon injustice and created by ruthless rapacity and carried on even yet with at time downright savagery not only to the human beings but valuable animals too, yet solvent and efficient and more than that: and not only still intact but enlarged, increased: brought still intact by McCaslin, himself little more than a child then, through and out of the debacle of chaos of twenty years ago where hardly one in ten survived, and enlarged and increased and would continue so, solvent and efficient and intact and still increasing so long as McCaslin and his McCaslin successors lasted...not the land but us, not only the blood, but the name too, not only its color but its designation: Edmonds, white, but, a female line, could have no other but the name his father bore; Beauchamp, the elder line and the male one, but black, could have had any name he liked.... (p. 111)

A mix-up all the way, the sole secret continues through generations...the beyond-record truth a cementing force, a linkage invisible...'patrimony to join him with lusts and passions, the hopes and dreams and griefs...' 'Carothers' grandfather had never heard'. McCaslin continues. A nationhood upraised in spite of anomalies endless in the process of blend. This nationhood kept them all united. India could not achieve that end, Rabindranath lamented this lack, but lacuna sought to be filled in by an age-old Indian concept 'Individual and the Universe'. But when he sought it to give a concrete shape in Nation against the concept of International he confused the original Indian view. The West did not enter into Indian subtlety—Nation is Nation, in conflict with another they stand firm united as one man, Islam has given it a faith-form. So there was a crusade. Indian abstraction leaves no scope for a crusade. War in the two Indian Epics is not a crusade, but a course of correction.

[6]

American civilization is growing as from the Abraham's stage of forming, and Indian a civilization well-formed disintegrating, so Naipaul's 'A Civilization Wounded'. Isaac McCaslin Nazarene, the boy, General Compson's recommended stay-graced, now attains New Testament Nazarene stage. His marriage too Isaac's kind of marriage, the young lady told him "His grandmother was my father's sister. We were the same as brothers" (p. 116). Secret blood-mix was providential as it were. Biblical Isaac's was decreed, not a Canaanite to marry, but one from Abraham's own land and tribe. The story's Isaac had to marry a girl who knew her father's sister was his grandmother. She was his Rebekah. Together they own the land, the bunglow was finished and they readied themselves to move. Her meeting was Rebekah's meeting with farm owner Isaac, even more: they missed the first night's supper, did not answer the bell, rather one asked the other to 'lock the door', the second bell got them in bed, no stir out to meal. Then the Biblical scene of knowledge, not Lawrence's rawness but restrained sweetness of ardour to know, even physically, Eden's Lord knew they were made so:

... 'he had never seen her naked before, he had asked her to once, and why: that he wanted to see her looking at him naked because he loved her but after that he never mentioned it again, even turning his face when she put the night gown on over her dress to undress at night and putting the dress on over the gown to remove it in the morning and she would not let him get into bed beside her until the lamp was out and even in the heat of summer she would draw the sheet up over them both before she would let him turn to her: [Landlady's rap on the door ignored] she said Take off your clothes': her head still turned away...he paused beside the bed so that he never paused but merely changed the direction of moving, downward now, drawing him still downward with the one hand down and down and he neither saw nor felt it shift, palm flat against his chest—and not looking at him now, she didn't need to, the chaste woman, the wife, already looked upon all the mean who ever rutted, now her whole body had changed, altered, he had never seen it but once and now... ' (p. 117).

Biblical knowledge, they knew each other, then 'Promise', which 'promise'? The secrecy of their knowledge? Yes! The author is inside the Holy Writ-context, he cannot trifle it over, over the promised, sacred bond. If 'She is lost, she was born lost. We were all born lost' (*ibid.*). Lord too decreed 'Be fruitful and multiply'—a nation is going to be born. The boy is a husbandman like Isaac in his own land, among his tribes. America is adventure itself. Huck Tom their forefathers in the right direction, Faulkner only idealizes it. The boy is their third generation progenitor: 'If this don't get that son you talk about, it won't be mine'—A promise.

Faulkner draws conclusion to his long short-story coming back to where he began—the woods and woodlanders; only industrial encroachment immediate; Sam and the Bear and Lion the mongrel are in their graves in the forest, their memory retained in love, the boy has more reason to do. The owner of the woods Major de Spain is too busy to join the party. The ownership of timber sold out to a city lumber company, new arrangement is already afoot, miles of rusted iron rods dumped, Hoke log-line junction changed, yet wood animals move about though movements arrested by industrial encroachment.

The wood is something different now to him though itself the same, memory the transmuting factor: "summer, and fall, and snow, wet and sap-rife spring in their ordered immortal sequence, the deathless and immemorial phases of the mother who had shaped him, if any had, toward the man he almost was, mother and father both to old man born of a Negro slave and a Chickasaw Chief who had been his spirits' father if any had, whom he had revered and hankered to and loved and lost and grieved; and he would may someday and they too would own for their brief while that brief unsubstanced glory which inherently of itself cannot last and hence why glory: and they would, might, carry even the remembrance of it into the time when flesh no longer talks to flesh, because memory at least does last: but still the woods would be his mistress and his wife" (p. 122).

This forest and those in it—all his. No man can shake it off however far removed he can be anywhere. Sam cannot forget his 'Grandfather the Chief', nor Isaac McCaslin, "feeling again as always the sharp shocking inrush from when Isaac McCaslin long yet was not" (p. 123). General Compson detected it quite early, school not his education, forest is. The third generation patriarch has the potency to drive successive generations for a towering nation from a husbandman-beginning close to the forest farm land working. Rebekah first met Isaac on his farm land working, she bashfully veiling her head.

Hemingway's is a very short story, characters only three, finally two in sharp contrast. These two waiters of a cafe, one quite young the other elderly; the third outsider their customer, an old man a week ago attempted suicide, his niece timely intervened and was saved. This customer old man is wealthy, why he attempted suicide and why he wanted to remain outside home late at night drinking more than he should is not clear. The younger waiter uncertainly accounted for 'he was lonely'; when this man withdrew the two waiters remained alone. The theme of the story is decided and defined by the interaction of these two characters, exactly not interaction, but intercourse between them. They talk and define their respective position: The younger with a wife was impatient to go home early and go to bed. The elder likes to stay "with all those who do not want to go to bed. With all those who need a light for the night".

The young waiter is very clear to his co-waiter "I want to go home to bed". An hour is important to him, it may not be to the elder; he jokes "you have no fear of going home before your usual hour?" The elderly waiter felt insulted. Just humouring him a little the younger declared, "I have confidence, I am all confidence. I am all confidence." The elderly waiter has no 'confidence', he is not so 'young' now. So they have their difference. Wife or no wife hardly matters, he is at his ease outside in a 'clean well-lighted place'. The young waiter is desperate to leave early for home 'to go to bed' as early as possible, home unclean and ill-lighted no factor for him. One is quite opposite to the other in taste and temperament. Their old customer preferred to spend as much time as he could at a Café, home had no charm for him, though a wealthy man and could afford to buy a bottle of drink to carry it home.

The home-centric young waiter has his reason to be home centred, he has no reason to suffer from insomnia. Though his colleague has enough reason to explain to himself his sleepless night just the cause of insomnia. The whole attitude is the sum total of the hard realities of his life, a man totally out of his moorings nestled finally in a void of his attitudinized existence—a clean well-lighted place. No bar is for him, no bodega either 'naday pues nade', his gospel. Out of nothingness an attitudinal cult is born, if purity—self-purity—that is also perverted. Better then to accept life with all its impurities and darkness. A notional perfection is no substitute for life. The young waiter lives it, he has no nausea, no sneer, no incapacity to steer through, no negative isolation. Cafe is as good for him as bar and bodega. He can sleep well, even in darkness. It is an attitude that represents America. America's is not purist passivity, Indian trend is, but performing adventurism.

Faulkner gives a brooding cast of the mind to his style while Hemingway's is a tinsel-twist to truth, otherwise plain. A home-truth hauled up to universally shared reality. What we call nothing is everything, so is the mystery of this creation.

Hawthorne's story 'Rappaccini's Daughter' follows a different style, not in sharp difference with the British style of writing, theme too love, depicted in its utmost restrained and refined romance, his is a grand British legacy in America, a British mind in proper American setting.

Bibliography

The Bibliography below follows a principle: detailed reference provided for those to locate quotations, for all the rest the readership is required only awareness how the subject is explored. Quotes from the Bear are from an Indian reprint, hence may not be reliable.

Austen, Jane

Augustine, St.

Arabian Night's Tale

Anglo. Saxon tradition—Thegn

Bacon, F.—*Wits*

Browning, R.—*Monologue*

Bronte, E.—*Wuthering Heights*

Bible: O.T.—Abraham, Noah, Ham, Eden Knowledge, Adam-Eve, Rebekah-Isaac, Nimrod, Genesis, Exodus, Solomon, Gomorrah, Sodom, Canaan

Corneille—N.T. La Cid

Conrad, J.—*Heart of Darkness, The Rescue*

Carroll, L.—*Alice's Wonderland*, Congreve, W—Wilde, O: *Wit* Coleridge, S.T.—*Chistabel*

Charvantes—*Don Quixote*

Defoe, D.—*Robinson Crusoe*

Dickens, C.—*David Copperfield, Oliver Twist, Great Expectations*

Darwin, C.—*The Origin of Species*

Eliot, G.—*Adam Bede, Middlemarch*

Faulkner, W.—*The Sound and the Fury 1929, The Bear*

Hemingway, E.—*The Old Man and the Sea, A Clean Well-lighted Place* (Short story)

Hawthorne, N.—*The Scarlet Letter, Rappaccini's Daughter* (Story)

Homer—*Iliad.*

Keats, J.—*Grecian Um.*

Lawrence, D.H.—*Lady Chatterley's Lover.*

Mark Twain—*Jumping Frog, The Adventure of Tom, Swayer 1876, The Adventure of Hucklebery Finns 1884.*

Morrison, T.—*Beloved* (1987) *Chatto & Windus, Vintage* (2007), *The Bluest Eye.*

Milton, J.—*Paradise Lost*, Pandemoniam.

Mediaeval Alligory—Pearl.

Naipaul, V.S.—*A way of the World, Half a Life, El Dorado, The Free State, A Bend of the River.*

Orwell, G.—*A Animal Farm.*

Rabindranath, T.—*Creative Activity (a concept).*

Richardson, S.—*Clarissa Harlowe, Pamela.*

Rushdie, S.—*Grimus, The Ground Beneath Her Feet, The Moor's Last Sigh, Shalimar the Clown.*

Shakespeare, W.—*Macbeth [witch], Hamlet [friends], Romeo and Juliet, Julius Caesar, Othello.*

Shelley, P.B.—Prometheus Unbound.

Sophocles—*Oedipus Rex.*

Sterne, L.—*Tristram Shandy* (Uncle Toby).

Scott, W.—*Ivanhoe* (Tounament at Ashbey). *The Heart of Midlothean* (Mob).

Tennyson, A.—*The Lotos Eater.*

Woolf, V.—*The Stream of Consciousness.*

Wollstonecraft, M.—*Feminism.*